THE SPECTATOR A
AUDIENCES IN
POSTM(

Spectators and audiences are everywhere in contemporary culture. However, even in conventional performance, whether in the theatre, in film or television, or at a sporting event, it is difficult to discuss spectators with any authority, since each of us experiences and understands the display in different ways and all methods of analysing spectators are flawed or unreliable. This book provides instead a series of investigations into specific types of performance activity, and how they relate to their audiences. Topics discussed include the relationship of audiences to the rise of the director, the avant-garde, tourism, gambling, the effect of cinema on live performance, and sport, including crowd violence. Spectatorship is an area of increasing importance in the field of theatre and performance studies, and this engaging study is a valuable contribution to the development of thinking about audiences and spectators.

DENNIS KENNEDY is Beckett Professor of Drama Emeritus in Trinity College Dublin. His books include *The Oxford Encyclopedia of Theatre and Performance, Looking at Shakespeare: a Visual History of Twentieth-Century Performance, Foreign Shakespeare, Granville Barker and the Dream of Theatre* and *Plays by Harley Granville Barker*. His essays have appeared in numerous books and journals, and he has lectured widely on performance subjects around the world. His own plays have been performed in many places including New York and London, and he has frequently worked as a dramaturg and director in professional theatres.

THE SPECTATOR AND THE SPECTACLE

Audiences in Modernity and Postmodernity

DENNIS KENNEDY

CAMBRIDGE
UNIVERSITY PRESS

CAMBRIDGE UNIVERSITY PRESS
Cambridge, New York, Melbourne, Madrid, Cape Town,
Singapore, São Paulo, Delhi, Tokyo, Mexico City

Cambridge University Press
The Edinburgh Building, Cambridge CB2 8RU, UK

Published in the United States of America by Cambridge University Press, New York

www.cambridge.org
Information on this title: www.cambridge.org/9781107403604

First published 2009
First paperback edition 2011

A catalogue record for this publication is available from the British Library

ISBN 978-0-521-89976-5 Hardback
ISBN 978-1-107-40360-4 Paperback

In Memoriam
Daniel A. Ritter

Contents

Illustrations

Credits. 1: Georges Seurat (1859–91), oil on panel 24.1 x 15.2 cm, Fine Arts Museums of San Francisco, museum purchase, William H. Noble Bequest Fund, 1979.48. **2:** Edouard Manet (1832–83), oil on canvas 208 × 264.5 cm, Musée d'Orsay, Paris, Photo © Réunion des Musées Nationaux / Hervé Lewandowski. **3:** Antoine's illustrated programme, Bibliothèque Historique, Paris (courtesy of Jean Chothia). **4:** Caricature by Giovanni Manca, *Il Pasquino* 11 (20 March 1910), private collection. **5:** Sketch by Charles Sykes, *The Bystander* (2 October 1907), © British Library Board, all rights reserved. **6:** *Mr Punch at the Play* (London: Educational Book Company, c.1907), private collection. **7:** International Shakespeare Globe Centre, photo John Tramper. **8:** Tom Holte Theatre Photographic Collection, Stratford-upon-Avon, © Shakespeare Birthplace Trust. **9:** Museum of Jurassic Technology, Los Angeles. **10–11:** photos Dennis Kennedy.

Acknowledgements

A large number of people around the world have contributed to the making of this book over some time. For invitations to speak or write on topics that prompted my ideas I thank Susan Bennett, Michael Booth, Michael Bristol, Alexander Chepurov, Fiona Fearon, Hirota Atsuhiko, Barbara Hodgdon, Andreas Höfele, Peter Holland, Jill Levenson, Dieter Mehl, Angel Luis Pujante, Maria Helena Serôdio, Kishi Tetsuo, Stanley Wells and Simon Williams.

I am deeply grateful to colleagues and friends who have advised me by answering questions, discussing issues or commenting on portions of the manuscript. They include Kalamandalam Ashokan, Rustom Bharucha, Sue-Ellen Case, Jean Chothia, Kathleen Coleman, Karen Fricker, Melissa Gibson, Wilhelm Hortmann, Vinod K. Josi, Erica Magnus, Minami Ryuta, A. K. Nambiar, Marianne Novy, Anthony Parise, Peggy Phelan, Thomas Postlewait, Janelle Reinelt, Thomas Rimer, Richard Schoch, Shen Lin, Sheila Stowell, Sun Huizhu (William Sun), Ron Vince, Yong Li Lan, Phillip Zarrilli and my colleagues in Trinity College Dublin, Chrissie Poulter, Paula Quigley, Brian Singleton, Antony Tatlow and Steve Wilmer.

Edward Braun and my colleague Matthew Causey have been especially helpful in critiquing some of the chapters. I thank them also for discussions over the years that have enlightened me and kept me from mistakes. Those that remain are my own.

Material assistance was provided by research grants from Trinity College Dublin and by the Meyer Fellowship of the National University of Singapore. Parts of some chapters have been published in earlier versions in *Theatre Research International*, *Theatre Journal*, *Shakespeare Jahrbuch*, *Shakespeare Survey* and in the following collections: *The Edwardian Theatre*, ed. Michael Booth and Joel Kaplan (Cambridge University Press, 1996), *Four Hundred Years of Shakespeare in Europe*, ed. Ton Hoenselaars and A. Luis Pujante (University of Delaware Press, 2003) and *Shakespeare, Memory and Performance*, ed. Peter Holland (Cambridge University Press, 2006).

PART I

The problem of the spectator

CHAPTER I

Introduction: assisting at the spectacle

A spectator is a corporeal presence but a slippery concept. Whether considering spectators in history or the present, in one's own culture or a foreign one, in film, television or any form of live performance from theatre or sport to mass political or musical gatherings, we are likely to drop quickly into intellectual quicksand. The reasons for the difficulty are apparent enough: audiences are not (and probably never have been) homogeneous social and psychological groups, their experiences are not uniform and impossible to standardize, their reactions are chiefly private and internal, and recording their encounters with events, regardless of the mechanism used to survey or register them, is usually belated and inevitably partial. Almost anything one can say about a spectator is false on some level.

Yet audiences are indispensable to performance and commentators cannot avoid them. In common speech people make generalized conclusions about reception they have observed (the audience hated it, or the fans went wild), while journalist-critics manage to divine group response from their own responses and from the reactions of those around them. In time their reviews may be given documentary status by performance historians. Film theorists established positions on spectators that widely influenced other fields. Sociologists of sport concern themselves mightily with fan psychology and behaviour. The television industry continues to take audience research very seriously, despite serious flaws in all methods of enumeration, since vast sums of money are connected to official audience ratings. Media scholars consider at greater depth and with a critical eye the same imperfect sets of observed or statistical calculations. Even the most methodologically exact theatre historian might now and then slip into the convenience of the first-person plural when discussing the reception of performances. Despite the plenitude of difficulties audiences present, analysts continue to deal with them and the world at large is curious about them. Notwithstanding the materiality of

3

spectators, comprehending them is a problem in metaphysics. Writing about them may border on the impossible, but it also seems necessary.

In what follows I have tried to evade the impossible. I do not assume that spectators react in similar ways to the same event, or that they are socially unified just because gathered, or that my own responses are indicative of those of other spectators, or that spectators in history have received performances the way spectators do today. My attempts to sidestep these difficulties have given the work four features worth noting at the start.

1. The book does not have a single argument but is a gathering of thoughts about specific historical or theoretical problems related to spectators. Though I have connected the chapters and arranged them thematically, they are investigations that draw upon different methods and sometimes different theoretical fields. They are literally *essais*: trials or attempts at dealing with the intellectual trouble that audiences bring, views of performance problems from the standpoint of the watcher. A fully reasoned book on the spectator would mistake the problem, as I see it. There are many tales to tell about spectators, but there is no single story.
2. I range across different performance modes – theatre, television, sport, ritual, tourism, gambling – in an effort to uncover elements of contemporary culture that shape spectatorial experience and how it may be construed. Generally I propose that the medium is not the message: the message, if there is one, is in the spectator's presence, and thus sometimes I blur the usual distinction made between live and non-live performance. At times I try to question the semiotic basis for understanding the process of spectation, wondering whether creating meaning for the audience is a necessary object of performance.
3. While my examples are various, the nature of the investigation prohibits a comprehensive look at the topic; spectators are too historically and culturally specific to permit a grand mapping. I use examples as I have come upon them and as well as I can understand them, not claiming they are the necessary illustrations. To do this I have sometimes moved outside my own field of theatre and performance studies, drawing as needed on some of the investigative methods of qualitative sociology, political history and economy, media studies, psychology and art history. I may not have done this very well, but the effort is necessary to avoid a closed-circuit approach.
4. In brief, I am more concerned with the philosophic issues that spectators raise than with their specific experiences.

It has often been noted that there is no word in English (or in most European languages) to cover the two main senses involved in greeting performance, seeing and hearing. *Spectators* (those who look) gives us the first, *audience* (those within hearing) the second, both derived from Latin, and arguments have erupted at assorted times over the best usage. The classical (and biblical) traditions insisted that hearing the word was primary to understanding: Aristotle called spectacle (*opsis*) 'the least artistic element' of tragedy, Ben Jonson followed him, for once agreeing with a Puritan position, and the negative use of the word today in English (e.g. 'an empty spectacle') continues this bias. The popular traditions, on the other hand, regularly elevated the visual as capable of more direct contact with an audience; though without the authority of an ancient philosopher, many artists and theoreticians have favoured the eye, from Aristophanes to Jonson's nemesis Inigo Jones, from Charles Kean to Edward Gordon Craig and Bertolt Brecht. There are circumstances when we are chiefly listeners (for a radio play) or chiefly watchers (a mime performance), but most of the time both senses are involved and it is not helpful to distinguish the two words on an etymological basis. In general I use *audience* to refer to a group of observers of a performance, while *spectator* refers to an individual member of an audience, including a theoretical spectator or one I have myself imagined.

The title of this chapter, 'Assisting at the spectacle', is of course a literal rendering of the French *assister au spectacle*, which means in colloquial English simply 'to be present at a performance' – to be a spectator or a member of an audience. I use the phrase in a larger or metaphoric way because it brings to mind one of the most persistent historical and theoretical issues: are spectators passive receptors, merely consuming what is offered, or are they active participants, adding something to the event? In what ways does a spectator assist the spectacle?

WHAT IS AN AUDIENCE?

As one person walks across an empty space, another watches, in Peter Brook's famous formulation at the start of *The Empty Space* (1968: 9). But if this were 'all that is needed for an act of theatre to be engaged', then any observation anywhere of one person by another would qualify. As a metaphor the formulation has its attraction, and there has been a long-standing reliance upon theatrical imagery to describe elements of our interaction with the ordinary. But Brook's idea does not help much in understanding an audience in the stricter sense of a group attending to a

performance in a theatre or cinema or stadium. Does the solitary spectator really constitute an audience? We might as well deal with this issue
first, as it affects the value I will place on spectator presence. Solitary
watching is most associated with television, though it is not a necessary
condition: many examples exist of communal TV viewing, from sports
bars to soap-opera parties. Further, in the case of broadcasts millions of
scattered viewers are watching alone or in small groups – for the World
Cup or the Super Bowl, hundreds of millions worldwide – and most of
them are aware of their simultaneous participation in this larger audience,
a circumstance that distantly resonates with the experience of the theatre.
John Fiske (1987: 80) claims that 'television provides a common symbolic
experience and a common discourse, a set of shared formal conventions
that are so important to a folk culture'. I would add that the knowledge
that one is watching the same programme at the same time as millions of
others is directly connected to the cultural commonality television can
provide and creates an audience, though an audience without presence.
A solitary spectator for a video on the same set, however, cannot be called
an audience in any sense, just as the proliferation of channels on cable and
satellite reduces the prospect of shared experience that characterized
television in its terrestrial era. As programme delivery mechanisms for TV
and the internet move toward on-demand downloads, private viewing
will probably become even more common, destroying the concept of a
'television audience' that network broadcasters have relied on.

   Though I am primarily concerned with theatre and other live events,
I must consider briefly how postmodernity and above all the electronic
media have affected the audience, in idea and actuality. I agree with Alain
Badiou (2004: xv) that 'postmodern' as an adjective has been 'evacuated
of all content' – he suggests his own work might be described instead as
'more-than-modern'. But the *condition* of postmodernity is definitely at
hand, whether it is conceived primarily as interdependent world economies, a set of interrelated communications systems or a psychosocial
state of being. As a historical epoch that defines culture, postmodernity is
palpable; it has what I call 'reality-in-the-world'. (I use this phrase, a twist
on Heidegger's *Dasein* – 'being-there' or 'being-in-the-world' – to avoid
confusion with Lacan's 'the Real', or with the historical movement of
realism and its adjectives 'realistic' and 'realist', which are descriptions of
a style.) For help on the spectator in postmodernity, I turn first to
Nicholas Abercrombie and Brian Longhurst's *Audiences* (1998), a work by
media sociologists which divides contemporary audiences into three
types: simple, mass and diffused. The *simple* audience is the traditional

one, spectators gathered together bodily for an event performed live in a theatre, concert hall, or sports stadium, those literally within hearing. The second type, the *mass* audience, is composed of the scattered spectators of television and other mass media; the authors include film in this category because of its mass distribution, though from the standpoint of gathering or presence, an assembly of people in a cinema is actually a simple audience. Their final type, the *diffused* audience, refers to dispersed spectators in media-saturated societies who are continually surrounded by representations:

The qualities and experiences of being a member of an audience have begun to *leak out* from specific performance events which previously contained them, into the wider realms of everyday life. Being a member of an audience becomes a mundane event (36–7).

In this condition, similar to what Guy Debord a generation ago called 'the society of the spectacle', the incursions of electronic simulations are so pervasive that there is no substantial difference between watching and not watching. Citizens in the capitalist world have little choice but to be part of the spectacularization of life, so that, as Abercrombie and Long-hurst put it, 'Everyone becomes an audience all the time' (68).

The distinctions among audience types are not absolute, and one spectator might participate in all three categories with the same event: in the daytime attend a football match as part of a simple audience, watch highlights of the game on the evening news as part of a mass audience, and record its broadcast for what the authors term a 'narcissistic' or private use of the video at a future date (I detail this Debordian process in chapter 8). The questions of 'liveness' treated by Philip Auslander (2008) become relevant here, and more complicated. He holds that the media-tized world has redefined the live, which can no longer be accepted as a given or natural state but must be seen only in terms of the simulated. Television, the 'determining element of our cultural formation' (2), has altered our perception of what performance is. True enough, though the issue is larger. If in the West and other so-called first-world countries we have reached a state where communications, entertainments and other electronic interactions are so pervasive and incessant that we cannot avoid them, and do not wish to, then perhaps we have moved into a new phase of human life, one in which it does not much matter whether an event occurs live before us or distantly in some simulated, recorded or heavily mediated form. Writing this at a computer in Dublin I am listening via the internet to a real-time broadcast of recordings from KCSM, a jazz radio station in California, while also on an internet chat line with my daughter in India. These events are happening 'live' in real time but so thoroughly mediatized that they might as well not be. Crucially, they involve the corporeal presence of one person only: myself. Perhaps I am on the way to becoming what Matthew Causey (2006) calls the 'posthuman spectator' with 'posthuman subjectivity'.

Auslander's book is important, though he is more interested in the legal implications of his topic than the philosophic ones. Yet I doubt that many spectators are as perplexed about the live as he implies. They may not care whether a news event or a TV show is broadcast simultaneously or delayed, or if a high-tech simulation is inserted in a live concert or theatre performance, or if a cinematic special effect is generated digitally, but they are likely to remark the distinction. At stadium rock concerts the giant video screens which double the musicians' presence may be 'the manner in which audience members access the performance' (Causey 2006: 23), but if so that occurs with force only because of the authenticating live manifestation of the performers' bodies. Walter Benjamin's famous assertion that mechanical reproduction has rendered the aura of the original work of art obsolete, for all its credibility in the 1930s and historical importance thereafter, must not be conflated with market value. The ready availability of cheap reproductions, or Baudrillard's exposure of the simulacrum, have not reduced the auction successes of Picassos and Rembrandts. The rapidly rising prices of famous works, and the excessive anxiety about their authenticity, even if driven by investment factors, suggest that the original has by virtue of its rarity achieved added monetary appeal. Perhaps this is true of the live as well, as Jill Dolan (2005) insists. To paraphrase Causey, what most distinguishes the live is the spectator's distant awareness of its true opposite, which is not the recorded or the simulated, but death. The death we carry within us is the perpetual ghost at the spectator's banquet, another reason for thinking that the presence of the spectator is more important than the presence of the actor.

A final point about the audience for electronic media: a number of commentators now assert that the standard notion of the TV audience as an observable phenomenon is a fiction made at the convenience of the television industry and too easily accepted by scholars. Related to judgements about the undominated uses of TV that viewers can make, itself prompted by Michel de Certeau (1984) on the resistant power of consumerism, writers such as Ien Ang (1991) assert that industry notions are completely detached from the actuality of the audience, that the industry lacks any interest in what spectators really think or do, instead presenting data to advertisers or state agencies that can convince them of the value of financial sponsorship. The television audience is inherently unstable, says Bird (2003: 3), because it is 'everywhere and nowhere'. We know quite a lot about reception, Katz holds (1996: 9); 'what we know least about is the psychology and sociology of the viewing experience itself . . . how viewers position themselves before the screen'. In Fiske's concise formula (1989: 57), 'There is no text, there is no audience, there are only the processes of viewing.'

CONSTRUCTING THE SPECTATOR

If there are major headaches in trying to understand the character of the diffused media audience, returning to film and live performance provides only limited relief. On what basis can we think of a simple audience in a cinema or theatre as any different from a mass television or diffused audience, anything more than a random collection of individual spectators, even if they happen to be in one space? If all spectation is ultimately psychological and personal, are we not forever trapped in conjecture and supposition?

The problem was first faced seriously in film studies, but partly deflected. In his early work in the 1960s Christian Metz presumed a linguistic basis for understanding reception, affected by Roman Jakobson's communication model of sender-addressee and transmitter-receiver. Metz's hypothesis was that the 'messages' of narrative film were primarily photo-realist and embedded in the product. As Thomas Elsaesser (1995: 12) summarizes, for Metz 'The spectator/receiver's job was merely to "decode" the message "correctly", which meant that "subjectivity" was located in the "phatic" dimension of the communication act.' In this semiotic (or telegraphic, or Saussurean) view, the film text, from shot to shot, already inscribes subjectivity. If an actual spectator diverges from the inscribed subject position, what has occurred is not a flaw in the theory but in the transmission, a 'failed reception'. Metz's later work (1982) developed a more sophisticated approach to subjectivity centred around the idea of scopophilia, and it is only fair to add that he never conflated the theoretical subject with actual spectators, but the structuralist basis remained.

A psycho-semiotic refinement of Metz, influenced by Lacan and most notable in France, attempted to realize a more complete account of subjectivity. The British journal *Screen* took up the call in the 1970s and 1980s, famously in Laura Mulvey's essay 'Visual pleasure and narrative cinema' (1975), which argued that the female spectator was excluded from classical Hollywood film because that tradition constructed the spectator in the male subject position, leaving no space for alternative response. Intended as a manifesto for change in film making, the article was actually more influential in the academy, especially through its theory of an inscribed 'male gaze' which dominates spectatorship. Despite its radical significance Mulvey's view was rooted in an assumption that the spectator's subjectivity is limited by the film's authority. Most oddly, given her topic, Mulvey ignored the prospect of spectator agency. Equally important was the application of the Lacanian concept of 'suture' by Jean-Pierre Oudart (1977–8) to describe the ways the spectator is psychologically 'stitched into' the world of the film through the oscillation of 'looks' organized by point of view. But the psycho-semiotic assumption that the film text governs spectator response, aside from its disconnection from actual spectators, further totalized Lacanian ideas into a monolithic theoretical model based on gender and sexuality. Imagining the viewer as stuck in Lacan's mirror stage, at the centre of an illusionary representation, as Baudry did (1985, originally 1970), supposes a spectator unable to recognize the line between fiction and certainty (reality-in-the-world). The *Screen* approach was challenged by various materialist critical moves and also by cognitive film theory, both of which focused on the conscious rather than the unconscious processes mobilized in viewers. Moving completely away from Lacanian theory were a set of reception studies of actual cinema audiences in history and the present, similar to the sociological approach to media audiences and subject to similar methodological difficulties.

In theatre studies we can identify parallel trends, though without the critical trap of a determined subjectivity. Of the books in the linguistic or semiotic tradition, most of them written in the 1980s, I mention especially Patrice Pavis (1982), Marco De Marinis (1993) and Marvin Carlson (1990) as addressing the two-way character of communication in the theatre. Live performance, with its multiple points of view and optional spectation procedures, does not encourage critics to presuppose a determining text, whether written or performed, nor a theoretical subjectivity for the recipient. Lacan nonetheless provided the basis for Peggy Phelan's *Unmarked* (1992), an investigation of the indeterminacy and ephemerality of performance. In Herbert Blau's *The Audience* (1990), a collection of essays about disappearing inspired by Beckett and Derrida as well as Lacan, the author chooses to speak for no spectator but himself. Blau approaches audiences by considering how playwrights and theatre artists have conceived them psychologically.

More concerned with a materialist consideration of gender are Jill Dolan's *The Feminist Spectator as Critic* (1991) and Sue-Ellen Case's *The Domain-Matrix* (1996), which have been broadly influential in reconfiguring ideas of subjectivity and have sparked a number of contributions on gender and the queer that are directly applicable to spectators. In a different vein, Susan Bennett's *Theatre Audiences* (1997), an essential book on the topic, relies on literary reception theory and circumvents the problem of subjectivity by not adducing specific audience results. It is difficult to expand upon Willmar Sauter's statistical exploration of contemporary audiences (2000) since it is circumscribed by data from middle-class Swedish theatregoers and does not take theoretical account of the biases of spectator surveys or the legitimate uses that might be made of them. Bruce McConachie's treatment (2003) of the psychology of Broadway audiences in the early Cold War period is filled with insight, though the support he uses, Lakoff and Johnson's research in cognitive psychology, is scientifically uncertain. McConachie is well aware of the problems the method poses but proceeds nonetheless on the assumption that a direct relationship exists between audience perception and the intellectual and emotional 'containment' characteristic of an age. He deduces spectator response through textual and performance analysis, but despite the cognitive frame the *process of deduction* is little different from that achieved in other structuralist theoretical frames such as the semiotic, Freudian or Lacanian approaches he rejects. A different advance in the study of historical audiences comes from Christopher Balme's *Pacific Performances* (2007), a book about European encounters with the cultures of the South Seas from the first contacts of explorers in the eighteenth century to contemporary touristic displays and diasporic re-imaginings. Looking at both the reactions of Europeans to the manifestation of Polynesia and Polynesian sights of the new arrivals, Balme places spectatorship inside intercultural encounter.

My examples are seriously incomplete; no summary account can manage the fact that the spectator is the unspoken topic of most work in theatre and performance studies, even if that spectator is a pale hypothetical inference of the commentator's imagination.

A deeper problem is that – McConachie aside – most analysis of performance supposes a semiotic configuration, with speaking subjects on stage (the transmitters) and more-or-less silent objects in the audience (the receivers). Even when the author is well aware of the indeterminacy and multiplicity of signifiers and the ungraspable shape of what they might signify, and attentive to the reciprocity of communication and the possibility of spectator resistance, it is difficult to discuss elements of any type of performance without recourse to a sender-receiver model. The very fact of its visibility tends to make performance stand for something else – in Peter Handke's wonderful phrase in *Offending the Audience*, theatre is 'a brightness that pretends to be another brightness'. The semiotic formula, which considers performance as an action by doers for watchers, has been at the heart of the social and financial contract that normally obtains between actors and audience. Certainly I have never managed to evade the inference that, whatever else they do, spectators read signs, especially when dealing with processes of the visual (Kennedy 2001), and some of the chapters which follow depend upon a similar representational paradigm. Even Hans-Thies Lehmann (2006), who says so much of value about how spectation has been revised in contemporary 'postdramatic' theatre, does not attempt to drive beyond the semiotic; the sophistication of his analysis is not matched by any sophistication of the linguistic model.

Perhaps everything to do with spectators in theatre and film can be related to a problem in semiotics. Yet when considering the spectator theoretically it is also important to consider the limitations of semiotic usage, which lie not only in indeterminate signifiers but also in the prospect that a spectator may hold no interest in messages, whether or not they contain thematic consequence. I do not mean that representation is absent from performance; the responses of spectators are always in part prompted by what is shown to them, even if they reject it or misunderstand it or give it back in an altered manner. But I do mean to point out that relying on a semiotic scheme to explain spectatorship is an incomplete procedure that takes insufficient account of interactivity and imagines the spectator chiefly as a recipient. Too often semiotically based analysis predicts an ideal spectator as reader, and thus can trap itself inside a moral conviction about proper or correct reception. For a spectator, legibility may not be the primary concern. A good deal of the history of audiences, especially after records improved in the eighteenth century, reveals that spectators often attended the theatre without attending to the play. They came to ogle an actress or another spectator, arrange an assignation, be with friends, create a ruckus, be noted at the event, watch a new scenic device, or for the sake of companionship, or simply because they were given a free ticket. We still arrive at the theatre with our agency intact. As I suggest in chapter 7, spectators in a proscenium playhouse may actually feel superior to actors on stage through the sense of voyeurism the architecture encourages. If a semiotic analysis inflects the stage with authority, a psychological one might reverse the power arrangement.

Similar motivations apply to other events. An individual spectator – let us call her Carole – doesn't especially like football but goes to Saturday's Chelsea-Tottenham Hotspur match because her partner Bill has season tickets and asks her to come along; she watches the fans suspiciously and thinks about Indian novels. Handy-dandy, that evening Bill resentfully accompanies Carole to a film she has selected; he replays the match in his head and halfway through takes fifteen minutes to buy popcorn. Next week they have complimentary seats at a production of *Macbeth* their friend Dennis has directed for a small theatre in north London; over a drink with him afterwards they say appropriate things but all three would rather have been at home watching the latest episode of *The Sopranos* on television. The unwilling spectator, the reluctant spectator, the spectator in a bad mood or feeling poorly, the accidental spectator, the snoring spectator: I cannot put statistics or proper names to this roll call but they are not fictitious creatures. Observable at many types of performance, they suggest that semiotics cannot tell the tale of what assisting at the spectacle means socially. If we can admit that an audience is a public assembly for an event larger than the performance, we should see that spectation is about more than reception.

THE AUDIENCE AND THE UNIVERSAL

I am stuck with the same question: what is an audience? When spectators congregate in public for a performance, live or recorded, does anything unite them? Among those disparate selves can anything 'universal' occur? Like Badiou (2004), I propose that the universal is not a transcendent or unanimous condition but rather a truth that has meaning only inside the set of conditions governing it. Let us assume for the sake of argument that a performance achieves whatever significance it may have for the audience by virtue of their spectation. Can it be said that anything universal happens to the assembled spectators? If a universal exists, it cannot be in the way spectators experience meaning in the event of performance, or the way they connect (or do not connect) the performance to their lives. For one spectator, tonight's production of *Hamlet* is a story of revenge, for another a playing out of spiritual crisis or political corruption, for a third a tale about a split subject torn between the sexualities of his mother and his girlfriend, while for any of them the most gripping feature might lie in the scenographic or performative rather than in a scripted or thematic element. The universal of the event cannot reside in the physical dis-position of the spectators, whether in a proscenium theatre or outdoors, whether standing or sitting, whether uncomfortable, in a state of heightened alertness or asleep. Any of those could alter *habitus* sufficiently to alter acceptance. Nor can the universal reside in how spectators respond with gestures such as clapping or booing, whether they laugh or cry, whether they will remember or forget, whether they will argue about the performance or get drunk in disgust at it.

No, if there is a universal in a gathered group it must be *the gathering itself*, in the simple act of being present, as simultaneous witnesses or participating observers, at an event offered for display *precisely for this group*. Then the random composition of the group is not significant, the repeatability of the event not the key, and the various undefined purposes or rationales for presence irrelevant. Even the living presence of performers is not essential. It is the living presence of the spectators that most matters and provides commonality to the event. Individual spectators do not become a mob or a pack or a single psychological entity; they make the group but the group does not make them. They become an audience by virtue of their cooperative attendance, nothing more.

This definition is simpler than Blau's assertion that 'what is universal in performance is the consciousness of performance' (1987: 171). Stressing the mysterious 'appearance' of the performer as central to all types of performance, Blau goes too far in implying reflexivity about performance is present also in the act of spectation. I doubt that it is essential for watchers to have consciousness about their watching, and certainly it is not necessary for them to hold similar notions about what their watching might mean, which must be the case if the condition of universality were to apply. Both those conditions would imply the spectator is mindful of an abstraction bordering on the metaphysical, and surely we cannot assume pre-existing, psychologically unified circumstances among those disparate selves any more than we can assume that all performance, or even *this* performance, tonight, adduces a unified set of responses. No psychological unity, no specific consciousness, can be supposed in a gathering of spectators. The only certainty is their presence.

Next, the issue of volition, and here I must distinguish two types of spectators. The first are those whose assistance at the spectacle is in some sense mandatory. Ritual ceremonies, whether religious or social, provide one set of examples, when they are considered essential to their participants' place in the cosmic or public realms: weddings or funerals, baptisms or bar mitzvahs, public punishments or moments of formal celebration. Juridical performances provide another group of examples: the law compels participation at a trial or investigation and can penalize absence. There are also occasions at an ordinary entertainment when social or professional responsibilities might render a person's attendance close to obligatory.

But under the conditions of capitalist postmodernity most performance is leisure activity, superfluous, play, a social excess, and thus most spectators are of a second type: volunteers at the spectacle. I do not mean that performance for them cannot comment on or even affect important areas of political, social or psychological life, but its address to its audience is usually in the realm of the voluntary. In the case of live performance, a further characteristic is impermanence. Because it dematerializes in the moment of its accomplishment, live performance gains its power before an audience from its vanishing, its being here and then not being here in the flow of the now, regardless of its memory traces whether public or private. What further unites these spectators at a live event, then, is not what they receive but their unnecessary presence at a disappearing act.

AUDIENCE GESTURES

> Give me your hands if we be friends
> And Robin shall restore amends.

Puck, in the epilogue to *A Midsummer Night's Dream*, itself drawn from the conventions of Roman comedy, connects hand clapping, a common gesture of audience approbation, to the handshake, a common gesture of friendship. At the end of Peter Brook's famous production in 1970 the actors scurried through the house to shake hands with the applauding spectators, equating friendliness with approval. Applause is friendly, and it ties together. It ties the audience to the actors, especially in the curtain call, and it ties spectators to each other, forming a temporary bond among them. In this view applause can be seen as a gestural gift that makes noise and also acts as a substitute for touching, an extension, through outstretched arms, of the spectator's body to the actor's body.

Applause is the most obvious indicator that miscellaneous spectators have become an audience. It is part of a larger set of social behaviours related to the reception of performance in the western tradition: cheering, shouting bravo or encore or *bis* and other approbative signs; booing, hissing, catcalls and other disapprobative signs; laughter and weeping. I will call them audience gestures. Some of them are more or less deliberate, like clapping and shouting; others tend to be involuntary, intuitive or spontaneous, like laughing or weeping, which can occur despite a person's exertion to suppress them. Audience gestures are not universal, they have histories as well as phenomenologies, they are temporally and culturally shaped. Yet some observable expression of esteem (or repugnance) is so common among spectators, and so frequent through time, it is surprising how little these gestures have been studied. Baz Kershaw (2001) goes so far as to suggest that this avoidance is rooted in an unwillingness to see applause as determined by the changing status of the stage. He notes the increasing habit of contemporary audiences in Britain to respond to mediocre performances with uncritical ovations, and relates the trend to the declining political power of theatre. This is an intriguing conclusion, but the larger historical point is that the protocols of applause have commonly been subject to alteration.

Roman audiences, for example, had an organized series of approbative gestures, ranging from finger snapping to hand clapping (*applaudere* means 'to strike upon') and on to some peculiar gestures from the period of the Empire like waving the flap of the toga or a special cloth. Martial records that spectators signalled with *mappae* ('napkins') their desire that a defeated gladiator should be granted a reprieve, and that on other occasions at the games the crowd would wave the large edge of their togas to indicate that a gazelle should be freed. But waving did not always mean approbation, it seems, since Ovid points to an example when spectators were asked to flap their togas in the circus to object to an unfair start of a race. The Roman secular traditions were strong enough to continue into Christian services. In the fourth century Eusebius writes that Paul of Samosata (200–75) encouraged the congregation to approve his sermons by waving linen cloths in the Roman manner, and it was apparently the custom in the Christian churches in the fourth and fifth centuries to cheer popular preachers.[1]

The stark contrast with the restrained manners expected in the more traditional Christian churches today shows how etiquettes of applause, which can be affected by spectators' class, gender and ethnicity as well as nation, are ultimately regulated by behavioural codes. Augustus curbed applause at huge Roman events by dividing the audience into two *chori*, each with a leader, attempting to control outbursts that might get out of hand. All gestures are subject to similar social regulation, spoken or unspoken. The law can forbid certain gestures in specific circumstances, such as giving the finger to a judge in court, but social custom is more likely to dictate rule. A note in a concert programme requesting the audience to refrain from applause until the end of the song cycle, even though justified by a sense of musical or narrative flow, is the same type of gestural constraint as the demand that children not fidget in church or that students follow a dress code; all are about decorum and authority over the bodies of others.

The acceptability of the type of applause also varies with the nature of the event; approbative gestures fitting a football match in an outdoor stadium, like the sounding of a gas-charged foghorn, are forbidden at a tennis match, not to mention a performance of *King Lear*. Applause can also be considered disruptive if it comes at inappropriate moments, as when an inexperienced concert-goer claps between the movements of a symphony and is hushed by his knowing neighbours. From its first performance applause was frowned upon during and after Wagner's *Parsifal* because of the religious connotations of the story; in Germany today act one still ends with silence, while acts two and three are applauded. Such precise behaviour conventions must be learned, a very distinct form of cultural capital, and those who do not know them can be marked as audience outcasts. It was common, by the way, to applaud between the movements of a symphony in the nineteenth century, and not uncommon for a movement to be repeated if demanded by the auditors. These examples recall that gestures are always social in meaning and subject to social regulation. As the anthropologist Jean-Claude Schmitt (1984: 2) writes, 'discourse on gesture is, in each period, a discourse on social order and its exclusions'.

Attempts to order applause are most evident in the institution of the claque. The claque – a group of supposed spectators hired by a manager to promote the approval of an event – is another practice with origins in the Roman Empire. It became important again in nineteenth-century Europe, and can help in understanding the shifting status of applause. The theory behind the claque was that an audience was a kind of machine, that its applause needed a starter or a crank to get it going, to maintain it and to resuscitate it when it started to fail or stall. (Television producers used to conceive of mechanical laugh tracks in a similar way, and nineteenth-century commentators often referred to claque-induced applause as mechanical.) In Italian opera moments for applause and for encores were composed in the music, even in the realist operas of Verdi and Puccini, and the claque leader had to learn the right spots. A claque supporting a singer or a composer could readily force an encore and thus stimulate the audience and the critics to think the work a success, just as an opposing claque could engineer a failure. To the end of his long life Verdi tended to measure success by the number of encores his audiences demanded.

The claque was firmly institutionalized in Paris. A *chef de claque* was paid between 300 and 500 francs a month in the latter part of the nineteenth century, and was considered as essential to theatrical experience as an actor. One reporter noted that rank-and-file *claqueurs* had big, strong hands; though their only payment was free admission, they went about their work with diligence. There were sixteen engaged each evening at the Comédie Française, and thirty at the much larger Paris Opéra. Following their leader's cues, *claqueurs* set about to engineer approbation. Applause was often scored in the prompt script, the types being distinguished by such terms as *acclamation, hilarité, tressaillement, redoublement* and the ultimate, *explosion indéfinie*.[2] Some managements during the Third Republic took considerable trouble to disguise the presence of the claque, suggesting that spectators were not often fooled by these *entrepreneurs de succès*, as they liked to call themselves; the goal was to encourage applause without giving the game away. The minor theatres in the early nineteenth century also employed *chatouilleurs* (literally, 'ticklers') to laugh at the jokes to stimulate a tired or grumpy audience, while at melodrama houses a number of women, Hemmings notes (1993: 108–10), 'were employed not to laugh but to weep'. He concludes that audiences were increasingly marginalized by professional applause, despite the antagonism of the public to the claque. Intriguingly the end of the claque in Paris was brought about by 'the new custom of extinguishing the houselights at the start of a play' (116), since a claque could function only if its leader's signals were visible. But the institution lasted much longer in some opera houses, especially in Italy, and Earl Wilson reported that the claque was still going strong at the Metropolitan Opera as late as 1944 (*New York Post*, 21 March 1944: 24).

If the claque shows one border in the management of applause, the curtain call uncovers another. The curtain call in its literal sense, players called before the act curtain to accept individual or ensemble applause, arose in the eighteenth century in Europe. With varying degrees of practice it remains in use. Singers in major opera houses take calls after each act, arranged by voices in a long awkward line across the stage, holding hands in front of the curtain. Opera accommodates this custom better than the non-musical theatre, which has been discomforted by it for some time in northern Europe and America. The rise of naturalism put a particular strain on the tradition, since the act curtain call broke the pretence of reality while the play was still in progress. At the beginning of the twentieth century frequent complaints appeared in the press about the absurdity of following a scene of murder and rapine, as one New York journalist put it, by 'a smirking line of actors stretched foolishly across the stage'.[3] Granville Barker tried to break the custom of curtain calls after each act by announcing in his programmes at the Court Theatre in London that the actors would take bows only at the end of the performance.

But curtain calls are generally staged, a reminder that the applause they seek is partially ceremonial as well as controlled. With actors bowing to acknowledge their debt to spectators as their employers, the curtain call consents to approbation but also lures it: its structure and protocols, despite variation from place to place, make it difficult for most spectators to refuse standard gestures of endorsement entirely. What is theoretically generous, a gift from the volunteers at the spectacle, can easily become an obligation. On the other hand, discarding the curtain call presents its own difficulties. The second half of the twentieth century saw significant changes in the practice, influenced by a number of material circumstances including the disuse of the curtain, modifications of stage architecture and the trend to smaller playhouses. Influential avant-garde attitudes, especially in the 1960s and 1970s, professed aversion to the customs of the bourgeois theatre and sometimes abandoned curtain calls, making the clapping audience feel foolish, uncertain of propriety, waiting for the actors to appear in a bow, wondering whether the play was really over. At the end of the first night of Brook's *US* in 1966 the London audience was confronted by a line of staring actors; after some minutes of silence Kenneth Tynan said to them loudly from his seat, 'Are we keeping you waiting or are you keeping us?' (Tynan 1987: 250). An extreme case such as the Living Theatre's *Paradise Now*, when spectators (at least in Brooklyn in 1968) were invited not to applaud but to strip and join the nude performers on stage in a communal dance, points out how important some organized opportunity for audience expression can be.

In a typical curtain call applause brings closure to the performance event in a way that is much stronger than the end of the drama itself. Borrowing Goffman's term (1967), we might call it an 'interaction ritual' that for the first time in a traditional performance gives the audience some measure of authority. Most opportunities for audience expression in the theatre have been attenuated or removed: at a sporting event spectators shout and scream encouragement or disapproval as the game proceeds, but at a playhouse they are expected to remain seated and take it in silence. At the curtain call, then, the audience formally acknowledges its pivotal position, its power to make the actors go or stay.

Thus applause makes explicit the predicament of theatre spectators in the West: they are assisting at the spectacle but their assistance has been regulated and commodified. They may choose not to clap, they may choose to boo or hiss, they may rise in protest and leave early, but the parameters of their conduct are regulated by the bourgeois origins of contemporary audience behaviour. Are they, as Kershaw complains of spectators overly predisposed to standing ovations, applauding themselves? In part, yes. But *they are applauding themselves for being present together*, for having achieved, if only for a moment, the condition of assembly.

PATROLLING THE AUDIENCE

So it is fair to say that the overt responses of spectators are shaped in shifting degrees by the performance text, the physical environment and social conditioning. Audiences for theatre, film, television or sport are notionally free to make use as they will of what is presented, but they are also ordered by the event. I'll call this division the free cats of Michel de Certeau as opposed to the caged dogs of Michel Foucault. For Certeau consumers under capitalism can adapt products and environments to their own purposes, as readers can 'poach' texts, while Foucault reminds us that consumers, obviously restricted to what is for sale, are patrolled by pre-existing economic and political systems. Is it possible to say anything about these cats and dogs that helps in understanding spectation?

We should first look outside Euro-American culture. If local variations can be observed in practices in the West, distant fields bring substantially more variety. In Indian dance-drama, for example, audience activity is affected by ceremonial customs and religious associations which regard terminal applause as out of place. In temple and shrine performances in Kerala spectators move in an uncertain disposition between traditions of belief and traditions of connoisseurship. At Kathakali performances, for example, spectators would be likely to give vocal encouragement during a scene, or indicate approbation immediately after a well-executed passage of singing, rather than clap the actors in anything resembling a curtain call. Yet performances of Kathakali in theatres in New Delhi, or even in tourist centres in Kerala, will commonly cater to the western idea of a curtain call. The farther one moves from the courtly tradition of Kathakali into the realm of Keralan ritual, the less likely any applause will occur. Clapping would disrupt the observance in the folk tradition of Teyyam, for example, or in the dance-drama of Krishnattam at the Guruvayur Temple.

Similar variations are noticeable in non-religious performance in East Asia. In China productions of Jingju (Beijing opera) are accompanied by shouts of *hao* ('good') from spectators pleased with a sung moment; curtain calls, if they exist, are perfunctory. Though most performances now occur in proscenium theatres, often recently built, the more expensive 'tea seats' closest to the stage, where tea and cakes are served at tables, still preserve the less formal audience attitude of the past. In an adaptation of traditional etiquette, it is common today for spectators to answer their mobile phones in the house, to walk in the aisles and to come and go as they please – since no intervals are taken, this is often a necessity – but climbing over one's neighbours in a row of fixed seats is just as disruptive as in the West.

A more intriguing example comes from Kabuki, the popular form developed in the seventeenth and eighteenth centuries in Japan, which today shows some tension between inherited modes of audience response and those affected by modernist European procedures. Kabuki was first performed on Nō stages, but around 1700 the bridgeway characteristic of Nō was extended into a long, slightly elevated ramp (*hanamichi*) running through the house, the audience sitting on the floor about it as well as in galleries above. Visual records, chiefly woodblock prints advertising the shows, indicate that spectators attended only partly to the play, since they are often shown talking, moving about or eating and drinking while the action proceeds on stage. Special moments called *mie* were designed to evoke approbation: at the climax of a scene the leading actor would stop and, in time with music, strike an exaggerated pose with neck extended and face muscles taut, while members of the audience would cry out his particular nickname called his 'shouting name' (*kakegoe*). Today in Japan Kabuki is likely to occur in proscenium playhouses with upholstered seats, the *hanamichi* leading from the stage to the back of the auditorium. Melodramatic exits are still conducted on the ramp and are still precisely staged to encourage audience reaction. But the *kakegoe* will be shouted by a specially employed person, a member of one of the *kakegoe* guilds, who is assigned for the performance to a specific actor. Three guilds in Tokyo control the practice; connoisseurs of the form, members receive free passes to the show as payment, as nineteenth-century *claqueurs* did in Paris. This procedure is an attenuated and regulated survival from the rough-and-tumble days of earlier Kabuki, and since the shouting name is different from both the actor's stage name and his birth name, *kakegoe* procedures now imply a sophisticated awareness of Kabuki traditions on the part of the audience. Curtain calls are not used (nor are they used in Nō performances) – though they are sometimes added in Kabuki performances given in the West.[4]

No such historical awareness restrains responses to mainstream films in India, according to Srinivas (2002: 155), who notes a 'participatory and interactive style of viewing' in some cinemas. Spectators are likely to 'cheer and whistle, shout out to characters on-screen, throw coins at the screen in appreciative display and sing along with the soundtrack'. They have been known to protest the content of a film by ripping upholstered seating with knives. The 'civilizing process' (Elias 1978) that has rendered public expression of high emotion rare in the West has apparently not affected Bollywood popular audiences, who may carry something of a premodern sensibility into the modernist technology of the cinema.

In the darkened cinemas of the West audiences act differently, usually even more quiescently than those in the playhouse, notwithstanding a relaxed ambience that encourages eating and drinking. Exceptions exist, of course, such as the ebullient mood at camped-up midnight screenings of *The Rocky Horror Picture Show* when spectators costume themselves as characters in the movie, talk back to the screen and quote lines in unison.[5] Spectator behaviour in such a case is imitative, almost ritualistic in its regulation, so that the text of the film is a pretext for the party, but the party is entirely dependent on the text of learned response. This type of audience behaviour, associated with the old Saturday movie serials in the US and Christmas pantomimes in Britain, is generally understood as appropriate for children, whose ignorance of proper etiquette frees them from spectator conventions. But in fact pantos not only encourage raucous behaviour, they actually demand it, build it into the narrative, as those audience-appropriated screenings of *Rocky Horror* now do, as football does and even as Shakespeare performance sometimes does at the new Globe Theatre in London (as we will see in chapter 5). Unconventional audience response can be commodified in the same way that tourist experiences are commodified. Elinor Fuchs (1996) describes popular live shows that accomplish this trick by promoting spectator interactivity in a playful way. *Tony n' Tina's Wedding*, for example, which has run in New York since 1988 and has been seen in over a hundred cities around the world, replicates the environment of an Italian-American wedding. Ticket-buying spectators are treated as invited guests. 'Audience members actually play the roles of Tony n' Tina's family and/or friends', according to the producers, who advise spectators to 'eat, drink, dance, converse and allow yourself to be caught up in the activities'.[6]

The opposite circumstance – audiences refusing to accept a performance as the producers intended – has been seen numerous times in theatre history, often accompanied by riots, and socially coherent audiences continue to assign alternative connotations even to film. An interesting set of cases involves the politics of minority audiences. In a small-scale ethnographic experiment at a homeless men's shelter in a church in an unidentified city in the US, Fiske and Dawson (1996) studied the residents watching a video of *Die Hard*, a melodramatic Hollywood action film of 1988 starring Bruce Willis. The homeless men, well aware of their social outcast state, were interested in the excessive violence of the film when it demonstrates oppositional power. They identified with the bad guys and turned off the TV when the plot moves to punishment and the restoration of the established social order, something they understood all too well and took no pleasure in. The authors cite similar studies of Native American homeless men watching Westerns who switched off at the moment of the Indians' victory, 'thus obliterating the restoration of white colonizing "law" in the second half of the narrative' (304). This conduct is enabled by viewing a private television and is not likely in a public cinema in the West, but the examples do suggest the maintenance of resistant power on the part of spectators, whether they act upon it or not.

Autocratic repressive governments routinely regulate the content and style of entertainments in all modes of delivery, but controlling audience acceptance is another matter altogether. Only the most intrusive of states can exercise absolute rule over public proceedings, as the Chinese Communist Party did during the Cultural Revolution when no more than twelve texts were authorized for live performance. The 'revolutionary modern dramas' (*geming xiandai xi*) approved by Jiang Qing, a former actress who was Mao's wife, were political melodramas intended to certify the rectitude of the state. In a situation where neighbours might inform on neighbours and children on parents, any overt dissent in a theatre gathering would have been impossibly dangerous. It is not surprising that the little evidence available about reception in those desperate years suggests that audiences joined in confirming the spirit of the stage event.

Illustrations of spectator resistance occurred in the East European socialist states in the two decades or so before 1990, when ideologically subversive theatre productions, or moments in productions, sometimes managed to escape censorship through clever performance strategies that were taken by audiences as coded messages. Shakespeare and other classic plays that were admired by the state could be used to convey undercurrents of resistance to authorized ways of thinking, chiefly by non-textual measures. When the news was thoroughly controlled or altered to support the state, as in Czechoslovakia and the German Democratic Republic, the theatre became the location for conveying truth. It is difficult to establish the nature of resistance in actual spectators, since speaking openly would have been contrary to the purpose, but there is general agreement that it occurred. In the 1980s in East Berlin I observed on more than one occasion laughter or applause at unexpected moments that pointed to political defiance in sections of an audience (Kennedy 1990). Of course if audience gestures unanticipated by the censors came to the attention of the police, the producers ran the risk of severe retaliation. In the Soviet Union after Stalinism a certain amount of theatrical resistance was tolerated in alternative theatres as a way of containing dissidence, as in the work of Yuri Lyubimov at the Taganka Theatre in Moscow from 1964 to his exile in 1983. Though some of his productions were heavily censored, Lyubimov's audiences understood the political delicacy of his position and had learned to see through the surface of stage events to surrogate meanings, as with his famous *Hamlet* of 1971 (Golub 1993).

A calculated endeavour to exploit anti-authoritarian spectatorship was devised by the Brazilian Augusto Boal in the context of South American dictatorships, gradually elucidated from the 1970s with different theatre and community organizations around the world. Initially based on his book *Theatre of the Oppressed* (2000, first published in Spanish 1974), Boal's objective was to transform the passive spectator/citizen into an actor/activist – his term is 'spect-actor' – by using interactive theatrical techniques to reveal the nature of oppression. Departing from Brecht's *Lehrstüke*, the procedures have something in common with avant-gardists such as Prampolini, Artaud and Grotowski, but by focussing specifically on the relationship of spectatorship to social action Boal devised methods that can be applied to several political circumstances. First a proposal or model performance about a local issue is presented, then the watchers, working within the same scenario, make changes that affect the protagonist of the narrative. The spect-actors are encouraged to use give-and-take to clarify their own social circumstances. The process marks the spectator position as passive and dominated, while the actor position is active and defiant. Boal sees this vector from compliance to resistance as socially liberating, triggered by the theatrical mode but, crucially, not limited to it. In his phrase it is 'theatre as a rehearsal for change'.

If the theory of the spect-actor were extended further, it would offer the possibility of a merger of watching with performing rather than the sequential process Boal proposes. That raises questions about the division of audience from actor, one of the most persistent and unresolved issues of theatrical modernism. I take up some of the modernist difficulties with reception in the next two chapters, which concern two classic issues of theatre history, the rise of the director near the end of the nineteenth century and the complications of the historical avant-garde at the beginning of the twentieth. In the second part of the book I deal with the politics of watching, with examples from the culture of Shakespeare performance from the start of the Cold War to the present, seen in light of political history, tourism, globalization and the effect of cinema on theatrical performance. A final part deals with the psychology and disposition of the spectator through sport, gambling, game shows and ritual, with an intermezzo on memory and museums.

The further we look the more fluid audience response appears to be. Differences arise from the diversity of performance forms, whether they are live or simulated, whether viewed publicly or privately, from the cultures in which they are situated, from the mental state of individual spectators, their gender and class positions, their ages and relative health, and so on almost to infinity. My examples, whatever their limitations, imply that assisting at the spectacle is not a stable condition but a process of negotiation among the self of the spectator, the other of performance, and a third order, the indistinct but powerful police force of the gathering. Perhaps Certeau's free cats and Foucault's caged dogs are more similar than first appears, and live together.

CHAPTER 2

The director, the spectator and the Eiffel Tower

Though directors have been central to theatre in the European tradition for more than a century, it is not easy to describe their function or explain fully what they do. Since they have not all done similar things, theorizing the office is a dubious enterprise. A director is not actually necessary in the process of making theatre, any more than a playwright is; nonetheless it is hard to imagine the disappearance of directors. Their cultural authority is embedded in the thinking of both the commercial and subsidized sectors in most countries in the world, including many parts of Asia; even if local circumstances determine their importance, directors remain fundamental to the way we comprehend and value theatrical work. Theatrical production in the modern age and beyond has been a complex endeavour: producing plays is an undertaking that calls for aptitude in interpreting texts that are often distant and difficult, for dedicated attention to historical as well as contemporary meanings, for knowledge of psychology and the changing nature of human desire, for an ability to communicate with actors and designers and a host of other skills that are difficult to master, including the skill of coping with budgets of both the financial and calendar kind. Yet the director, as Delgado and Heritage (1996: 1) note, 'is still a strangely undefined and shifting role with a range of responsibilities that require someone who is an artist, philosopher, actor, pedagogue, procurer, coach, linguist, midwife, technician, and administrator'. We might add literary critic to the list. Contemporary figures describe directing in such varied ways as 'cooking, shopping, deciphering, conducting, cultivating bacteria, giving birth and tossing salads'. No matter if we consider directors the creators of a distinctive art form, or simply enunciatory managers subject to communal forces, the director stands as the icon of the successes and failures of modern theatre. But despite their centrality, very little attention has been paid to what directing means on the social or cultural level, and especially what it means to the spectator.

NEGOTIATING MODERNITY

During the course of the past century a portion of the authority of the writer and the actor was transferred to the figure of the director through a variety of historical circumstances, some engineered by directors themselves, some following from increasingly sophisticated scenography and technology that require highly specialized knowledge to control and aestheticize. It may seem odd that in the era of the death of the author the power of the stage director should grow greater, but, to paraphrase Mark Twain, the report of the author's death was always an exaggeration. The high status of both author and director relies on the concept of the individual subject which never disappeared from the art industries or the popular imagination. How directors gained the power to establish or control the aesthetic and social experience of the theatre is a complex historical issue. It is normally explained by detailing the growing demands of realistic and naturalistic production in Europe and North America after 1850, the spectacular demands of both romantic and urban melodrama and, crucially, the rise of a theatrical avant-garde in the 1890s that emulated the avant-garde in literature and the visual arts and wished to transform the nature of the spectator's experience. In this narrative the significant assumption was that modernist approaches – most clearly formulated by Edward Gordon Craig – were fundamentally conceptual and scenographic, based on the need for a controlling eye to forge the messy aspects of theatrical production into the unified vision associated with a painter or sculptor. In a thoroughly masculinist manner, the director was proposed as a subjective master who was not required to justify technique or purpose, which were subsumed into the larger enterprise of creating novelty, coherence and formal exactitude.

But it is not so simple, surely; the standard treatment is particularly flawed in its tendency to underplay larger social issues. Patrice Pavis (1992: 171) gives us a broader understanding. The introduction of the director, he writes, 'is linked to the historical development of western culture: the decline of classical performance traditions, the disappearance of a strong form, the culmination of a bourgeois individualistic tradition, the formulation of a theory of the subject and the author, in this instance the stage subject'. That list is a useful countermeasure to accounts that focus on discrete aesthetic innovation, particularly the reminder that the director as controller was enabled by the retreat of traditional theatrical styles and the enlightenment idea of the bourgeois subject. These conditions paralleled the development of European capitalism and were requisite to it. To put this succinctly, we might see the director not as a creation of modernism but rather as a logical result of modernity.

What do I mean by modernity? In a history of modern art T. J. Clark (1999: 7) writes that we use the term in an easy way assuming that

> most readers know it when they see it. 'Modernity' means contingency. It points to a social order which has turned from the worship of ancestors and past authorities to the pursuit of a projected future – of goods, pleasures, freedoms, forms of control over nature, or infinities of information.

Clark defines modernity not by recourse to an industrial or economic model but to a temporal one, a 'projected future' that involves commerce (goods) but implies personal freedoms and satisfactions. We can direct this to the theatre by saying that when there is no longer a dominant sense of what performance should look and sound like, because there is no longer a hegemonic conception of the social or spiritual purpose of the theatre, then the way is open for a self-defined style or fashion or method from someone with the talent to make it and a theatrical institution willing to endorse it, always aimed at a free-floating idea of the spectator as consumer. Add to this an expanding discourse from Paris concerning oppositional movements in painting, sculpture and photography, starting as early as the 1860s, and the ground was prepared for a genetically modified art production. I think that is what happened in the last third of the nineteenth century as Europe pointed itself toward imperial capitalism: the director filled the space left vacant when the old gods of theatre departed, driven away by the ascent of the long run and the attendant decline of the repertory system in the major centres. Behind it all, of course, was the huge urbanization of audiences that enlarged opportunities in the theatrical marketplace and that transformed the class basis of spectatorship. In areas where the old system continued side-by-side with the new, as in central Europe, it did so only through direct intervention by royal or state power.

Much of subsequent theatrical experimentation and change has been at the urging of stage directors, who soon began to function as authors of productions. This was possible because early modernist directors insisted on relatively lengthy periods of rehearsal under their express supervision, during which the problematics of theatrical collaboration could be renegotiated. It is revealing that, with the great exception of Meyerhold, most major auteuristic directors have tended to foreground those aspects of production immediately in their control, such as mise-en-scène and conceptual framework, rather than the more collaborative elements of acting or spectator response. Similarly, after the wave of playwrights' theatres before the First World War, few star directors have founded their careers working with living authors, whose superior status in copyright law jeopardizes the director's power. From this standpoint the director might be considered 'a sign of the weakness and decline of the modern stage', as Peter Stein puts it; or, as Declan Donnellan says, a necessary evil (Delgado and Heritage 1996: 8, 11). It is a bit disingenuous for major directors like these to be so self-deprecating, but following from that my first task is to offer a revised analysis of the office of the director as developing from another consequence of modern capitalism. My major point is that directors, despite the aestheticist traditions of modernism, can be seen as inheritors of nineteenth-century industry, both the theatre industry and the manufacturing industry. As such their task was to attract spectators while at the same time denying they were pandering to the public.

HISTORIES OF THE MODERN

Make It New, advised Ezra Pound, tersely summarizing the central myth or *grand récit* of modernism. There have been a number of modernisms, of course, but in its early theatrical form modernism found the director a godsend whose interventions provided a method for limiting the multiple possibilities of scripts and styles into a synthetic order – paradoxically called 'organic' – that was plausible in the moment. The dominance of theatrical modernism was assured by the loss of the popular audience to film; what began as an elite bourgeois alternative to the regular play-houses, between the wars became the elite bourgeois mainstream. But its ascendancy came about also because of its own discourse, since from the start modernism included both 'art practice and a way of thinking about it' (Wood 1999: 12). Until fairly recently most histories of modern theatre have complied with modernist values, a move probably influenced by art history (and well articulated for modernism in general by Puchner 2005). Characterizing the trend in the 1960s and 1970s was a series of structuralist approaches from the United States that proposed the rise of the director as an evolutionary inevitability: the introduction to Cole and Chinoy's *Directors on Directing* (1963), Brockett and Findlay's *Century of Innovation* (1973) and Eric Bentley's *The Theory of the Modern Stage* (1976). Because they rely on documents written by modernist directors and designers, they tend to conflate manifestos with practice: what the theorists said should happen was taken as what did happen, even when it did not. Further, they underestimate the significance of the director in the commercial or mainstream theatre. Read by three generations of drama students, these volumes codified modernist doctrine as the primary and proper message of the twentieth century, leaving no doubt that the director was the necessary force behind theatrical innovation.

But if we ask questions about innovation we are likely to get different answers than if we enquire about continuity. For example, if we take the standard view that Duke Georg of Saxe-Meiningen was the first true director in European theatre because he neither wrote nor acted in his productions and controlled all their elements, we are underplaying the facts that he was chiefly interested in fixing a conceptual interpretation by means of design, did not supervise rehearsals and left most of the details to his stage manager, Ludwig Chronegk, whom he elevated to Intendant of the court theatre in 1884. From 1871 it had been Chronegk who actualized the mise-en-scène, accompanied the Meiningen Players on those tours that influenced Irving, Brahm, Antoine and Stanislavsky and hired and arranged supernumeraries into the crowd scenes that are often cited as Georg's major contribution. Georg was proceeding not so much as a modern director as a theatre owner in the German tradition of Franz von Dingelstedt, while removing himself from the daily operations not appropriate for a prince. We can see Georg as a modern director only by intellectual back-formation, though it must be admitted that he originated the *idea* of the director and the integrated production.

Similarly, in recounting the rise of symbolist theatre in Paris in the 1890s it is insufficiently noted that Aurélien Lugné-Poe, the director of Théâtre de l' Œuvre, played in most of his own productions in the actor-manager tradition. The mise-en-scène was hardly the unified whole of the later modernist ideal, since on stage Lugné-Poe 'favored a long frockcoat with a high, stiff collar buttoned under the chin, no matter what the production' (Carlson 1972: 212); additionally 'guest actors would not always follow their director's style'. Frantisek Deak (1993: 217) notes that 'the semantic gesture' of Lugné-Poe's productions 'derived not from a director' but chiefly from 'symbolist poetic concepts'. Granville Barker acted in his own productions from 1900 to 1911, sometimes even in scripts he had written. And Stanislavsky, who taught the twentieth century how to rehearse by defining the director as an objective and independent coach for actors, acted major roles in most of his own stagings from 1898 to 1915: Løvborg in *Hedda Gabler*, Ivan in *Ivan the Terrible*, Stockmann in *The Enemy of the People*, Satin in *Lower Depths*, Ratikin in *Month in the Country*, Argan in *The Imaginary Invalid*, Salieri in *Mozart and Salieri*, the list goes on. Most significantly he took leading parts in all four of the Chekhov productions through which he defined the Moscow Art Theatre, Trigorin in *Seagull*, Astrov in *Uncle Vanya*, Vershinin in *Three Sisters* and Gaev in *Cherry Orchard* (the playwright wanted him to play Lopakin, but Stanislavsky found the role too coarse for his refined directorly self). In truth it was the customary practice of the actor-manager or owner-manager that dominated early modernist practice until after the First World War. Meyerhold was again an exception: he stopped acting in his mainstage productions after 1908.

In fetishizing the new, modernist histories also tend to underplay how useful the director was to commercial theatre. On the deeply industrialized stages of the United States, it can be argued that the director had appeared in the last quarter of the nineteenth century, well before modernist reforms reached those shores. Since the plays favoured by the Theatrical Syndicate and other theatre trusts demanded growingly precise realizations, 'the old-fashioned acting manager who kept order, marked positions, and arranged the constantly changing repertory lost his authority as touring companies and long runs became the prevalent mode of production.' The commercial side demanded closer control; the trusts forced traditional actor-managers out of business so that financial imperatives joined with the realist aesthetic in finding the director useful. 'Specialists in production were needed to process shows' because the trusts were omnivorous in their desire to supply the market. Thus the first professional directors in America 'did not think of themselves as masters of a distinctive art'; they were journeymen workers in a trade (Chinoy 1971: 129–32). Intriguingly, long after the triumph of modernism directors in the commercial theatre were still being accused of invidious industrial practice. Norris Houghton, speaking of the 1940 Broadway season, held that 'most of our good directors today are like able locomotive engineers, whose first job is to keep the train on the tracks and whose second is to bring it in on time' (in Carra 1971: 160).

THE EIFFEL TOWER

I am not proposing that the reformers in the late nineteenth and early twentieth centuries were creating the same type of work as the commercial theatres or appealing to the same audiences. Nonetheless the first modernist directors were closer in function than they would admit to the commercial theatres they wished to reform or supersede. The admiration of Chronegk and Craig for Henry Irving is a well-known example.

Another admirer of Irving will be my case study: André Antoine, whose first moves in 1887 in acting and mise-en-scène already seemed to demand all-embracing control. Yet up to 1906, both at the Théâtre Libre and the Théâtre Antoine, he behaved virtually as an actor-manager. He effectively owned both companies, organized the repertory and the casting, designed the settings, performed in almost every production and in the bills of short plays generally in every separate piece. It is true that he often took small roles, but if his intention was to deny the custom of the actor-manager the effect was counter-productive: as Jean Chothia (1991) notes, the audience was disconcerted because out of habit they assumed the small parts had a larger significance and looked for a plot turn that would reveal their covert substance. Antoine and a number of the other early directors in Europe differed from actor-managers less in their exercise of control than in their institutional position and the conception of the production as an artistic synthesis.

Yet whether or not we now consider Antoine a part of the Parisian avant-garde, for his audiences, both hostile and friendly, he was clearly at variance with the regular theatres. Like Zola he was engaged in a major social project that, despite attempts to make the stage the location of the actual, was not limited to a literal naturalism. In fact those infamous sides of real beef in *Les Bouchers* and the working jet of water in the fountain in *Chevalerie Rustique*, which startled spectators in 1888 with their immediacy and caused a minor scandal, were intensely troubling for naturalist theory, especially considering that *Les Bouchers* is written in verse. Antoine (1921: 117) complained that people came to see the novelty effects and not the plays, just as Reinhardt would later complain that his audiences were interested above all in the real trees on stage in *A Midsummer Night's Dream* (Kennedy 2001: 66–7). Neither director seemed to understand that extreme examples of actuality only increase the gap between the physical sign and its basic referent, exemplifying how easily breakdowns of transmission can occur between director and spectator, especially when novelty is foregrounded in an avant-garde manner.

Despite the convenience of the term *avant-garde*, the idea of an advance army of artists charging into battle is hopelessly flawed; as Baudelaire noted, writers who use military metaphors appeal to a belligerence they would quickly dodge from if it became actual.[1] The self-regenerating avant-garde was another of the heroic impossibilities of modernism, like the belief in inevitable social progress or the self-deception that one could innocently use the processes of modernity to critique modernity. I will leave this complicated issue for the next chapter, except to repeat Clark's notion that the true history of the avant-garde is the history of those who escaped from it. Definitely applicable to Antoine. Instead I wish to consider Antoine's early work as an example of the connection of the Parisian avant-garde to industrial development.

In his second full season at the Théâtre Libre, Paris was thoroughly occupied with another series of innovations, the 1889 Exhibition Universaire. Like the fairs in London and Paris that had preceded it, the world exhibition was calculated to show its host country magnificently endowed with material and industrial wealth and that its commerce placed it in the rank of the great imperial nations. 'World exhibitions are places of pilgrimage to the commodity fetish', wrote Benjamin (1999: 7); they 'glorify the exchange value of the commodity.' The chosen year celebrated the centenary of the storming of the Bastille. After the defeat of the Second Empire in the Franco-Prussian War in 1870 France became a republic again, at a time when most European countries were still monarchies. The exhibition organizers sought to justify the Revolution by creating an unprecedented display of republican modernity, and mandated that pavilions be built only of the progressive materials of iron or steel. Among the marvels was the Galerie des Machines, with its 110-metre single-span roof, the longest ever. Its contents included the latest bicycles, displays of electrical lighting, telephones, Edison's phonograph and other models of industrial strength.

But it was the tower designed and engineered by Alexandre Gustave Eiffel that proved the most remarkable innovation, 300 metres high, by far the tallest man-made structure in history, not topped until the completion of the Chrysler Building in New York in 1930. As a celebration of the Revolution and of French industrial might the tower was unparalleled, and within a very short time it became synonymous with Paris, transforming its physical and mental landscape. It is not often remembered that it was built so that it could be dismantled twenty years later – the fate of the Galerie des Machines – or that it was violently hated. Guy de Maupassant, one of the many artists who signed a protest in *Le Temps* in February 1887 against the plans, later used to lunch at one of the tower's restaurants, even though he did not much care for the food: 'It's the only place in Paris', he liked to say, 'where I don't have to see it.' As Roland Barthes notes in a famous essay, the Eiffel Tower, 'an object when we look at it, becomes a lookout in its turn when we visit it'; it is 'an utterly *useless* monument' and therefore a 'pure signifier, i.e., of a form in which men unceasingly put *meaning*...without this meaning thereby ever being finite and fixed' (Barthes 1997: 3, 5).

The tower thus achieves its glory not because it is empty of meaning but because it has the meaning of pure display – a work of silent theatre. It was built without any purpose other than to demonstrate that it could be built. It was and is a show, and from its height the cityscape is a show. Its relationship to visitors is always touristic and always spectatorial. Like the theatre of perspective, it is based on visual illusion, in that its graceful curves are created entirely from straight sections of iron beams bolted together (if you want to know, by two and a half million rivets), the original Meccano or Erector set. In the first year almost two million visitors took the lifts to the top, making a theatre out of the city; for the first time Paris became 'a map of itself' (Hughes 1991: 12, 14). If we cease thinking of it as a signifier, empty or not, and accept it as a performance of iron, we might see it as utterly non-representational. It stands for nothing other than itself. Of course one can imagine all sorts of meanings, as Barthes says, from a symbol of industry to a rupture of the Parisian skyline, but these meanings do not derive from a specific referent, much less a mandatory one.

The exhibition planners expected the tower to lose money but it rapidly recovered its costs and continues to make a profit, with an average of over 5,000 tourists a day, the longest theatrical run in history. It has more visitors per year than the Louvre, even though the tower does nothing and contains nothing, aside from restaurants and gift shops. It has resisted many attempts – some by Eiffel himself – to adapt it to practical purposes, except as a broadcast standard, though clever entrepreneur that he was, Eiffel helped finance it by selling broken and spare parts to a firm making its mementos and models. He was a scientist and engineer with no artistic pretensions, but the tower in 1889 was the greatest avant-garde project yet produced. Its construction materials dictated its form, denying the relationship between mass and space which had been the basis of monumental construction from the beginning of human time, the adamant ontology of iron fusing with an optimism about the transformative power of the machine. Architectural aesthetic thereafter became synonymous with the industrial, and the tower became a subject for avant-garde painters and photographers while still under construction. Hugely improbable, desperately naïve, it was the most heroic achievement of early modernism, designed above all to overwhelm its spectators.

The building of the tower framed Antoine's early work. Its plans were published in the month before the opening production at the Théâtre Libre, which took place on 30 March 1887. The most notable of the short pieces of that soirée was an adaptation of Zola's *Jacques Damour*, about a communard who 'returns after the amnesty to find his child is dead and that his wife, believing him drowned, has remarried' (Chothia 1991: 7). The play used only the story's characters and structure, creating a fifteen-minute skeleton of emotion that required much more spectatorial participation than Zola's original. Despite famously putting his mother's furniture on stage and turning his back to the audience, *Jacques Damour* did not have the trappings of scenic completeness that marked Antoine's later work on stage and in film. In 1887, partly out of financial necessity, suggestion was everything, the props in Antoine's promptbook noted precisely as only '2 coffee cups on round table' and '1 bottle of wine and 4 glasses on buffet'. As Henry James wrote of the London tour, 'when the appointments are meagre and sketchy . . . the spectators' observations of the way [the actors] rise to [their challenge becomes] a pleasure more intense' (Chothia 1991: 7–8). Like Eiffel's plans for the tower, Antoine was working with framework alone, drawing the spectator into a visible world through buoyant evocation. And like Seurat's small painting of the incomplete tower (1889, illustration 1), Antoine used a pointillist technique that attempted to reconcile 'the idealist tradition with scientism'.[2] He shared the desire to alter and control audience perception with the Parisian avant-garde painters, but participated just as much in the goal of Parisian mercantile industry, materials in both cases visibly dictating form.

Exactly two years after *Jacques Damour*, at 1.30 on Sunday afternoon 31 March 1889, Eiffel climbed 1,710 steps to the third level of his frame and unfurled the tricolour to a twenty-one-gun salute. Twelve days before that Antoine unveiled his own revolutionary commemoration, a play called *La Patrie en danger*, at the Menus-Plaisirs on Boulevard Strasbourg, a pleasant walk of an hour and a bit from the tower. Written by the Goncourt brothers in 1867, it had been rejected by the Comédie Française as politically unacceptable to the Second Empire and waited twenty-two years for performance. *The Motherland in Danger* presents a series of five episodes from the fall of the Bastille in 1789 to Danton's attack on the Tuileries in 1792. Anticipating docudrama, it relies on records, transcripts, letters and actual speeches, though structured conventionally as a political melodrama and with some tedious monologues. Antoine was aware of its limitations and placed his hopes on the mise-en-scène, ideas for which he borrowed from the international theatre industry: from Irving's *Macbeth*, which he had seen in London a month before, and from the Meiningen tour to Brussels of the previous July. Antoine intended the crowd scenes to carry the weight of the production, and despite the

Illustration 1 Georges Seurat, *The Eiffel Tower* (oil on panel, 1889)

poverty of his company he managed to get 200 extras on stage. He arranged them as groups of individuals rather than a single mass, spilling out into the wings, implying the circulation of fictive life offstage. He lit individual faces in the crowd with spots during extended speeches, so that the attention of the audience would be directed to the social effects of great political events.

The crucial matter, however, was rehearsal. He wrote to Edmond de Goncourt that he intended to rehearse the crowds 'some ten or fifteen times' (Chothia 1991: 68), a considerable deviation from the French custom of hiring the unemployed or underemployed from the street for a few hours on the day of performance. In practice he normally dealt with 80 extras at a time, breaking them into units of a dozen, each with an experienced actor as leader, and then blended the full complement of 200 in dress rehearsals. The demands of directing massive crowds, of constructing individual extras into a graceful curve, meant that, most unusually, he could not afford to perform himself – too much ordering was needed, too much industry-like attention to detail – so the company's second actor, Auguste Mévisto, took the leading role and the director worked with the players and as many of the extras as possible until well after midnight for a month, damaging his bronchial tubes in the process, according to Goncourt. Antoine 'used a foreman's whistle to train the crowd to quick responses', at one point even firing a pistol shot to show how a 'disparate rabble would respond as one to a sudden sound'. The mass spectacle worked well but Paris did not care for the play itself and the planned twenty-five performances were reduced to five, leaving him with a large deficit (Braun 1982: 32). Despite the lack of public success, his contribution to the World Exhibition became, like the Eiffel Tower, a celebration of modern efficiency, a Taylorian experiment, bolting together a production made up of supernumerary workers and a text made up of fragments. Early in the history of directing, Antoine's work demonstrated that the centrality of directors to theatre would be ensured by their industrial effectiveness.

SYMBOLS AND SPECTATORS

And by their effectiveness in commerce. The avant-garde Paris directors made a point out of their separation from the boulevard theatres (which were entirely commercial) and the official theatres (subsidized by the state and managed by bureaucrats, like the Opéra and the Comédie Française). Economically the distinction was manifestly correct. The financial existence of independent companies was always precarious; Antoine funded his initial productions out of his salary as a clerk in the gas company, and within a few years had incurred substantial personal debt. He never managed to make a living from running the Théâtre Libre, which remained a part-time avocation for the seven years of its life. I pick this up in the next chapter side by side with the theory of the avant-garde. For now I want to stress a related issue about consumerism and stage signification. From Robert Jensen (1994) we learn a good deal about how early modernist painting was established as a respectable category and marketed in Europe, though its artists often managed to appear disdainful of commerce. Sally Debra Charnow (2005) has usefully applied Jensen's insights to the marketing undertaken by Antoine and his colleagues, revealing in the process how the social and economic conditions of Paris at the end of the century were altering class positions. Antoine (born 1858) and Lugné-Poe (born 1869) were sons of clerks who had no land or shops to bequeath them; free of established ties, whether peasant or bourgeois, they were without a stake in the past. Their promotion, were it to come, would be through education and breaking with their fathers' occupations (19). In accomplishing this feat through the theatre, they used the most important tool of consumer capitalism, novelty or innovation.

They were also the children of Haussmannization, which in the 1850s and 1860s took the pickaxe to great swathes of medieval Paris, areas occupied by decrepit tenements long the province of the poor, to make way for the grand boulevards of the Second Empire. In addition to facilitating traffic to the rail stations, and precluding rebellious barricades in the narrow medieval streets, Baron Haussmann's civic remodelling gave Paris 'a distinctly middle-class, commercial character' (23). Between 1853 and 1870 Haussmann's projects, with the full support of Napoleon III, forced as many as 50,000 working-class citizens out of the centre. Nonetheless the total population of the city continued to grow, expanded by lower middle-class workers who were gaining wealth. The rising petits bourgeois – clerks, salaried employees, government functionaries – were transforming the social aspects of the capital as well. Between 1880 and 1914, for example, the circulation of the daily press grew by 250 per cent, reflecting the increase in literacy and the interest this population took in their surroundings, and attendance at all types of theatres rose greatly, as in London. Curtain times grew later to accommodate working hours, advancing from 5.30 or 6.30 p.m. in 1840 to 8.00 or 9.00 in 1885, further persuaded by Haussmann's civic lighting scheme which made the streets safer for pedestrians (Hemmings 1993: 48). The new social group began to displace the traditional bourgeoisie in cultural significance, providing new literati interested in innovation in the arts.

It was to them that Antoine directed the Théâtre Libre. His marketing tactics were a clever exploitation of their desire for cultural improvement and personal betterment. Since the enterprise was not licensed for public attendance and could not sell tickets in the normal manner, Antoine made his first evening's bill free to all, and worked hard to ensure the presence of a number of notables, including Zola. His gamble paid off in esteem if not in money; the success of the Théâtre Libre, guaranteed by an excited press, had been made possible by a marketing strategy that loudly proclaimed it was placing art above commerce. Antoine's procedure was parallel to that of the impressionist painters, who, having been rejected by the Salon jury, set up their first group show in 1874 to the grave annoyance of journalists and the ordinary public ('impressionism' was a term of abuse coined by a hostile critic). Though subsequently framed by a discourse that continued to oppose art and money, in fact the impressionists succeeded in establishing 'an elite showcase for their art' (Jensen 1994: 89). Over the next dozen years similar impressionist exhibitions created a market for oppositional work by refusing to market it in the traditional way, thereby appealing to the growing public intrigued by the new. The 1874 Salon des Indépendants, which included early work of Monet, Renoir, Pissarro, Degas and Cézanne, pictured modernity through bold colours and forms suggesting direct (i.e. non-academic) experience felt 'instantaneously' (without apparent reflection), a major rupture of the traditions of nineteenth-century painting, a model for the rupture Antoine sought in his initial years as a director.

The relationship of innovation to art is a complex historical one, and certainly was not created by modernism, but novelty achieved new value in the industrial age. For citizen-consumers novelty meant technological advance, plain to see in the mills of the towns and the architecture of the city and in the canals, railways and ships that connected them. In a world becoming saturated with images and objects, novelty promised consumerist satisfaction, ever illusive and thus ever in need of rejuvenation. Novelty contributed to the economic and social betterment of citizens of major nations, prompted nationalist pride and colonial adventures, themselves contributing in turn to the cycle of manufacture and sale of goods. Finally, novelty encouraged a sense of the importance of style and fashion in the rising classes. Consumer capitalism today operates along the same social lines, ever-expanding markets, competition and product innovation. But Paris, Benjamin's 'capital of the nineteenth century', the crucible of international modernism, was from the 1870s the particular home of novelty in literature, architecture, painting and theatre.

By attending in his early work to the exact details of daily life as perceived by his spectators, Antoine established one of the most important lines of authority for a director, the authentic display of environments that act upon the world as normally perceived and sometimes conceal it. Even when he turned to a quasi-symbolist mise-en-scène, as with *The Wild Duck* of 1891, it was precision of stage image (along with ensemble acting) that most distinguished his productions at the Théâtre Libre. His stylistic eclecticism, Charnow suggests (2005: 34), was itself 'a marketing strategy to build a potential audience', on the one hand refusing to restrict himself to a single fashion or single segment of the population and on the other appealing to the existing eclecticism of the bourgeois marketplace. As early as the 1850s the etiquette and fashion writer Constance Aubert promoted the notion of eclectic consumerism for women and the household, arguing that 'the free mingling of styles of all eras distinguished the modern middle-class home from the uniform period style of the aristocrat's *hôtel particulier*' (Charnow 34). Antoine and the other Paris directors, emphasizing the particularity of signs as commodities in themselves, were part of a larger reformation of social status.

Consumerist concerns led in a straight line to another persistent issue of modernism, also with its origins in Paris, the uncertain status of visual signifiers. The mixture of aesthetic novelty with the new bourgeois society was already apparent in Manet's *Le Déjeuner sur l'herbe* (1863, illustration 2), a classically inspired treatment of couples on a picnic. Two men in conversation are dandily dressed, one woman in a shift in the centre background bathes in a small pond, while the second woman, who has abandoned her clothes, sits by the men but alone stares at the spectator. It is easy enough to create a narrative for this, as Zola did, explaining that the second woman's nudity is justified because she has finished bathing and is drying her body in the air.[3] But that is not a necessary explanation, nor does it explain her gaze. The shocked reactions of the public had less to do with the sexuality of the image – which appears entirely lacking in concupiscence – and more to do with the uncertainty of the picture's meaning. Manet's *Olympia* at the regular Salon two years later was even more notable, the nude prostitute's celebrated stare displacing 'the spectator from his accustomed imaginary possession of the work' (Clark 1984: 79–80) and causing, a contemporary critic wrote, daily disturbances, 'laughter, mockery, and catcalls' among its original crush of viewers. The impressionists openly fastened upon this idea,

Illustration 2 Edouard Manet, *Le Déjeuner sur l'herbe* (oil on canvas, 1863)

regularly distorting nature and objects in order to disrupt the relationship of vision to conventional signification. During the period of the Théâtre Libre, Georges Seurat, with *A Sunday Afternoon on the Island of La Grande Jatte* (1886), another picture about bourgeois leisure, and *The Eiffel Tower* (illustration 1), a picture that idealizes industrial development, worked with points of colour to form a beautiful 'essence of things' not apparent to the unmediated eye. Seurat forced impressionism into abolition by isolating the meaning of the thing from its sign.

In the theatre, Ibsen provided realist and symbolist plays with visions of social and psychological circumstances activated by a textually determined mise-en-scène. His work appealed to the early naturalists because it offered extended opportunities to alter the way spectators viewed stage action through images of clarified reality. The symbolist directors, departing from the naturalist mode, sought images that were evocations of the ineffable. They also drew upon Ibsen but the textual guide was the medieval mist in Maeterlinck. These fabrications of alterity were matters of great significance for the theatrical avant-garde because they suggested

a reformed experience of spectation. Though the text of *Ubu roi* is more
satiric than symbolist, Jarry's work supervising the direction and design in
the 1896 production at the Théâtre de l'Œuvre provided the clearest
example of how adjusting the nature of stage representation could alter
the nature of spectator experience. I presume this is what W. B. Yeats
(1953: 210) felt at that famous dress rehearsal, half riot and half laughter,
when he worried that the final result of poetic reverie and symbolism
would be the descent of 'the Savage God' he had glimpsed on stage.
Watching the actors playing as 'dolls, toys, marionettes' and 'hopping
like wooden frogs', with Firmin Gémier waving a toilet brush as Ubu's
sceptre, Yeats was reacting to a shift in performance consciousness
brought about by radical manipulation of signifiers.

    Though they disagreed about what constituted reality, the naturalists
and the symbolists were closer in approach than the rigorous discourse of
the time would suggest. Both experimented with assigning reality-
meaning to unconventional symbols. I said above that Antoine complained that spectators were overly fascinated with his working fountain
and sides of beef. 'It was an entire meat stall', said one journalist of *Les
Bouchers* in 1888 (Charnow 2005: 87). Like Zola, Antoine hoped that his
extreme examination of representational images would suggest the
proximity of the ordinary to the tragic, the one infusing the other. He
expected the naturalist mise-en-scène, even the meticulous reproduction
of a well-known Paris café in act 1 of *Boubouroche* (1893), to be taken *as
reality*, with the same quotidian unremarkability (illustration 3). But what
his spectators saw were novelty effects of such power that the ramifica-
tions were excluded. The signifiers were so greatly innovative that they
destroyed the intended objectives. On one level this only underlines the
well-rehearsed idea that the ordinary on stage is never the ordinary of life,
and that material signs are never entirely free of interpretive misdirection.
But on a deeper level it suggests that the modernist desire to guide
reception by means of the unconventional or unexpected could disengage
the audience's competence entirely.

    The problem of the relationship of art to reality was more urgent for
the symbolist directors. Since they sought to conjure on stage the mystical
and unutterable, they had to rely on indistinct or imprecise symbols that
hinted but could not index. Lugné-Poe did not possess the stage technology nor the directing skill to accomplish this with conviction, but for
the plays of Maeterlinck and Ibsen in the 1890s he found silence and
emptiness to be salient substitutes. The director encouraged a very slow

Illustration 3 The reproduction of the café in Antoine's production of *Boubouroche*, as revived at the Théâtre Antoine, Paris 1897 (originally produced 1893)

delivery and long pauses, a somnambulist style, that wished to release spectators from the mundane. In the opening production of the Théâtre de l'Œuvre in 1893, Maeterlinck's *Pelléas et Mélisande*, the dim lighting from above, grey mask-like makeup, and costumes that blended with the scenery caused the critic Sarcey to describe the actors as 'creatures from a dream' (in Charnow 2005: 112), the exact effect the playwright wished. But Sarcey derided the style as impossibly pretentious, as did others in print and volubly in the house. Segments of the audience were not prepared to accept such an extreme redefinition of theatrical signs, any more than segments of Antoine's audience could accept the naturalist mode without bother. Unintentionally, the naturalists and the symbolists both relocated the referent for stage signifiers away from the back and towards the front: they detached the sign from its representational purpose and displayed it to the spectator *as absolute symbol*.

For the outrageous spectator this was ideal. Deak (1993: 250) notes how the followers of symbolism, men and women alike, flaunted dandyist versions of themselves in public. Some came to the theatre in medieval costumes, some as romantics, some as heroes or heroines from Wagner or Maeterlinck. Women copied dresses from the paintings of the Pre-Raphaelites, Puvis de Chavanne or Moreau. In Deak's words:

The symbolist actor, devoid of all traces of individuality and personality, ideally a depersonalized sign, was gazed upon by individuals with an overabundance of personality: an audience that dressed and behaved very much like fictional dramatic characters ... Viewed in traditional terms, the acting, even in some sense 'the theatre,' [was] happening in the auditorium instead of the stage.

This was an unexpected development of theatrical modernism directly connected to the world of the *flâneur*, the world of taste and style and leisure exhibited through clothing, attitude, domestic objects and other consumer items displayed publicly, that so fascinated Walter Benjamin. Dislocating the stage from its reality referent, a result that could be achieved only through the director's newly assumed power, both Antoine and Lugné-Poe participated in the advance of the bourgeois subject in a world in which the display of material objects and personal style had become a crucial mark of the self.

THE PERSISTENCE OF MODERNISM

Avant-garde theatres by definition rarely last long. They disappear through spectator neglect or lack of resources or the fatigue of their founders, their most useful reforms becoming absorbed into the larger theatrical establishment. The moment of the Théâtre Libre was over by 1894, that of the Théâtre de l'Œuvre by 1899, both driven out of business after a few years through debt. Of course future directors continued to create innovations in theatre practice, though revolutionary ones like Meyerhold or Reinhardt have been rare. Most good directors may ultimately be just good amalgamators, drivers keeping the train on the tracks. Whether with the flow or against it, the innovations of directors are always bound by the current theatrical apparatus, as Brecht pointed out, which is normally local in nature. Indeed Meyerhold and Reinhardt were successful because in very different ways they responded magnificently to modernisms tied to rapidly changing social and political circumstances. Trade issues like systems of finance, theatre organization, actor training and unionization, along with shifting audience majorities and the incursions of mass media, establish the base on which the superstructure of directing must operate. So my alternative history is not so much a replacement for the received view of the director as a counterpart to it. For example, when we note that the greatest influences on directing in the second half of the twentieth century came from writings in the first half by Craig, Copeau, Artaud and Brecht, we should also note that none of them actually directed very much or for very long, and, with the exception of Brecht, when they did direct often encountered reluctance to their strategies from actors or hesitations from the theatre industry.

If we are to have artists of the theatre, Craig insisted, we must allow the individualist director to proceed unabated. But directors including Craig seldom exercised Craigian power unless they also exercised managerial control as producers or artistic directors, replicating the condition of the nineteenth-century actor-manager. The growth of institutionalized theatres after 1945 boosted the general authority of directors more than their artistic accomplishments; the careers of Giorgio Strehler, Jean Vilar, Roger Planchon, Peter Stein, Yuri Lyubimov, Peter Hall and Trevor Nunn are inconceivable without the subsidized companies they led. Their theatres incidentally made a place for star directors who did not wish to be managers, such as Peter Brook before 1970. In general, the higher the subsidy the more authority granted to the director as auteur; protected from the box office the director is free to become an artistic dictator. Some organizations, accepting avant-garde doctrine, continued the tradition of the director in the heroic mould. Here is Charles Marowitz, writing as late as 1986 (xvi):

Anyone who denies the power drives of the director . . . is deluding himself. The director is a self-obsessed colonizer who wishes to materialize power through harnessing and shaping the powers of others.

Authoritarian modes of direction have been increasingly challenged by collaborative developments, the autobiographical and body-based procedures of performance art, and co-directing and other strategies that have emerged from feminist interventions. Perhaps the coercive and aesthetically subjective traditions of the director inherited from high modernism are waning. But though notions of mastery and unity may be in retreat, directors have retained much of their force; it is a great irony that the diversity, eclecticism and cultural inclusion of what is usually called postmodern performance often require even more aesthetic management, as in the productions of Robert Wilson, Frank Castorf, Jan Fabre, Reza Abdoh or Elizabeth Lecompte.

Even the interventions of collaborative theatre, devised theatre and physical theatre, which propose democratic or team-based models of organization, have not fundamentally affected the authority of the director. This can be destabilizing for the spectator, who is given conflicting messages about artistic control. Ariane Mnouchkine took the same salary as the rest of the members of the Théâtre du Soleil and was seen by spectators to share the cooking and sweeping, but no one doubts that she was the leader of the pack. Other unconventional troupes follow similar patterns: Simon McBurney of Complicité, Robert Lepage of Ex Machina, Romeo Castellucci of Socìetas Raffaello Sanzio, Ong Keng Sen of Theatreworks Singapore, all have placed unmistakable personal stamps on their allegedly collaborative companies. As Joanne Akalaitis said, 'there is no such thing as a totally open collaborative situation, and at some point in the directing process you're in a position where something needs to happen that cannot happen by direct appeal' (in Bartow 1988: 9). In fact postdramatic theatre places more stress on the office of the director, whose responsibility might now include domains formerly in the hands of the playwright or designer. In such a circumstance it is hard to maintain a fully collaborative structure. As Lev Dodin said of his ensemble at the Maly Theatre in St Petersburg, 'I may consider myself to be the father of the family but some actors may think of me as a son of a bitch' (Delgado and Heritage 1996: 73).

But for many spectators the director is only dimly attendant in the performance anyway. There are few parallels in the arts to the role. Choreographers, of course, but they are directors by another name – body directors, we might say. Film and television exist through substantially different fabric, dictated by the camera and post-production, so that while directors in those modes might still be acting coaches they are primarily arrangers of shots and editors of what has been recorded. Otherwise the closest in function is the conductor of an orchestra: a regulator who does not normally make the music but who guides or coaxes or cajoles individual musicians to perform as a group and realize an interpretation of a written score. But the spectator perceives the conductor through the stylized and rhythmic movements of the conductor's present body: crucially, in a space dedicated to the production of sound, the conductor is the one performer whose presence is exclusively visual. The stage director, on the other hand, is almost always unseen, an invisible mediator. Exceptions such as Tadeusz Kantor and Richard Foreman are quite rare, and even in those cases the onstage control was in some measure dramatized. In general terms, theatre directors are artists whose art disappears into the bodies of actors and the mise-en-scène. If a spectator does not look at the printed programme, phenomenally speaking where does the director exist? In many countries the director refuses to appear in the curtain call, even on opening night, so that awareness of him or her is removed entirely from the physical. For the audience the director remains partially concealed, a mysterious beast whose leadership must be taken on faith, more like a nameless sports coach than a musical conductor.

On a theoretical level directors customarily organize and filter meaning; they are active intermediaries between the scripted text and the embodied text. Because this is a conceptual position, it has been convenient for theatre studies to privilege directors, as it has been in film studies. Directors provide commentators with a method of intellectual and historical organization, borrowed from literary examinations of authors, enabling discourse about the development or stylistic unity of a career, affiliation to movements or comparative analysis with others. The approach is useful industrially as well, since celebrity directors can readily become brand names with marketing potential. (The model also comes from film: after the successes of directors in the French and Italian New Wave, Hollywood realized an economic advantage from the promotion of trademark directors.) This has played out well in the contemporary remains of the theatrical avant-garde, the major festival circuit. Here spectators, who by definition are cultural tourists, are likely to be informed about theatre practice, and as a result organizers commonly promote productions by directors' names. Festival audiences, like wine buffs, know the important marques, the heady Bordeaux reds of Wilson and Brook, high in tannin and with a long bin life; the Côtes du Rhône of Ninagawa Yukio and Deborah Warner, elegant and peppery; the white Burgundies of Lepage and Dodin, redolent of citrus fruits and summer flowers; the vintage champagne of Pina Bausch; the Beaujolais Nouveau of Calixto Bieito and Peter Sellars, cheeky little wines indeed. Making decisions based on reputation, festival audiences may attend performances with a deeper awareness of the director's role than is usual, which can also be true in locally subvented repertory institutions. The more professionalized an audience, the more likely it will be fragmented into specialized groups which identify with specific brands of performance. And those elite audiences tend to justify themselves as co-producers, effectively applauding themselves as the elect, so that their relationship to the director is likely to be more knowledgeable and perhaps more forgiving.

But most of the time the relationship of the director to the spectator is both distant and theoretical. A spectator can be generically aware that someone has organized the elements of the event without being very interested in who that person is or which specific tasks she or he has performed. The immediacy of acting and mise-en-scène is normally more commanding than how they have been activated. Indeed the comprehensively collaborative nature of performance tends to moderate specific contributions to the process. And directors have a similar distance from actual spectators, unless they choose to speak to them after the show. On their part, directors continue to presume that their role in rehearsal is to be the ideal spectator, but that is a creature who cannot exist outside the director's imagination.

Relocating the director's position within an industrialized and audience-centred position is a corrective to the historiographic traditions that have idolized directorial innovation. It is clear that modernity shaped the director, less clear what postmodernity will do about that, if anything. But given the number of theatrical institutions that out of economic necessity are now organized along lines employed by commerce, and how often theatre budgets are constrained by rehearsal periods shorter than ideal, it seems likely that directors will continue to apply the efficient industrial methods they inherited in the early history of their art.

CHAPTER 3

The avant-garde and the audience

It is impossible to define the avant-garde adequately. Since presenting oneself or one's work as 'advanced' necessarily is an oppositional position, the accuracy of definition is always obscured by the self-proclaimed identity of the artist, normally expressed in negative terms: whatever I am, says the avant-gardist, I am not what has gone before. I am far ahead of custom, I deny the pressure of the market, and I disdain the common audience who cannot be expected to understand my work since I am part of the future. Like the office of the stage director, avant-gardism is an intimate result of modernity, especially modernity's implication that industrial development and the expansion of goods point toward T. J. Clark's 'projected future', a future that promises ever more liberality yet is ever receding. The contradictions inherent in avant-gardism can be taken for granted, especially its insistence that it must be evolutionary, a new avant-garde regularly replacing the old. Massimo Bontempelli, writing in the 1920s, held the spirit of such movements to be

sacrifice and consecration of the self for those who come after . . . the avant-gardes of the first fifteen years of the century have in general submitted to the fate of military avant-gardes, from whom the image is taken: men destined for the slaughter so that after them others may stop to build (in Poggioli 1968: 67).

Despite the violent form of its expression, this is the standard nineteenth-century notion of progressivism, now outworn in every way except in commerce and aesthetics. Such an attitude can operate only in dialectic, when one side of a debate on value condemns an avant-garde while another side, normally including the artists, acts as its promoter. An avant-garde can only exist when surrounded by a discourse about avantism. Some respectable theatre commentators continue to use 'avant-garde' in an uncritical way, by and large referring to stylistic innovation or to the fact that the artists concerned appear out of the mainstream, and without reference to the theoretical repercussions of the term, its

49

economic implications or whether the concept must be reordered in postmodernity. While I hope to use the term more precisely (and more historically), I will not attempt to judge whether particular artists actually deserve the appellation or rate them on a scale of avantism. Instead I will ask questions about how specific avant-gardes have positioned their potential audiences and how those audiences have responded.

For the historical avant-garde in Europe, loosely gathered in the period from about 1880 to 1933, reception was the main theoretical and practical difficulty. An important goal of most modernisms, whether or not considered avant-garde, was the reformation of the bourgeois audience, even if that meant temporary financial hardship for the artist. A number of avant-gardists actively scorned or reviled their audiences or potential audiences, attempting to force a relationship between art production and social and political life. Instead of working within profitable styles and subjects that ratified habitual attitudes, they privileged novelty over custom and unease over solace. This was one of the reasons for the general modernist preoccupation with form, especially the persistent concern for expressing the nature of the representation in the work itself. Modernists regularly transferred their disquiet over modernity to their patrons, eventually turning the bourgeois concept of the audience upside down, especially the assumption that art should have a comfortable, one-for-one relationship with the tangible facts of the everyday world.

The optimistic or social engineering battalions of the theatrical avant-garde army which appeared after 1918 addressed some of these audience problematics, shifting avant-garde thinking away from the purely aesthetic into the realm of the social. The celebratory socialist work of Meyerhold for mass audiences is the most obvious example of a new deal for audiences. But that settlement, dependent on social management of the arts under direct subsidy conditions, could occur with any force only in the Soviet Union, and even there only for the dozen years or so before Stalin liquidated the idea of the avant-garde as antithetical to a collectivist state. In post-Versailles Germany, under the exhilarating but chaotic Weimar Republic, the devastations of the war and its economic aftermath forced artistic contemplation of the moral failures of the Kaiser Reich and bourgeois industrial culture. Brecht's challenge to bourgeois spectators to distance themselves from empathetic psychological identification with a character in order to contemplate the underlying economic cause for actions (*Verfremdung*) might in time have worked a radical change in Germany, but that move was ended when he lost connection to his audience in 1933. In another vein Brecht's 'teaching plays' (*Lehrstüke*, written 1929–31), designed for workers and amateur theatre, radically revisioned both the spectator and actor positions. Both Meyerhold and Brecht, in their very different ways, wanted to change the institutions of art. Ultimately they asked their audiences to change the social structure that even in the Soviet Union still privileged ideas of beauty inherited from the enlightenment.

But most other avant-gardists, working inside capitalist political economies, had no idea how audience reformation could be accomplished except by their own example. For many writer-directors, from Jarry to Marinetti to Artaud, the resistance of the mainstream spectator only strengthened resolve to soldier on within coteries. The fact that such artists gathered small or antagonistic audiences proved they were on the right track, assemblies of the self-appointed demonstrating, somewhat tautologically, the advanced status of the work. Beckett, after the Second World War still in the tradition of the historical avant-garde, admitted that he offered *Waiting for Godot* to Roger Blin because Blin's production of Strindberg's *Ghost Sonata* had been notable for two reasons: 'the fidelity to the author and the near emptiness of the theatre' (in Gussow 1996: 32).

A THEORY OF THE AVANT-GARDE

I return to the realm of painting, where the problematic of an audience for modernism was first apparent. The affronts to convention that took place in the latter part of the nineteenth century – the early-modernist movements of impressionism and post-impressionism, culminating in the full-blown modernism of cubism just before the First World War – posed serious challenges to the traditional alliance between artist and viewer. The breakdown of the aristocratic patronage system had forced painters in the nineteenth century to cultivate buyers. At least some industrialists and merchants with nouveau cash did not have an established or inbred method of verifying the value of art; they could be seen as deficient in cultural capital or knowledge of standards. For new pictures the gap was theoretically closed by the official academies which, through their juried exhibitions, also provided the place of mediation between buyer and seller. Economically, galleries were sites of transaction; socially, they were sites where art was authorized.

In France the authorizing power of the Académie des Beaux-Arts derived from its official state status and its right of exclusion: painters and paintings not admitted to its annual exhibition, the Salon de Paris, were denied conventional approbation and ready sale. We have seen already how the 1874 impressionist exhibition, organized after its painters had been passed over by the Salon jury, created a new market for the work, but the revolutionary movements in modernist painting date to an earlier rejection. In 1863 the Salon jury discarded seventy per cent of submissions, including work by Whistler, Pissarro, Cézanne and Manet's *Déjeuner sur l'herbe*. The outcry from artists and press was so great that Napoleon III, seeking to end the turmoil by compromise, viewed the rejected works and agreed they should be shown publicly in a separate 'Salon des Refusés'. The affair also prompted the government to reform the Salon, taking selection out of the hands of the Academy (Mainardi 1987: 124), but vindication of the repudiated works was less significant than the profitable result: artists who were marked by rejection now discovered that rejection was marketable. The refused artist became the advanced artist.

As Peter Bürger points out in his influential *Theory of the Avant-Garde* (1984), the major quest of mainstream European art in the nineteenth century was for independence from 'life praxis'. Having lost the patronage of the church and of the aristocracy, bourgeois art began to claim the status of an organic entity, idealist in nature, complete in itself and subject only to its own laws. It privileged form over content by insisting on art's autonomy from cultural forces external to its artists, justified by the romantic demand of freedom from aesthetic rules and social restrictions. Emphasis on the signified gave way to emphasis on a coherent set of signifiers, often sentimentalized; meaning receded and art became 'about' itself and the artist who made it. No longer a servant of the aristocracy, the artist in a commodity society became a maker of independent objects. But as Russell Berman (1989: 48) notes, 'the autonomous work is, from the start, not only autonomous but also an object to be possessed; the idealist description of art also aims to make art a pure commodity'. At the end of the century, however, more self-conscious avant-gardists rejected the bourgeois blueprint – not by finding new patronage in the aristocratic model, but by disavowing the hold on art exercised by the purses of the middle class.

The chief technical strategy for accomplishing the avant-garde project was the insistence that art is a cultural artefact. Bürger's summary is useful: 'The European avant-garde movements can be defined as an attack on the status of art in bourgeois society. What is negated is not an earlier form of art (a style) but art as an institution that is unassociated with the life praxis of men' (1984: 49). The avant-gardists created art that self-consciously looked like art in order to re-establish art's position within the social order, thus permitting their work to comment on and critique that order. Avant-garde art denied the succour of realism in order to call attention to its own artifice, its manufactured-ness (what Bürger calls *montierte* or its 'fitted' quality), deliberately attempting to shock the bourgeoisie by contradicting trustworthy expectations. 'The organic work of art seeks to make unrecognizable the fact that it has been made', he writes. 'The opposite holds true for the avant-gardiste work: it proclaims itself an artificial construct, an artefact' (72). Cubist painting, with its emphasis on 'reality fragments' forged together in montage fashion, is one of the clearest examples. But avant-garde painters, by definition attacking commodity society, still lived in a commodity society and still found their clients among the bourgeoisie.

In the theatre, with its need to attract spectators assembled in groups, the issue of an audience for the avant-garde became even more para-doxical. The reform movements that originated in Europe in the last decades of the nineteenth century refused the established theatrical system which treated plays as commodities and audiences as consumers of product, what Brecht would later call the culinary theatre. In different ways these movements attempted to find not traditional theatrical success but rather to take their audiences into a new kind of seriousness. Here we join the well-known tale I introduced in the previous chapter, the foundation of most of the narratives about the revolutionary nature of fin-de-siècle theatre: Nora slamming a door, Antoine pushing a handcart across Paris filled with his mother's furniture, Yeats shocked by the toilet brush in *Ubu roi*, the Freie Bühne and the Independent Theatre Society avoiding the ban on *Ghosts*, the nocturne of tea-drinking by Vladimir and Konstantin as they argued in Moscow over an art theatre. These were the reigning theatre myths of the twentieth century, deeply inscribed in standard histories. Indeed much of the subsequent discourse for mod-ernist theatre was shaped as early as 1914 by the rather peevish tone in the writing of Edward Gordon Craig, that ultimate example of the *refusé*, who was confident that the nineteenth-century audience was ignorantly trapped by the fussy over-decoration and inflated acting of the regular theatres.

He was right in many senses. But it has not much been noted how thoroughly the reformers were convinced that audiences were like child-ren who needed to be led. The avant-garde artists of the end of the nineteenth century expected to lead audiences into a social and aesthetic promised land that would cast off the mendacity and the habits of intellectual compliance they associated with the burgher's life. *La Vie de bohème* contained a huge and unacknowledged dilemma: though reformers disdained middle-class values and tastes and sometimes revelled in that disdain, their hope of success lay with middle-class audiences, whether established or emergent. *Epater le bourgeois* was a self-defeating motto: consumers normally will not pay to be offended.

Of course avant-gardists strove to transfigure the notion of the audience as mere purchaser of product. They sought to change the spiritual or interior aspects of middle-classness, not necessarily to change the economic and social group that bought their pictures, listened to their music, read their books or watched their plays. Stephen Dedalus intones at the end of Joyce's *A Portrait of the Artist as a Young Man* (written 1914–15) that his purpose was 'to forge in the smithy of my soul the uncreated conscience of my race'. Extending the romantic notion of the artist as priest and saviour, his formulation was continued through the modernist period. Indeed a powerful notion in the twentieth century was that artists of high seriousness should *not* be popular or financially successful. This means, in effect, that until the revisions of the commodity status of art in postmodernity, the perception of advanced art in the West accepted the avant-garde premise. To simplify: avant-garde art equalled small audiences and something close to financial failure. If the audiences got too large, or the monetary rewards too great, by definition the work was not on the cutting edge.

Obviously this is a limited view of the serious artist's relationship to the public. Prior to romanticism western culture found no necessary relationship between penury and artistic greatness, and many serious artists in the twentieth century maintained a double position regarding financial success, from Pablo Picasso to Andy Warhol, from Bernard Shaw to Woody Allen. It is therapeutic to recall what Harold Clurman frequently said, 'all artists dream, and when they dream they dream of money'. Another way of stating Clark's principle is that the real history of the avant-garde is the history of those who escaped from it. Bürger, in his desire to separate the avant-garde from modernism in general, underplays the ways in which avantism used its advanced status to sell itself. Robert Jensen (1994: 10) notes that modernist rhetoric tended to reiterate endlessly a 'distinction between authentic art and commodities', a distinction central to Bürger's definition of the avant-garde which will not hold up well for either modernism or avantism. Jensen notes that even archetypal alienated artists like Egon Schiele had learned by 1910 that 'alienation sells, that to be alienated was as much a role, a way of establishing professional identity, as occupying a position in the academy'. Picasso used to say that people didn't buy his paintings, they bought his signature, a commodity idea confirmed in a thoroughly post-avantist fashion in 1999 when the Picasso estate did sell his signature: to the French automaker Citroën, who put it as a brand on one of its cars.

THE PLEASURE OF BEING BOOED

In chapter 2 I treated the uncertainty of signs in the theatres of Antoine and Lugné-Poe as a problem of representation. It can also be seen as a crisis of spectation. It was not so severe a crisis as to alter the spectator's conventional position nor did it cause a breakdown in the customary doer-watcher relationship, which remained generally unaffected by theatrical modernism. It was by no means as severe a crisis as that occurring more recently, when the very ground of spectation has been shaken by cinema directors like Jean-Luc Godard and Alain Resnais, by theatre directors like Tadeusz Kantor, Jerzy Grotowski, Richard Foreman and Romeo Castellucci, by performance art and by the onslaught of digital culture. Nonetheless some historical avant-gardes from Craig to Artaud did pose significant challenges to the spectator which, when combined with doubts about the meaning or force of stage signifiers, suggested that new options for audience commitment might be found. The fact that avantists generally failed to exploit them does not diminish the significance of the attempt. The most intriguing of these, and certainly the most immediate, were connected to disorder in the house.

There is of course a long history of unrest and mayhem in the theatre. Before polite behaviour became the norm, rowdy sections of audiences regularly erupted over the play, its politics or the price of admission. A goodly amount of trouble was caused not so much by objections to the performance itself as by opposing sects of spectators who were primed for conflict over an issue the performance was taken to symbolize. Certainly that was the case with *Hernani* in 1830, when Victor Hugo anticipated discontent from the traditional audience at the Comédie Française and dismissed the claque in favour of stacking the auditorium with friends and supporters of romanticism, to ensure a fair hearing for his play. When his supply of complimentary tickets ran out after three nights, the inevitable occurred and the remainder of the record number of thirty-nine performances were filled with partisan shouts and serious disorder. Jarry followed this strategy three-quarters of a century later when (it seems) he organized a group of spectators to protest against his own *Ubu roi*, a kind of volunteer oppositional claque, so that his sympathetic faction had a group to react against. Of the first performance Yeats (1953: 210) wrote, 'the audience shake their fists at one another ... feeling bound to support the most spirited party, we have shouted for the play', as if it were a kind of game, which it may have been for most spectators. (Though typically not as violent, these examples suggest a similarity to football riots discussed in chapter 8.)

Engineering disorder for the sake of publicity became the pattern for the avant-garde movement that most sought arousal in the house, the Italian futurists. The founder of futurism and leader of the Milan group, F. T. Marinetti, a genius at self-promotion, recognized that theatres were logical sites for large-scale dissemination of ideas, necessary conditions for his endorsement of art for political ends. Even though he and his colleagues were not men of the theatre – though they were all men – they made the playhouse their base of operation. The first futurist evenings or soirées (*serate*, in the singular *serata*) were events far removed from traditional plays, even avantist ones, consisting as they did of declamations of futurist manifestos and poems, nationalist speeches in favour of war and violence, organized sound from 'noise machines' and the display of futurist paintings on stage. As Martin Puchner (2005) convincingly shows for the futurists and for other movements of the historical avant-garde, the manifesto was not so much a prelude to an imagined new form of art but was the work of art itself. Marinetti became quickly notorious and audaciously exploited his celebrity in a series of *serate* between 1909 and 1911 in cities from Turin to Naples, always ensuring that advance publicity would create dissension. Often the futurist performers would be met by crowds at the station or their hotel, sometimes with a joyful welcome, sometimes with showers of abuse. The theatres were packed and the response of spectators highly agitated, whether in approval or condemnation.

The futurist programme boiled down to hatred of the past and faith in a renovated future. Depending on location and circumstance, specifically this meant a nationalist cry to rid northern Italy of Austrian rule, a denunciation of inefficiency and inept government, a call for war to rid the country of corruption and tradition and religion, or a condemnation of bourgeois apathy and old-fashioned art, always with the underlying motif of the unstoppable power of technology and the machine. Its insistently bellicose policies, masculinist mode, association with the Fascist Party and the questionable nature of its art have tended to obscure the futurist movement's radical experiment with the idea of an audience. Because they sought controversy at all cost, the early futurists considered an event successful if it created uproar. 'It does not matter whether we are booed or applauded', Marinetti said in 1910. 'What matters is that our programme is surrounded by a lot of noise and notoriety' (in Berghaus 1998: 101). 'Futurists must teach all authors and performers to despise the audience', he claimed: selling tickets for the same seat to more than one spectator or gluing an unsuspecting spectator to his seat (Goldberg 1988: 16). On one level this is merely juvenile. On another it identifies the most consistent problem of the theatrical avant-garde: how to force spectators out of complacent consumption of the show into an active engagement with its purpose.

Günter Berghaus concludes that the early *serate* were weapons 'in the political and artistic fight for a total renewal of Italian public life', and that the most effective weapon in the arsenal was provocation. The declaiming of poems and manifestos was not about the 'appreciation of an artistic creation' but rather 'the main task of the declaimer was to challenge the spectators and to provoke them into reactions of an unpre-meditated kind' (Berghaus 2005: 33). The spectator became the antagonist to the performer, audience reaction the text of the performance.

The prime example of theatre as combat occurred in December 1913, nine months before the outbreak of the actual war, in what became known in futurist mythology as the Battle of Florence. To coincide with an exhibition of futurist paintings, Marinetti's supporters organized a *serata* at the Teatro Verdi which prompted more interest and hostility than any preceding event. Contemporaries estimated that between 5,000 and 7,000 people crammed themselves into the auditorium, with nearly as many left outside. They were noisy and restless with anticipation, ready for a good brawl. When after a two-hour delay the futurists appeared, 'all hell broke out' according to Ardegno Soffici, one of the performers. Another described the banners he saw in the dress circle: 'Perverts! Pederasts! Pimps! Charlatans! Buffoons!' (Berghaus 1998: 123). Then from the balconies the barrage of missiles began, onions, carrots, potatoes, eggs, tomatoes, apples, cauliflower, polenta, chestnuts and chestnut pudding, house keys, light bulbs – one struck Marinetti on the eye – accompanied by screeches and screams, catcalls, whistles, stamping feet, trumpets and a car horn. If we are to believe the newspaper sketches of other *serate* (illustration 4), the gifts included shoes and boots, paper airplanes, water (or urine), walking sticks and burning paper, stink bombs or firecrackers. In Florence not all the projectiles reached their target. Soffici wrote that some hit 'the bald heads and shoulders of gentlemen in dinner jackets, the elegant hats of the ladies down in the stalls, where they provoked violent

Illustration 4 Spectators attack a futurist *serata*, Turin 1910. F. T. Marinetti
stands on stage with arms crossed watching the missiles arrive

protests and screams' and fisticuffs among groups of spectators (125).
Jammed in seats and crowded into standing room, no one left. The
declaiming went on, and the futurists returned the abuse and some of the
missiles. A man in the house offered Marinetti a pistol, suggesting he
commit suicide. 'If I deserve a bullet of lead', Marinetti replied, 'you
deserve a bullet of shit!' But little of this or any part of the performance
could be heard.

From the standpoint of provocation the Florentine *serata* was a magnificent success. 'We Futurists managed to unleash the best forces that lay hidden inside you', one participant wrote in an open letter; 'only in confrontation with us could you find the best in yourself.' Berghaus (1998: 126) claims that the spectator had been turned into 'an active collaborator in the communication process'. But in such chaos what communication could possibly occur? In the end this event was not about communication: it was about disdain for the audience from the stage and a reaction to that disdain from the house. The audience had been primed to respond violently by the futurists' own programme, and did so in a ritual drama that had nothing to do with what was actually heard or seen. Operating out of behaviour learned through newspaper reports and word-of-mouth, the audience used the occasion to object – but their objection was the performance the futurists desired, a perfect demonstration of the limits of audience participation. These participants did not abandon the spectator position. They assisted at the spectacle by fulfilling their assigned role: the curtain rose and the missiles descended. For hours they stayed in the house and those with seats stayed in them. It was astonishingly disorderly, but it was not a riot: spectators were doing exactly what was expected of them.

'The Pleasure of Being Booed' is the 1915 title of Marinetti's pamphlet known in a shorter form in 1911 as 'Manifesto of Futurist Playwrights'. But after the Battle of Florence Marinetti came to realize that being booed in such an extreme fashion was not aiding the futurist cause, since no exchange of ideas was possible. He began to avoid large-scale *serate* in favour of smaller, more sympathetic groups and in the 1920s turned to writing avantist drama. The vegetables did not stop flying entirely – that would not be helpful either – but he had learned something important about audience behaviour. Treat spectators as stupid fools and they may end their complacent passivity by acting as stupid fools: audience involvement is always double-edged. It was a lesson that had to be learned anew by the New York avant-garde. When in 1968 the Performance Group under Richard Schechner staged *Dionysus in 69* and sought audience participation, some male spectators seized upon the orgiastic scenes and the close physical environment to undress themselves and fondle the actresses. As Arnold Aronson (2000: 100) notes, the 'performers demanded that Schechner restructure these scenes more rigidly' to prevent spectators taking sexual advantage. If spectators were to participate, 'they too needed some sort of script'.

As we have seen, the organizations devoted to theatrical renovation began small, usually as restricted clubs. Constituting themselves as private societies rather than as commercial ventures, they achieved a number of cultural goals at a stroke: they normally eluded the censor's power and other licensing restrictions; they insured a determined audience, sometimes financially committed to the project by prior subscription; they rationalized an irregular production schedule; and they validated their own advanced status by controlling the admission of the general public. But it was extremely difficult to survive under the harsh financial regimes forced on these troupes, which helped to promulgate the notion that art in the theatre was bound to be a losing proposition. Antoine's Théâtre Libre was a one-man operation: 'I am like the little, well-established shopkeepers who cannot afford to keep a clerk', he said. 'I sweep the shop and carry the letters myself' (in Waxman 1926: 174). There were 349 seats available for his first performance, too small an audience to sustain a company even if he had been allowed to charge for admission. In 1894, after seven years of intermittent productions, Antoine was bankrupt. As early as 1888 he expressed a desire to continue the Théâtre Libre for two more years only and then gain a subsidized theatre from the government for a much larger operation with 600 subscribers (Charnow 2005: 49). Which is what happened, though not so quickly. When he reappeared on the scene in 1897 it was in a sustainable public theatre which he called the Théâtre Antoine, and eventually he gained the directorship of the Odéon (1906), a heavily subsidized one. In the Berlin version, Otto Brahm dissolved the Freie Bühne less than five years after its founding in 1889, when he moved on to the stability of the Deutsches Theater where financial problems were alleviated. The Moscow Art Theatre was an exception to the rule of the impoverished free stage, as its first years were secured by a munificent private subsidy.

    In England, a country without a national theatre or a tradition of subsidy and with a theatrical system attuned to commerce and the long run, circumstances were even more difficult for the alternative societies and their audiences. Nor did the London equivalent of a theatrical avant-garde have before it models like Antoine or Lugné-Poe. In the seven years of its life the Independent Theatre Society (1891–8) never had more than 175 members. Its founder, the transplanted Dutch critic J. T. Grein, wrote that 'the income was barely £400 a year during the whole of its existence' (*Stage Society News*, 25 January 1907), and he remained convinced during the Edwardian period that advanced drama could not prosper on the regular London stage. The Stage Society, offering more varied plays and with better rehearsed productions, was substantially more successful. It limited membership to 300 in its first year, and performed only on Sunday evenings. In his memoirs of the period Alan Wade (1983: 4) recalled that Sunday performances, officially prohibited in the United Kingdom, 'caused considerable nervousness to theatre lessees' who agreed to hire out their houses only when assured that there would be no advance publicity or reviews in the press. Even so the police arrived at the Royalty Theatre for the Society's first event, Shaw's *You Never Can Tell* in 1899, to question the legality of even a private performance on a Sunday, forcing Frederick Whelen to keep them 'adroitly involved in a long argument' until the play was over. The single Sunday performance meant that the Stage Society was able to take advantage of professional actors working in the regular theatres on their one night off. The small membership was meanwhile authenticating itself as the vanguard of dramatic art.

In its second season the Society was pressured to raise its number to 500 and to give an additional performance of each production on Monday afternoons. In the interests of the actors who were working for next to nothing, newspaper critics were now invited; the legal worries over Sunday performances had apparently receded. By 1907 the Society had increased its rolls to about 1,200. The expansion spoke well for the growing interest in what was called the New Drama, but put a severe strain on accommodating the membership for popular events. When Granville Barker's play *Waste* was refused a licence that year, for example, the Society hurriedly stepped in to mount two private performances. There was great trouble securing a venue, as theatre managers were reluctant to offend the Lord Chamberlain by staging, even privately, a script his Examiner of Plays had banned; the Lord Chamberlain might retaliate by withholding renewal of the manager's operating licence. By a stroke of luck the Imperial Theatre in Westminster became available; since it was about to be torn down, the usual fear was eliminated. The controversy surrounding the play insured a heavy demand for tickets, which could only be obtained by becoming a member; it may have been the *Waste* affair that artificially inflated the Stage Society's membership. The secretary, A. E. Drinkwater, was 'a firm disciplinarian', according to Wade (1983: 19), 'quite impervious to blandishment, and it was reported at the time that Henry James and two duchesses had to be content with seats in the gallery'.

Despite its modest size and modest programming, the Stage Society established the model for the New Drama and the new audience in London. In 1903 Barker wrote to William Archer with a plan to take the Court Theatre for 'a stock season of the uncommercial Drama' – he was thinking of Hauptmann, Sudermann, Ibsen, Maeterlinck, Schnitzler, Brieux and Shaw. Barker's chief justification was his belief in the potential for an expanded new audience:

I think there is a class of intellectual would-be playgoers who are profoundly bored by the theatre as it is. Matinée productions don't touch these people (who are all workers) and Sunday evening is expensive and incapable of expansion . . . I think the Independent Theatre – the New Century – The Stage Society – have prepared the ground, and the time is ripe for starting a theatre upon these lines, upon a regular – however unpretending – basis (in Salmon 1986: 41–2).

The audience would be greatly expanded, though still small, as the Court had only 614 seats. Barker knew that subsidy was necessary (he suggested a start-up fund of £5,000) and that subscription sales were important. But he also knew that if the advances made by the Sunday societies were to be consolidated, the theatre had to be a public one, accessible to all. Barker even suggested that the highest price should be five or six shillings, which would have been a great bargain in the Edwardian period, about half the cost of a standard ticket for the stalls, which was ten shillings and sixpence.

In the event most of these goals were not reached in the famous Vedrenne-Barker seasons at the Court Theatre (J. E. Vedrenne was Barker's business manager). When the venture began in 1904, performances were on Tuesday, Thursday and Friday afternoons only. These were days on which the regular theatres did not hold matinées, so that gainfully employed actors could be used in the manner established by the Stage Society. Rehearsals were squeezed in whenever possible, often lasting until the small hours. Only gradually and cautiously did the new management expand into evening performances. A small guarantee fund was established, most of it donated by Shaw's wife Charlotte, and favourable rental terms for the theatre were provided by its lessee, but no large subsidy was obtained. The tickets cost the same as they did at the St James's Theatre or at Drury Lane. The subscription scheme was completely unsuccessful; at the end of the second season, when the venture had achieved significant fame, only twelve subscriptions had been sold (Borsa 1908: 113). Antoine, who also concentrated in his first years on an audience from literary and artistic circles, did little better; he managed to enrol thirty-four subscribers by October 1887 but the sum raised (3,400 francs) did not cover his expenses (Charnow 2005: 35–6).

'The plain fact is', said *The Referee* (16 April 1905) during the first Vedrenne-Barker season, 'Mr Vedrenne has succeeded in drawing to the theatre a class of playgoer for whom too scant consideration is shown by the theatrical managers; playgoers, I mean, with a purely artistic taste for the theatre.' But who were these people with a purely artistic taste? Shaw boasted they were 'not an audience, but a congregation' (A. Henderson 1932: 444). The 'great British public', Mario Borsa (1908: 112–13) wrote, 'artless, coarse-minded, and dull-witted – does not frequent the Court . . . The Court audiences are composed of persons of culture and students, with a goodly percentage of society people.' In an interview in 1907 Barker said his audiences were mainly women, male sentimentalists who had not obtained majority and older people who hadn't grown up (*The Theatre*, 7 September 1907: 235). Perhaps he was joking, but most contemporary comments reinforce his assessment. It is a new audience, *The Bystander* (10 January 1906) noted:

The Court Theatre is now become a cult. The matinée-goers are an audience apart. A decade ago they would have been termed 'Soulful.' But the elect who crowd to the productions at the Court Theatre are bizarre, not so much in appearance and dress as in point of view . . . Outspokenness brings no blush to their cheek. They are mostly women.

F. C. Burnard, the editor of *Punch* (13 December 1905), went to one of the first matinées of *Major Barbara* and found that 'the female element in the audience proponderated over the inferior sex by something like twelve to one'. This was not an ordinary matinée audience of women, he thought, for it 'had not a theatre-going, but rather a lecture-going, sermon-loving appearance' (illustration 5).

Matinées were not new to the regular theatres when Barker instituted his reign at the Court. They had grown during the 1870s and 1880s as the popularity of the theatre grew among the leisured classes and were used for both regular productions and for untried plays. The persistent audience for matinées during the late-Victorian period encouraged managers to experiment with more unconventional fare and probably paved the way for the Ibsen movement of the nineties. But the big point about matinée spectators, the point Barker emphasized in his letter to Archer, is

Shavians at the Savoy

(1) In the Stalls (Half a Guinea)

(2) In the Circle (Seven and Sixpence)

(3) In the Pit (Half a Crown)

(5) One of our future Monuments?

(4) In the Gallery (A Bob)

Illustration 5 The audience at Shaw's *You Never Can Tell*, Savoy Theatre, London 1907. A sketch by Charles Sykes shows the preponderance of women spectators, as well as class demarcations in dress and physical attitude in different sections of the auditorium

obvious: they were not workers, whether from the working class or the middle class. In fact the female matinée audience seems a marvellous demonstration of Thorstein Veblen's theory of vicarious leisure: wives and daughters of hard-working men of commerce sent out in daylight in flagrantly impractical dress to proclaim the freedom from drudgery for women bought by their masters' successful toil. Unable to afford the leisure of the aristocracy themselves, male merchants showed off women as surrogates of wealth.

And the matinée hat, that extreme example of sartorial provocation, was a leisure-marker of great cultural resonance. These hats, which 'spread in a vast radius around the head' and were 'piled high with ornamentation of birds, flowers or fruit', were very difficult to set on straight, requiring a mirror, an assistant and a number of remarkably long hatpins (Macqueen-Pope 1958: 167). Removing them, therefore, was an action of major consequence, not to be undertaken merely for the convenience of lesser mortals who happened to be seated behind them in the theatre. Critics railed against their absurdities to little avail; Shaw (1931, II: 77–8) started a campaign in the press as early as 1896. As a private club, the Stage Society could require ladies to remove them; even George Alexander got some of his clientele to consider their fellow spectators at the elegant St James's Theatre through a combination of discreet good manners and a free cloakroom.

As to the Court, reported *The Tatler* (21 December 1904), 'the hat question is very rife there because the stage is unhappily unusually low, and in the back rows of the stalls it is very difficult to see over mountainous hats'. Still, it was with considerable surprise that critics noticed at the very first Vedrenne-Barker matinée in 1904 that the new management had induced all but 'Three Ladies' to remove their hats. 'Cheerfully conforming to the new Edict' (*The Referee*, 23 October 1904), these bareheaded spectators were proclaiming membership in a new class of playgoer, separating themselves from Borsa's 'great British public' and from the mindless members of the middle class. Of course manners changed with resistance. A columnist for *The Lady* (8 December 1904) who called herself 'Cuckoo' attended a matinée of *Candida* and objected to the new policy: 'We were aghast at having to tear our hats off our heads as best we could, for at the Court it is a rule to prevent "matinée hats" obscuring the view of those behind, and I must say that most people looked dishevelled and untidy in consequence, for hats do disarrange the hair and flatten the front waves, etc., in a way that no man can understand!' (see illustration 6).

Illustration 6 Mr Punch's patent Matinée Hat, equipped with binoculars.
The note in the hat reads 'Drop 6d in the slot, and I will keep my head still'

Convinced that audience manners and attitudes had to be changed, the management urged compliance in other new ways as well. It attempted, for example, to regulate the anarchic habits of applause that survived from the nineteenth century. Some programmes announced that actors would not take curtain calls at the end of each act, but only at the conclusion of the performance. This desire to make audience habits conform to a more serious approach to drama connects Barker to the general modernist desire to control the nature of perception.

It was not only leisured women who attended the Court matinées, especially for the Shaw plays. A number of politicians were present for the premiere of *John Bull's Other Island* in October 1904 and Prime Minister Arthur Balfour sat in the royal box with Beatrice and Sidney Webb on 10 November. At a special evening performance in March, King Edward VII, the heavy embodiment of the unreformed theatregoer, royally sat there and laughed so hard that he broke his chair. This much-repeated story, which insured the success of the first Vedrenne-Barker season, was actually the wrong signal for the new audience Barker was seeking. In any event the King never made it to a matinée. By the time *Major Barbara* was in matinées a year later the nature of the audience had been well established and the critics were regularly commenting on its distinctiveness. Balfour, who saw *John Bull* three times, was in the box for the new play with the Webbs and Sir Oliver Lodge, 'heading a brilliant and intellectual audience' (*The Stage*, 30 November 1905). 'There was intelligence – alert and expectant – on both sides of the footlights at the Court yesterday afternoon', said the *Daily Chronicle* about *Major Barbara* (28 November 1905); 'the house was crowded to the doors' with 'a gathering altogether of quite surprising people' who were exceedingly responsive:

They leapt at every utterance; they laughed long before the bright lines came; they said 'hear, hear' at each twist of the argument, in low solemn voices, like the 'amens' of a prayer meeting. There was, indeed, something almost oppressively solid about this spirit of Shaw-worship that was spread abroad. 'Colossal!' 'The greatest mind in Europe!' Such were the hardly apt phrases that were bandied about in the entr'actes.

On the same day *The Standard* added that the enthusiasm of the audience 'almost succeeded in outlasting the severe long-windedness of the last act'.

Matinées clarify one of the chief issues about the advanced Edwardian audience. After its first precarious months, the Vedrenne-Barker seasons shifted into a different and more prosperous mode in which new productions were given six matinées and if financially successful were moved to evening performances. This procedure was much closer to Barker's original intention, as it allowed people gainfully occupied during the days to attend at night. But the plays that succeeded in the evenings were chiefly those by Shaw, the mainstay of the Court repertoire, and some of the more accessible realist works. The poetic dramas of Maeterlinck, Yeats and Masefield, for example, which helped to establish the versatility of the Court experiment and tied it to its European counterparts, never made the transfer. Gilbert Murray's translations of Euripides, which gathered much positive attention in afternoon performances, did very poorly when they became evening fare. In its original six matinées in January 1906, *Electra* took in an average of almost £100 per performance, a respectable box office for what was surely a minority taste. Of the first performance *The Era* (20 January 1906) said 'That theatre of the intellectuals – the Court – was filled on Tuesday afternoon with a highly cultured audience.' Yet when the play ran for two weeks in the evenings in March, the six performances in the first week averaged only £26 each. 'The business so far is suicidal', Barker wrote to Murray; 'it is all the fortune of war, war with the public.' *Hippolytus*, which did very well as the first Vedrenne-Barker matinée in 1904, did even worse than *Electra* when it was tried at night in April 1906.[1] The audience with a 'purely artistic taste for the theatre' was notably limited. The story went about that one night a man was refused admittance by the box office attendant because he was drunk. 'But of *course* I'm drunk', he countered. 'Do you think I should come to the Court Theatre if I was sober?' (Steir 1927: 277).

'I prefer addressing minorities', Barker (1909: 491) wrote; 'one can make them hear better.' The unconventional spectators attracted to the Vedrenne-Barker seasons constituted a self-defined and distinct culture. They matched the elitism of Barker's theatrical reform with a sense of their own superiority. They did not like the transfer of the Court operation in 1907 to the larger and more commercial environment of the Savoy Theatre, where they felt ill at ease and assimilated, and made their objections quite plain. The best example relates to printed programmes. At the socialist Court the programmes, beautifully printed in red and black ink on heavy linen paper, were single-fold pages that contained no advertisements or other distractions. Like the Stage Society programmes, they suggested seriousness of purpose; they contextualized the performances with an uncluttered elegance of design and a complete absence of commercialism. In most of them a large notice was printed in red, announcing there were 'No Fees' at the Court. Edwardian theatres were inconsistent about this issue, some assessing extra charges for programmes and for cloakrooms, others not. At the Savoy, Barker's business manager accepted ads and then made the mistake of selling the programmes. Some of the committed audience, a precarious coalition of Shavians, Fabians, feminists and theatrical pioneers, thoroughly disapproved of this mercantile consequence and took their revenge. When Barker made his first appearance as Sergius in *Arms and the Man*, he was greeted by an organized demonstration from the gallery, 'a loud chorus of shouts of "No Fees!" ' (*Pall Mall Gazette*, 31 December 1907). It was not the carrots and chestnuts Marinetti endured, but it was a clear expression of audience disapproval.

LOATHING THE AUDIENCE

The failure of the Savoy venture, and the failure of Barker's experiment with repertory scheduling at the Duke of York's Theatre in 1910, suggested that the new audience, no matter how committed and vocal, was not large enough to support an art theatre that was self-sustaining (Kennedy 1985). Here we notice the largest difference between conditions in England and on the continent. Antoine in Paris and Brahm in Berlin, after their few years of apprenticeship in poor theatre, moved on to the security of external subsidy. Barker in London did not: he never escaped the avant-garde. His subsequent attempts to create a repertory theatre seemed to be getting somewhere, but very slowly. The Little Theatre in Adelphi, where he and his wife Lillah McCarthy established management in 1911, was a severe house that looked like a lecture hall; it was all stalls except for seven boxes in the back and sat 278 people. The Kingsway in Great Queen Street, where they operated in 1912, held but 564. The three revolutionary Shakespeare productions at the Savoy, which brought larger total audiences, were made possible by a private subsidy, and the two that were successful paid for themselves through the kind of long runs that violated Barker's repertory principles.

Of these enterprises, the most intriguing occurred at the St James's Theatre in 1913. Here Barker's attempts to create a repertory theatre, and to move beyond the confines of his original Court audience, met their severest test. The St James's, the most fashionable theatre in London, had been the home of society drama since A. W. Pinero's *The Second Mrs Tanqueray* in 1893. Its location in Piccadilly, its repertoire of plays by Pinero, H. A. Jones and Oscar Wilde that made Ibsen's issues palatable, and the extreme etiquette of George Alexander's management, all these colluded to attract society, the haute bourgeoisie and the petite bourgeoisie who admired their betters. Alexander, who was elected to the London County Council in 1907 as a Conservative, operated his theatre like an expensive club. It 'exuded the same gracious dignity as himself', Macqueen-Pope (1958: 167) wrote, and the audience 'felt it as soon as they entered'. Even the box office manager wore a tall hat when on duty.

Complementary tickets were special cards reminding the bearer that evening dress was imperative for admission.

Evening dress was regularly worn in the stalls and dress circle everywhere in London, even for Shaw's plays, as is apparent in illustration 5. It is hard for us in a culture of prodigious informality to imagine the strict protocol this imposed on the audience in Victorian and Edwardian London. The resolute distinctions between classes, plainly marked by their degrees of dress, separated the audience into discrete areas of the auditorium. J. T. Grein recalled that on his first visit to London as the critic for a Dutch paper, he did not know the rules and arrived at the Lyceum wearing tweeds to see Henry Irving in *Faust*. Irving's business manager, Bram Stoker in the flesh, barred the way like Count Dracula, pointing to the notice on the ticket, 'Evening Dress Indispensable', and escorted the shamed foreigner to the family circle, tenth row, where, he said, 'I saw little and heard less' (Orme 1936: 44). The wealthy classes, 'shirtfronts and sables' as Macqueen-Pope called them, established a tone for the entire audience similar to that expected at their own tables and drawing-rooms.

The St James's was the very opposite of a socialist theatre attempting to reform the stage. Alexander did not want reform, he wanted continuance. He wanted a stage world that reflected the manners and dress of his leading spectators, one in which they could see themselves righteously manipulating the status quo. The wealthy members of the audience and the actors portraying wealthy figures on stage were engaged in a reciprocal semaphore in which dress was the flag: a semiotic view of spectatorship is helpful in this case because it moves into the realm of the social. Even the advertisements in the programmes reinforced the mentality. In 1913 they were dominated by elegant clothiers: furs from Revillon Frères of Regent Street, 'French Model Gowns' from the Elite Company of Grosvenor Mansions, Paquin designs, theatre gowns from Liberty's.[2]

Alexander insured that decorum went beyond the walls of the theatre, insisting that his actors who played society people on stage also dress like society people in their private lives. Once early in the century he caught Henry Ainley and Lilian Braitwaite walking together in Bond Street on their day off. Ainley wore a Norfolk jacket and a floppy hat, while his friend had on a tweed outfit. Alexander spoke magisterially, addressing them in the third person: 'I would remind them that this is Bond Street and at the fashionable hour, and that they are members of the St James's theatre company. Membership of that company entails certain sartorial obligations. I need say no more' (Macqueen-Pope 1958: 168). Alexander kept up his standards even during the war. In 1917 he sent for Godfrey Tearle over the same issue:

Tearle, I am told that you have been seen walking in Piccadilly in the forenoon incorrectly dressed. You wear a lounge suit and that is not the right attire for a young leading man in my company. The correct dress for a gentleman in the forenoon is a morning coat and top hat. You will have to rectify this error or I shall take it that you wish no longer to be a member of the St James's company (Quayle 1990: 313).

So the St James's was not the obvious venue for the leader of the New Drama to premiere Shaw's *Androcles and the Lion*, a Fabian extravaganza with feminist overtones. Alexander had taken his sartorially correct company on provincial tour in the autumn of 1913, and from the first of September to Christmas Barker rented the theatre for another repertory experiment. The disturbing merger of the old and the new was readily apparent. Shaw's portrait inside the front cover of the opening night programme was placed opposite an ad for the International Fur Store, Britain's leading vegetarian staring at an enticement for 'charming new designs made in Russian Sable, Chinchilla, Natural Musquash, and other fashionable furs'. Suffragists took the persecution of Christians in the play as a reference to their own cause and to the government's ridiculous insistence that suffragist prisoners on hunger strike were answerable for their force-feeding, not the authorities. When Ben Webster as the Roman Captain said on stage that Christians have only themselves to blame if they suffer, he was interrupted by 'suffragette cheers from the gallery'. Yet the critic reporting the demonstration also noted that spectators from the stalls were overheard using words like 'vulgarity', 'blasphemy' and 'childish' to describe the play (*Manchester Guardian*, 2 September 1913). When Shaw's Lion first came through the forest and shook his mane, one young blood in the stalls, probably thinking he had come to an Alexander production, 'screwed his monocle into his eye and muttered "God! What have they got Hall Caine in it for?" ' (Duncan 1964: 287). Strangest of all, Barker had placed a sign near the box office window – that same box office whose manager always wore a top hat – that read, 'We should like our patrons to feel that in no part of the house is evening dress indispensable' (*The Standard*, 3 December 1913).

I do not know if many people took up Barker's offer to violate the class code so flagrantly, but I doubt it. The problem of the new audience in

England was not just that it was too small to sustain the kind of theatre its
leader wanted. Nor was it simply that it lived inside a larger theatrical
community that did not want a reformed stage at all. In addition to those
external difficulties, Barker had created a further one. Like the European
avant-gardists, he thought that his spectators also needed reform. Both
Barker and Shaw, despite their mildly socialist agenda, or perhaps because
of it, believed that the audience required management. If spectators were
to rise to a higher level, they would have to be pushed there. Some of
them were like children, some of them were drunk. Since there was no
permanent subsidy to underwrite the cost, spectators would have to pay
for their improvement themselves: the bourgeoisie was again being asked
to fund a theatre that wanted to destroy the bourgeois position. The
desire to lead London to a promised land of the stage was eminently
socialist, the Fabian permeation theory applied to art. Barker on the left,
Marinetti on the right: both wanted the theatre to change the nation. Like
Marinetti, Barker lacked Shaw's patience to wait for slow change. Or
perhaps Barker grew to see that permeation was an insufficient weapon in
the face of the swift and incontestable alterations forced upon English
society after 1914 that moved the theatre farther away from the conditions
he sought.

In any event, he never got over a rather distant and slightly disdainful
attitude to the audience and its unwillingness to be led. In 1917, just as he
was deciding to retire from the stage, Barker wrote: 'I do believe my
present loathing for the theatre is loathing for the audience. I have never
loved them' (in Holroyd 1989: 175). More than any other characteristic,
that loathing for the audience tied him to the early avantists. Barker
escaped the trap of the avant-garde only by marrying a rich American
divorcée and abandoning active theatre work for the life of a leisured
writer. Meanwhile the issue of popular success eventually split twentieth-
century theatre into two parts: the larger part got the audiences but little
lasting attention, the smaller part got the critical and historical acclaim.
The schizophrenic problem of the avant-garde and the audience is still
with us.

PART II

Shakespeare and the politics of spectation

CHAPTER 4

Shakespeare and the Cold War

I begin four chapters on the politics of spectation with a consideration of how modernist approaches to the audience were extended after the Second World War in the context of new international tensions. The obsessive concern with hearts and minds on both sides of the Iron Curtain cast curiously tinted shadows on the arts in two principal ways: through a large increase of state subsidy and through the assertion of biased political content, or its mirror opposite, the apparent lack of political content. In the theatre, where a rise in public financial support was particularly noticeable, Shakespeare performance provides the most obvious entry point to the issue because Shakespeare crossed political borders with greater ease than any other dramatist and because his plays seemed capable of lending support to both sides in the venomous debate. The history of the interpretation and performance of Shakespeare in the postwar period is itself a complex subject but I am concerned here with only one portion, if a neglected one: the relationship of the English national dramatist to the international situation in Europe in the years from 1945 to 1964. My chief point is that Shakespeare was used in western and central Europe as a site for the recovery and reconstruction of values that were perceived to be under threat, or already lost – though often both the supposition and the proposed manner of recovery were a long way from logical, and tended to implicate spectators in an unusual way. In this chapter, however, I consider not individual spectators but rather how the audience was conceived and constructed by producers and directors in the throes of the Cold War.

SPECTATORS IN THE RUINS

The crucial year is 1947, when plans for material recovery in Europe were well underway and intellectual awareness of the vast amount of work remaining began to sink in. I will get to the political situation in a moment, but on the cultural front the most significant development was 'The Week of Dramatic Art in Avignon', the first attempt at the Avignon Festival, inaugurated in September 1947 only weeks after the first Edinburgh International Festival opened. Avignon was founded by the great French actor and director Jean Vilar, who oversaw it until his death in 1971. Vilar thought of theatre, in his own phrase, as a 'public service in exactly the same way as gas, water or electricity'. For him drama transcended class barriers and political differences by celebrating timeless themes, and Avignon gave him the opportunity to test his thesis on a large scale in a country still shocked by the years of occupation and the psychic and material devastation that accompanied the Liberation. If Sartre and Camus were devising an existentialist response to the human condition in the face of the war, Vilar proposed to use the festival setting to retrieve a classical equilibrium. He thought the project important enough to put up 300,000 francs of his own money, more than a quarter of its total capital in the first year, the rest coming from the city and the state (Vilar 1975: 471). Avignon was a utopian scheme, but one that took seriously the warning that civilization as Vilar understood it might have been destroyed, and that French bourgeois culture might still be destroyed in the aftermath of war. He spoke about his founding motivations in an interview in 1964:

In 1947, the year of the first Avignon Festival, we said that the theatre lacked oxygen. We had suffered the pain of war, of occupation. We still had rationing. Transportation by rail, by bus, by car was still very difficult . . . Whereas the theatre under the occupation had been a meeting place for Parisians, filled with a fervent public, ready to welcome the young and all their work (as authors, performers, directors, painters, etc.), suddenly after the Liberation it had to find a new reason for being, and not only artistically. The theatre, a much-loved social centre for the French, became once more just a place like any other. Theatres rapidly became the object of exploitation pure and simple . . . The Liberation had liberated the people; it did not liberate professional institutions [*les métiers*]. (Vilar 1975: 468, my translation)

From Vilar's perspective the Avignon Festival was a scheme for the maintenance of memory, a recreation of a European past.

For that recreation he chose as his first production in September 1947 the same play that Rudolf Bing had used in August at Edinburgh, *Richard II*. The venue at Avignon helped in selecting the text: outdoors in the Court of Honour of the Papal Palace, with 3,000 seats in front of monumental fourteenth-century walls, under the warm nights of Provence. Despite the evocation of the medieval papacy, this would be a classless place, Vilar thought, without the trappings and the divisions of the nineteenth-century playhouse. Performance there depended on large-scale vocal delivery and gesture, rich period costumes and a sense of ritual that resembled High Mass. The opulence and ceremony on stage could have heartened an audience aware of themselves as survivors in a ruined world. And aware of themselves, in Vilar's view, as inheritors of high art: 'theatre is only of value, like poetry and painting', he said, 'when it does not give way to the dress, the tastes, or the ordinary social needs of the masses' (472). Spectators were to be treated seriously, but would them-selves be asked to treat the event seriously. The Papal Palace heightened the meaning of a play about a royal history from the same era, collapsing the past upon the past in an uncertain present. *Richard II* served the purpose well, playing in Paris, on tour and reappearing at Avignon every summer for the next six years. It even went to Edinburgh in 1953.

Vilar was not an aesthetic interventionist. He thought a director should never interpose himself between text and audience, though his acting in the title role was powerful and many critics thought it the greatest part of his career. But his emphasis was on the humanity of the main character. Harold Hobson noted that the King was 'of no more account than any other human being; the emphasis is laid not upon him, but upon the whole human race . . . it comes out of M. Vilar's hands almost a new play and one of great imaginative power' (in Leiter 1986: 573). As Jean Jacquot (1964) says in his history of Shakespeare in France, choosing a Shakespeare history play in 1947 was Vilar's response to the need of the time for some kind of faith in the future. His belief in the reconstructive potential of the arts is further apparent in his early desire to include lectures, discussions, poetry readings, cinema, music and dance in the festival. The festival idea spread widely under Vilar's influence, so that by 1960 there were some fifty arts festivals in the country (Jeffery 1992: 18–19), while his lead in staging plays with historical settings in ancient surroundings was followed in the 1950s all over the south of France. And in Italy as well, where Giorgio Strehler opened the Piccolo Teatro di Milano in 1948 with *Richard II*. Luchino Visconti directed *As You Like It* that same year in Rome, designed in surrealist style by Salvador Dalí, and in the summer of 1949 *Troilus and Cressida* in the Boboli Gardens in Florence, designed by Franco Zeffirelli with 'unparalleled magnificence of costumes and circus-like pageantry' (Praz 1950). Cultural reconstruction lent itself to the idea of the festival, a self-congratulatory celebration of the amount of recovery already accom-plished, while the ancient ruins spoke of a romantic continuity with the past.

What was it about Shakespeare that encouraged these theatrical institutions to use him so flagrantly as a banner? Art in the classic mould
appealed to many people after the war because it represented an imagined
continuity with a calmer, more ordered world. Shakespeare, and particularly a play like *Richard II* with its dependence on artifice and ceremony amid cold-blooded politics, engaged precisely what seemed to have
been threatened or lost, a sense that some human endeavours moved
outside of time, some elements of life might be free of the harsh taint of
history, some values could transcend pain and death. The liberal democracies felt they had narrowly escaped the destruction of the humanist
values that they had claimed as central to their wartime cause. The defeat
of the Axis had been couched in moral terms but building a peace and
rebuilding Europe needed commitment to something more than survival.
Reviewing the assaults on humanity from unprecedented aggression,
national leaders could easily conclude that Europe must return to solid,
well-tested, Christian values, values traditionally claimed to reside in high
art, or to be supported by it. The right-of-centre governments that led
France, Italy, West Germany and some of the smaller states for much of
the postwar period positioned themselves as custodians of those values.
Even when their parties were racked by scandals of corruption or espi-
onage, they managed to suggest that they were inheritors and preservers
of the past.

The worries over reconstruction were enough in themselves to foreground high principles and high art, but the perceived threat to Europe
by the Soviet Union added immensely to the purpose. In the first years
after German surrender, when the fronts were 'congealing' (the term from
the era), a mounting desperation overtook the victorious western powers.
As Eric Hobsbawm (1994: 230–1) writes, the Cold War was based on the
western belief that 'the future of world capitalism and liberal society was
far from assured'. This thought may seem 'absurd in retrospect but [was]
natural enough in the aftermath of the Second World War'. Many
observers expected a worldwide economic crisis after 1945, and Wash-
ington, which of course set the foreign policy agenda for the West for the
next half century, feared large-scale trouble because 'the belligerent
countries, with the exception of the USA, were a field of ruins inhabited
by what seemed to Americans hungry, desperate, and probably radicalized
peoples, only too ready to listen to the appeal of social revolution and
economic policies incompatible with the international system of free
enterprise, free trade and investment by which the USA and the world
were to be saved'.

The year 1947 was crucial in international politics as well. In March the US president outlined the Truman Doctrine, which effectively constructed the frame for the Cold War: 'At the present moment in world history nearly every nation must choose between alternative ways of life', Harry Truman said. In a clear reference to Soviet moves in Europe, he announced that henceforth US policy would 'support free peoples who are resisting attempted subjection by armed minorities or outside pressure' (in Saunders 1999: 25). In June General George Marshall, Army Chief of Staff during the war and now Truman's Secretary of State, offered a plan to deal with the 'great crisis'. In a ten-minute address at the Harvard University commencement – he was receiving an honorary degree along with Robert Oppenheimer, General Omar Bradley and T. S. Eliot – Marshall held that the world and 'the way of life we have known is literally in the balance' and proposed that only the US could provide the necessary financial credit and material assistance that would ensure the continuation of a free Europe. 'There is widespread instability', he noted; 'there are concerted efforts to change the whole face of Europe as we know it, contrary to the interests of free mankind and free civilization' (24). The US, which he held to be 'an integral part' of European culture, had a moral obligation to step into the breach. The Marshall Plan (officially the European Recovery Program), with its massive aid for recuperation from war, was to be the carrot. Less than two months later the stick came along, when the National Security Act of 26 July 1947 created the Central Intelligence Agency.

When Stalin installed satellite governments in Eastern Europe and tried to close off Berlin, when Mao ordained a revolutionary people's government in China and supported a parallel revolution in Korea, official US opinion had concluded by 1950 that godless communism was in quest of world domination. Some of the obsessions and paranoia of the Cold War were directly attributable to an American presidential dread not so much of Stalin's belligerence as of a loosening of the alliance which kept anarchy and revolt off the streets of London, Paris and Rome. It is doubtful that politicians in western Europe were as unnerved by the Soviet threat, especially in light of the rapid demobilization of the Red Army, reduced from almost twelve million in 1945 to three million by late 1948 (Hobsbawm 1994: 232). But certainly many Europeans shared the fear that social upheavals could disrupt the international capitalist system. Indeed the frightening harvest of 1946 and the horrendous winter of 1946–7, the worst on record, conspired to increase those fears and to drive western Europe more firmly into NATO, the American camp and the rhetoric of the

Cold War. By 1952 the Marshall Plan had transferred some $14 billion to the western European countries in food, raw materials and currency, sealing the bargain. (The Soviet Union rejected the project – 'dollar imperialism', Molotov called it – and kept the eastern European countries out.)

The rhetoric grew harsher in the US of the 1950s, driven by the House Un-American Activities Committee and the persecutions conducted by Joseph McCarthy in the Senate. Nixonian red-baiting became a vital element of national politics for a decade of paranoia, set off with the first atom bomb test by the USSR in 1949, compounded by the hydrogen bomb in 1953 and the launching of Sputnik in 1957. Though it is clear that nuclear war was the last thing either superpower wanted, even a sophisticated thinker like John Kennedy knew that with his disadvantage as a Roman Catholic he could win the presidency only if he out-Nixoned Nixon, the current vice-president and his campaign opponent. In retrospect Kennedy's electioneering speeches in 1960 seem vastly out of touch with the actual state of the Cold War, as when he claimed that 'the enemy is the communist system itself – implacable, insatiable, unceasing in its drive for world domination... This is not a struggle for supremacy of arms alone. It is also a struggle for supremacy between two conflicting ideologies: freedom under God versus ruthless, godless tyranny' (Walker 1993: 132). I grew up in that nerve-racking environment and can attest that when I was studying Shakespeare at the University of San Francisco in 1960 there was a clear and palpable sense in the classroom that we were engaged in a battle against the world: escape from Civil Defence drills, bomb shelters, canned goods and bottled water in the basement, and Mutual Assured Destruction.

American Shakespeare studies in the period were dominated by an ideology of retreat from the present. To Hardin Craig, for instance, Shakespeare was a refuge; he promoted the view that the dramatist was aloof from or even diffident to any cause, and that the job of the present generation was to perpetuate his timelessness. In 1948 Craig claimed that Shakespeare's genius, like Chaucer's and Goethe's, was thoroughly objective:

His works are written from the point of view of general humanity, which means that they have in them the minimum of affectation, formalism, dogmatism, egotism, and prejudice. They are about life, about people and about recurrent human situations (in Bristol 1990: 158).

In the introduction to his complete edition of the works, which I used in university those many years ago, Craig (1951: 13) wrote that Shakespeare 'gives us in his plays life patterns that are continuous in the history of the human race'. Hope for a better future, and even for the defeat of world communism, was grounded in the permanent values in Shakespeare; a sixteenth-century playwright would show the way out of postwar materialism and malaise, the loss of spirituality and the alarums of the Cold War. To take an example with a different effect, Cleanth Brooks and Robert Heilman produced criticism with an 'aura of necessary trafficking with a corrupt world' (Grady 1991: 129) which helped make sense of the era of McCarthyism by insisting that it was possible to back away from taking sides in reading Shakespeare's politics: a kind of abstract expressionism of criticism, a subjectless idealism of withdrawal. American Shakespeare discourse often was in congruence with American Cold War discourse, and both found their way forcefully into Europe. To some commentators, Shakespeare was a cultural Marshall Plan.

UNREAL CITY

Though in 1922 Eliot did not list Berlin among his unreal cities in *The Waste Land*, he certainly might have done so in 1945. Like all great cities Berlin has two existences, a material form and a form in the imagination. Cities acquire their imaginary life from the cultural products that memorialize them: in depictions in paintings and photos, in novels and films and television shows set in them and songs about them. It is as spectators that we know them, or as readers, or as Certeau's walkers. No great metropolis survives without its invented echo or fantasy double, its parallel municipality, its dream of itself. On an international scale the imaginary Berlin was first formed in the 1920s, a city of freedom and excess and of breathless life on the run. The 1930s came as all the more of a shock to world popular imagination because the Nazis inverted Weimar Berlin's relationship of sex to death, as Marlene Dietrich's black-mesh stockings became SS black-leather boots. Berlin in May 1945: unreal city, the darkest heart of Europe. As Alexandra Richie writes in her monumental history *Faust's Metropolis* (1999: 605–9), 'There can be few places as haunting as a vast city on the day of its surrender', a city that on that day contained one-seventh of all the rubble in Germany. Under what Marshall Zhukov called the 'severest occupation', the Soviets set Berlin clocks to Moscow time and erected Russian street signs, making the city 'an extension of the Soviet Union'. With its citizens scrambling for the barest survival, the city moved almost entirely into an unreal life.

One of the most remarkable circumstances combined the imaginary with the material: the Renaissancetheater, which had escaped destruction, reopened two weeks after the surrender. Six more theatres were operating before the year was out, mounting an incredible 120 new productions. The next year, the city still a wreck, 196 plays and operas were available (Farr 1992: 165). In a study of the cultural and intellectual life in Berlin immediately after the war, Wolfgang Schivelbusch (1998: 63–4) recounts that in its first season the bombed-out Deutsches Theater in the Soviet Sector mounted ten productions under Gustav von Wangenheim, including *Hamlet* in December 1945. By April 1946 more than 100 theatres were operating in the Soviet Zone of Germany, most of them run by provincial or municipal authorities. Strict guidelines for repertoire were set by the occupying power, emphasizing progressive older works, anti-fascist plays, Russian classics and Soviet dramas. Repertories were regularly reviewed by the Soviets and unprogressive managers were replaced. Russian anti-American plays were also encouraged, despite protests from the US Occupying Forces that such activity violated Allied Control Council regulations. But the Soviets were only doing more openly what the western powers did, for the victors on both sides had assumed a high cultural mission, to re-educate the German people and force 'a radical break with the reactionary past' (Naimark 1995: 424–8, 398).

The rapidity with which *Hamlet* was staged prefigured just how consequential Shakespeare was going to be in the cultural reconstruction of the two German nations. Though it is usually assumed that the reasons were different, in both the Federal Republic and the German Democratic Republic Shakespeare was seen as a method of connecting with prewar culture. That was more apparent in the West, where much of official politics and culture hoped to retrieve the life lost after 1930, to retrieve that Berlin already deeply in dream form. As Wilhelm Hortmann (1998: 175–6) puts it in his history of Shakespeare in Germany, people sought the same thing in the crowded theatres as in the crowded churches: 'reassurance, guidance, spiritual orientation, some form of hope, not flat confrontation with the unthinkable and ineffable'.

The strategy had disadvantages in the struggle for hearts and minds; as early as 1947 western political officers in occupied Germany complained that the Soviets' deep commitment to their own culture 'produced an atmosphere of excitement and accomplishment', while the West could offer only a rather staid pre-Nazi version of high culture as alternative (Naimark 1995: 399). Nonetheless Konrad Adenauer's fourteen-year term of office as Chancellor from 1949 set out on a quest for restored humanity.

The theatre sought not revolution as after the First World War but wished instead 'to regain lost humanist traditions', and the regeneration would be a safe and conservative one. When Brecht returned to Berlin in 1948 – he called the city that 'pile of rubble near Potsdam' (Farr 1992: 163) – he saw this desire as an attempt to carry on as usual, repressing all the huge falsity of the time. In one of the most telling analyses of the postwar situation, he said that 'everybody is afraid of the demolition without which reconstruction is impossible' (Hortmann 1998: 179–80). Audiences flocked to Shakespeare. From 1945 to 1955, the annual average was about 1,000 nights of performance for Shakespeare compared to less than 150 for Brecht. In the two decades after 1955 Shakespeare was undoubtedly in first place among playwrights in the number of productions and total performances. Schiller was considerably behind, and only after 1971 did Brecht begin to gain on his Elizabethan model. It is not surprising that West Germany evaded both the totalizing mentality and specific social implication in its use of Shakespeare in the 1950s. As an emergent liberal democracy it had much to prove and much to make up for; Adenauer Restoration was above all fixed on rebuilding Germany while convincing the victors that it was not the same old Germany. Ideas were dangerous, and for a while West German thought and art could pretend to avoid them.

Obviously things were very different in the East. In the GDR ideology was constantly foregrounded; artists without proper and approved analysis were deemed reactionary and could be condemned. Yet we find that a similar concern for established values dominated Shakespearean issues in the first decades after the war. Since Shakespeare was officially important in the Soviet Union, his position in the new German workers' state was doubly assured. Leninist orthodoxy maintained that Shakespeare wrote at the cusp of historical change from feudalism to capitalism, and that his characters often show a dawning awareness of the threats to humanity the new order will bring: a humanist reading based on materialist analysis. Theatre was valued in the GDR, somewhat paradoxically for an anti-bourgeois state, because it referred to a grander and more generous scale of human endeavour. It was a place for teaching, but also a home for what was elevated in the spirit. Thus a number of productions at the Deutsches Theater and elsewhere remained relatively free of overt political statements and often, like the Wangenheim *Hamlet* in 1945, took refuge in a generalized Renaissance-ism. As Maik Hamburger (1998: 372) puts it, 'Restoration of humanist values on a rationalist, atheist basis was, in fact, the main concern of subsequent Shakespeare productions in East Germany through the 1950s.'

The crucial period lay between the construction of the Wall in 1961 and the quatercentenary of Shakespeare's birth in 1964. Now the geographical centre of the Cold War, Berlin became a city of the imagination in this struggle, a Shakespearean double agent. Piscator's *Merchant of Venice* (1963) at the Freie Volksbühne, for example, sought on the western side to critique the anti-Semitic past and the disturbing signs of its continuation in the Federal Republic. It was a long way from Kortner's *Twelfth Night*, a production from 1957 that played in West Berlin at the Schillertheater in 1962, which seemed to deny all social or political forces in the text. Piscator's *Merchant* was part of the radical change in interpretation that Hortmann (221) dates from 1964, the move from a Christian Democrat view of theatre to making Shakespeare a battleground for thought, 'anything but a museum or high altar'.

In the eastern city the *Hamlet* by Wolfgang Heinz at the Deutsches Theater (1964) presented a fairly standard Marxist view of the prince as a failure because he refuses to grab the moment of history, allowing the fascist Fortinbras to take over the kingdom, but Heinz played this out in front of a triptych background of the nightmare paintings of Bosch, showing a world clearly out of joint, or the hellish landscape of Hamlet's mind. But the most important Shakespeare production in Berlin at the time was the Berliner Ensemble's *Coriolanus* in 1964, which applied Brecht's theatrical techniques for class analysis to Shakespeare for the first time in the GDR. Until then German theatres were not fully equipped, methodologically speaking, to present fully Marxist interpretations of the work. Only after *Coriolanus*, and the publication of Robert Weimann's book *Shakespeare und die Tradition des Volkstheaters* in 1967 (English version 1978), did the techniques useful to a materialist explication of Shakespeare in performance become widely known in Germany.

INSTRUCTING THE AUDIENCE

Shakespeare lived in a different world in Britain, more secure, continuous with the presumption of national greatness, appealing to the mentality of timelessness Vilar promoted in France but with the added assurance of the English language. Even Laurence Olivier's film of *Henry V* (1944), made under difficult conditions as his bit for the war effort, suggested a mythic politic rather than a *Realpolitik*. But the prewar inclination to keep social issues off the stage in the land of Shakespeare's birth started to wither in the face of the changes that were part of the cost of victory. With important foodstuffs and fuels still rationed until July 1954, many shortages continuing beyond that date, and a difficult economy on the horizon, it would have been very strange if all performances of Shakespeare in Britain ignored the harsh life and uncertain future audiences had endured since 1940. At the same time a sense of celebration and optimism often accompanied public events after the war, most notably in the Festival of Britain of 1951, in which the international-style architecture of the pavilions and buildings on the renovated South Bank of the Thames continued the traditions of high modernism (the Royal Festival Hall is the one remaining example). It might be argued that the Cold War extended the grip of theatrical modernism too, at once providing an opportunity to explore untapped potentials in the Shakespeare texts and certifying the notion that theatrical producers knew what the audience should need.

In the almost continuous rise in the number of Shakespeare performances since the war, one of the most notable features was the enlargement of the theatrical canon. Coincident with the final elevation of Shakespeare as the national poet, the Old Vic Theatre had begun this process in 1915 by a commitment to produce every play in the First Folio (1623), the first time any theatre anywhere had undertaken such a venture. Completed at last in 1923 as a 300th birthday present for Shakespeare's book, the project was caught between the desire to celebrate Shakespeare's status and the obligation to include even theatrically despised plays like *Troilus and Cressida*, *Love's Labour's Lost* and *Titus Andronicus*, all of which were saved for the final season. The last of these had for centuries been ignored on stage in Britain, its immature verse and cannibalistic plot too far removed from the sensibilities of the audience. Because *Titus Andronicus* appears so unShakespearean, many people thought it could not have been written by Shakespeare. Samuel Johnson in 1765: 'the barbarity of the spectacles, and the general massacre which are here exhibited, can scarcely be conceived tolerable to any audience'. T. S. Eliot in 1927: 'one of the stupidest and most uninspired plays ever written, a play in which it is incredible that Shakespeare has any hand at all' (Kennedy 1998). So the critics in 1923 were pleased that the play had been mounted at the Old Vic with some delicacy. 'It does not make you vomit in your stall', one wrote, though 'as a sensitive product of the twentieth century' he nonetheless asserted his right to be sick over *Titus*. Tamora does not 'gobble up her sons with unction' but 'pecks at them daintily, leaving the coloured electric light to do the rest'. Another reported considerable laughter in the house at the end, with the deaths of Tamora, Titus, Lavinia and Saturnius occurring 'within about five seconds, as in burlesque melodrama'.[1]

The next major production, by Peter Brook in 1955, was the epitome of a modernist move to recover inferior works. Still only thirty years old, Brook had already made his mark as a director of undervalued Shakespeare texts, and for *Titus* he set out to create a stylized world where the loathsome horrors of the play could be taken seriously by the audience at Stratford-upon-Avon; to effect the necessary aesthetic control he also designed the sets and costumes and composed the music. 'I can authoritatively deny,' wrote Bernard Levin, 'that he is also the man who tears the tickets in half' (*Truth*, 26 August 1955). The programme called attention to the text's marginal position by noting that this was its first performance at Stratford and only the third performance in Britain in a hundred years. Despite his belief in the play, the inappropriate laughter and gruesome melodrama from the Old Vic production were much on Brook's mind and he took considerable trouble to staunch their flow. His chief method involved conveying the physical horrors through beautiful estrangements, as in the well-known appearance of Vivien Leigh as Lavinia after her rape, de-tonguing and manual dismemberment, with streamers of scarlet and white ribbon flowing from her mouth and wrists accompanied by *musique concrète* played on the harp. Laurence Olivier's performance as Titus, universally praised, accented a powerful but controlled anguish, just as Aaron's evil was submerged into Anthony Quayle's exotic beauty.

Heavily influenced by Olivier's playing, the critics frequently compared *Titus* to *King Lear*, legitimizing its new status. 'This inferior and disputed tragedy has been admitted to the canon', one review noted; 'we have, in effect, acquired another Shakespearean play', said a second; while the headline of J. C. Trewin's notice read 'A Despised Play Set on High.'[2] Looking through the reviews of the production and its 1957 revival in London, I was struck chiefly by the witnesses' awe over a historic moment. They expected an embarrassing show, they got a major theatrical event. The critics were also much more aware of audience response than usual, frequently taking the trouble to describe what they call the mood of the auditorium or the reaction of spectators to a specific scene. A number of papers noticed a self-conscious anticipation in the house before the curtain on opening night at Stratford, usually ascribing it to a kind of queasy expectation about the inferior text and its frenzy of blood. Many commented on the absence of laughter, though some said there was sporadic nervous laughter, implying it came from people insufficiently in control of their emotions. As Trewin wrote, 'Titus, in some minds, was pre-judged as a joke . . . But the laughter dies at birth. Throughout the house was held by its throat.' Brook's modernist endeavour to recover the text is clearly in evidence here, since preventing or limiting inappropriate laughter was the absolute first step in claiming a higher value for an inferior script, and the critics apparently accepted that premise as just and proper.

A few astute commentators dared to admit that after the war and the mundane terrors of Belsen, the Britain of 1955 was in a position to understand the Elizabethan fascination with cold bloodshed. Harold Hobson, for example, remarked that *Titus* 'comes disconcertingly near to the current standards of political behaviour' (*Sunday Times*, 21 August 1955). This sense of the play's relevance – to use the term that Peter Hall would claim as the foundation of the Royal Shakespeare Company (RSC) in 1960 – or of the play's presence in the living world, was much more noticeable on the continent. In between its startling premiere in Stratford and its triumphal entry into London, the production went on tour to Paris, Venice, Belgrade, Zagreb, Vienna and Warsaw. In Europe, Brook (1968: 47) thought, 'this obscure work of Shakespeare touched audiences directly because we had tapped a ritual of bloodshed which was recognized as true'. In the easternmost of those cities it was seen by an academic and theatre critic who wrote that '*Titus Andronicus* has revealed to me a Shakespeare I dreamed of but have never before seen on the stage.' He was Jan Kott (1966: 353). Kott and Brook met in a crowded and smoky Warsaw bar and began a discussion about the innate cruelty of Shakespeare's themes that would lead to Kott's book, *Shakespeare Our Contemporary* and to Brook's production of *King Lear*, both of which appeared five years later.

In many ways Brook's position on recovering inferior works for the modern audience was the turning point in the postwar use of Shakespeare in general. The Cold War reading of the texts, influenced by Brecht as much as Kott, that was to dominate the RSC and most European production for the next generation, was created in part by the boldness of Brook's treatment of the most neglected Shakespearean play. Lying disused, without any reliable tradition of performance, the marginal works were therefore more manoeuvrable and more directable: their audiences responded with less resistance to the imposition of foreign methods and new meanings. The pitiless brutality of *Titus* made it an especially effective weapon in the battle over the ownership of Shakespeare's texts that Brook and Hall waged against traditionalists. Recovered for a stage adamantly contemporary in nature, Brook had uncovered a wealth of opportunity for other plays, both lesser and greater ones.

In his delightfully sardonic way, Kenneth Tynan caught the spirit of this movement early. After he saw the London revival in 1957 of Peter Brook's

Titus along with Peter Hall's production of *Cymbeline*, he wrote that 'these two young directors should at once go into partnership'. He suggested a business card for them:

Hall & Brook, Ltd, the Home of Lost Theatrical Causes. Collapsing plays shored up, unspeakable lines glossed over, unactable scenes made bearable. Wrecks salvaged, ruins refurbished: unpopular plays at popular prices. Masterpieces dealt with only if neglected. Shakespearian juvenilia and senilia our specialty: if it can walk, we'll make it run. Bad last acts no obstacle: if it peters out, call Peter in (Tynan 1984: 265).

When the RSC was formed three years later, Hall and Brook did go into a kind of partnership, and their distinctive shared trait at Stratford remained an engagement with recovery. Even when directing the well-known and established plays, they continued to bring to Shakespeare a spirit of reinvention, revelation and disclosure: you may think you know these texts, their productions of the 1960s would say to the audience, but we're going to show that you do not. To put it another way, they treated the major plays – *Lear*, *Midsummer*, *Henry IV*, *The Tempest* – as if they were marginal works needing rediscovery.

SHAKESPEARE AS COLD WARRIOR

The Brechtian mode was first developed for Shakespeare in France and Italy, notably in the productions of Roger Planchon and Giorgio Strehler. Both had seen the Berliner Ensemble and met Brecht before his death in 1956, and both immediately saw the potential for Shakespeare of his general method. In 1957 Planchon staged an adaptation of *Henry IV* in Lyon which used Brechtian devices effectively to comment on the power struggles in the text, and particularly to reveal the social and economic distinctions between the proletariat, foot soldiers, nobles and the church. Mimed scenes were interpolated that showed the suffering of the common people and the cruelty of their rulers. The play was entirely deromanticized: Hotspur was stabbed in the back while Prince Hal was fighting him in the front. Strangely co-incident, just a few days later Strehler opened *Coriolanus* in Milan in a modernized translation; the production also emphasized essentials through a reduced visual field that gave the audience time to think – each fragmented scene was identified by a placard that commented on its significance. In the title role Tino Carraro played a dictator with paranoia, suggesting a political tragedy with thoroughly modern applications.

The populist dramaturgy begun by Vilar in 1947 had a decade later become an overtly Marxist one and was used more and more as a dissident exclamation in the capitalist countries of Europe. Nowhere was this more surprising than in England, where Peter Hall, overwhelmed by the power and clarity of the Berliner Ensemble's productions in London in 1956, founded the RSC four years later with Brecht's organizational model and performance methods as his cornerstones, only a year before the Berlin Wall was built. It seems particularly strange that a company sponsored by the Queen should mark itself as so politically engaged, and there is huge doubt that it ever was. The Royal Shakespeare Company, as the joke went at the time, has everything in its name but god. Nonetheless important productions in the first years clearly placed social issues in the foreground, even if they often remained ambiguous about what conclusions should be drawn from them. And the RSC was not alone in preferring Shakespeare. An era of unprecedented prosperity saw a significant increase in the number of Shakespeare productions everywhere in Europe, enabled by huge increases in public spending.

Of course Shakespeare had been presented before the war in a variety of Marxist clothes, especially in the Soviet Union. What was different about Marxist Shakespeare in the 1950s in Europe was the echo of the Cold War, which lent any criticism of the West made from within a heightened voice and contextualized it with the knowledge that an alternative to the capitalist system was living next door: as Coriolanus says, there is a world elsewhere. Why did liberal governments in the West fund companies that presented work critical of the capitalist order? In a sense they were trapped into it, or embarrassed into it, by the fact that it was being done in that elsewhere. East and West, arts councils were locked in a cultural arms race. If John Le Carré is right, the Cold War was a 'looking-glass war', in which the enemies stared at each other across the front and saw only their own reflections. The greatest irony of the period was that a figure of high-art status like Shakespeare was enlisted into the socialist cause by West European Marxists while after 1968 or 1970 certain directors in the Eastern Bloc would be using him to critique and undermine the socialist system in place there. 'Dissident Shakespeare' had different meanings depending on where you were, but on both sides of the Iron Curtain it was likely to be well funded.

East of the Elbe the new authorities continued the long practice of state support for high-art ventures, a duty that now conveniently combined continuity of the past with propaganda about the virtues of socialist government. Though Austria, West Germany and France also had long traditions of public subsidy, it was only after the war that countries like Italy, Britain and the US began to take seriously the notion that financial support for the theatre might be a national task. There is little doubt that the sums spent on the arts by the governments of western Europe were at least in part designed as counter-propaganda for the East, and designed to support bourgeois notions of freedom. Ironically western nations relied on a quasi-socialist redistribution of wealth to arts organizations in order to bolster the virtues of a free-market economy.

It is well known by now how deeply implicated the secret services were in cultural financing. In her exhaustive study *Who Paid the Piper?* (1999), Frances Stonor Saunders detailed the extraordinary extent of the CIA's involvement in European cultural affairs, funding, always indirectly, intellectual journals (most famously *Encounter*), book publication, conferences, travel, writers, orchestras, recordings, films, tours of ballet, theatre and jazz groups, radio broadcasts and the networks of the Voice of America and Radio Free Europe. Most of the American payouts in Europe were channelled through or connected to the Congress for Cultural Freedom, a strange and often opaque organization first located in Berlin, then headquartered in Paris in the 1950s. The Congress had almost limitless money to promote artists, critics and events sympathetic to American policy, or somehow indicative of the virtues of the western way of life. I am not claiming that the CIA paid for Shakespeare performance; in fact the work CIA funders preferred was usually American, modernist, experimental or populist. But I do suggest that the large support for Shakespeare in western Europe during the Cold War was part of a web of government spending, overt and covert, local and American, that had as its object the promotion of the superiority of liberal democracy and the capitalist system.

In 1962 Kenneth Tynan presented a parody of the Congress for Cultural Freedom on *That Was the Week that Was* on the BBC. Saunders (1999: 340–1) presents it thus:

'And now, a hot flash from the Cold War in Culture,' began the sketch. 'This diagram is the Soviet cultural bloc. Every dot on the map represents a strategic cultural emplacement – theatre bases, centres of film production, companies of dancers churning out intercontinental balletic missiles . . . a massive cultural build-up is going on. But what about us in the West? Do we have an effective strike-back capacity in the event of an all-out cultural war?' Yes, the sketch continued, there was the good old Congress for Cultural Freedom, which, 'supported by American money, has set up a number of advanced bases in Europe and elsewhere to act as spearheads of cultural retaliation. These bases are disguised as magazines and bear codenames – Encounter, which is short for "Encounterforce Strategy" '. A 'Congress spokesman' was then introduced, who boasted of a cluster of magazines which were a 'kind of cultural NATO', the aim of which was 'Cultural containment, or, as some of the boys like to put it, a ring around the pinkoes. . . . I'd say we had a historic mission. World readership . . .'

West Berlin flourished through parallel subventions from the Federal Republic, which provided assistance for daily life and for the arts. Air ticket subventions, tax concessions, hotel subsidies, funding for two universities, for first-rank housing projects, for the Deutsche Oper, the Philharmonie, the Freie Volksbühne and the Schaubühne, all designed to draw visitors and impress them with the culture and politics of a free town in the middle of a hostile country (Tusa 1996: 354). Less than a decade after the war the unreal city had become a very real 'showcase of capitalism meant to prove the superiority of the West and to dazzle those in the Soviet zone' (Richie 1999, caption to 1953 photo). Later Peter Stein had only to suggest that he might leave the city for the West Berlin Senate to agree to build the Schaubühne a new home that cost over 100 million Deutschmarks (Patterson and Huxley 1998: 229). But by 1961 Khrushchev found the open door unacceptable and contemplated forcibly annexing West Berlin; in the end the Americans accepted the Wall as an expedient way out of a dangerous situation. 'It's not a very nice solution', John Kennedy said at the time, 'but a wall is a hell of a lot better than a war' (Tusa 305). Feeling abandoned by the world and desperate for recognition of their plight, West Berliners latched onto Kennedy's eventual visit in June 1963 as a decisive moment: *Lasst sie nach Berlin kommen*, he said of those in the West who wished to compromise with the Soviet Union, 'Let them come to Berlin.' And that was just what West Berliners wanted to happen, let the world come to see the lethal line in the sand of the Cold War.

In the larger frame, the turning point in the Cold War history of Shakespeare came in the very year of the Wall with the publication of Jan Kott's *Shakespeare Our Contemporary* in Polish, followed the next year by a French edition and in 1964 by translations into English and German. If the Cold War had been lurking in the shadows of Shakespeare studies and performance since 1945, with Kott's work it entered without disguise and with a new language. His book made the divide in approaches apparent. Brecht's followers saw Shakespeare as a force for social change in the present; Kott saw him as our contemporary precisely because, in his view, the world does not change. Not for Kott the Marxist belief that progress is possible through the actions of human beings; Shakespeare showed us, he claimed, that we could not escape the cyclical nightmare, the beast within our sexuality or the 'grand mechanism' of history. Abandoning his Marxist background after the Soviet invasion of Hungary, Kott became in his critical work a supporter of the dominant western belief in individualism. As John Elsom (1992: 78) astutely points out, by retaining the old trust in the universality of Shakespeare but moving it directly into the realm of the 'contemporary', Kott hinted that directors in the East could use the mask of Shakespeare to 'comment on current affairs without fear of censorship' from Stalinist regimes.

Kott's influence on Shakespeare productions in the 1960s and 1970s was enormous. The most famous, of course, was Brook's *King Lear* for the RSC in 1962, which was overwhelmingly driven to convey a world without affect, a world of universal annihilation. Kott's most widely read chapter, 'King Lear or Endgame', called upon Beckett's play to explain the clownish atrocity of Lear and Gloucester. *Endgame* (first produced in Paris in 1957 as *Fin de partie*) is the quintessential Cold War drama, showing a remnant of life in the 'shelter', an entropic universe, a metaphorical and theatrical space made up of absences. The disintegrating body and the closure of narrative are its most significant features, where the blind Hamm who cannot stand and the sighted Clov who cannot sit are doubled images of Cold War impotence that is not quite able to end. 'Outside of here it's death', says Hamm. *Endgame* became for Kott a model for understanding the absurd within Shakespeare's tragedy, and Brook seemed to swallow the idea whole. Brook himself wrote that '*Lear* is for me the prime example of the Theatre of the Absurd, from which everything good in modern drama has been drawn.' Certainly Brook gave the ultimate compliment of a cold warrior when he added that 'Kott is undoubtedly the only writer on Elizabethan matters who assumes that every one of his readers will at some point or other have been awoken by the police in the middle of the night' (Brook 1987: 89, 44).

Though the production was at pains to use a number of Brechtian devices, from its anti-illusionist creation of the storm scene to bringing up the house lights during Gloucester's blinding in an attempt to implicate the audience, these were apolitical in implication. Brook's *Lear* was focussed on the individual, not the social group. It assumed Kott's existentialist premise, the anti-Marxist premise that the world is a cold and unchanging place, that human progress is not possible since men and women are beasts at heart. Nowhere did this theme resonate more loudly than in Eastern Europe, where many people living under Stalinist regimes felt powerless to alter their lives and lived in fear of repression and retaliation. Admitting that his *Lear* did not connect with spectators on its tour to the USA in spring 1964, where audiences felt remote from its themes of absence and loss, Brook (1968: 21–3) noted that earlier that same year 'the best performances lay between Budapest and Moscow'. The production must be acknowledged as one of the first – perhaps the very first – major performance of Shakespeare that appeared in the socialist countries which used Kott's coded method to critique, implicitly and only half-intentionally, the politics of the Iron Curtain. Brook's *Lear*, born of the Cold War, produced in the year of the Cuban Missile Crisis, visually indicating holocaust and devastation, more than anything else evoked for its audiences East and West the policy of Mutual Assured Destruction. One of the greatest productions of Shakespeare of the modern era, it was a cultural phenomenon, almost an oddity, enabled by its moment.

Despite subsequent growth in the number of Shakespeare performances, it is highly unlikely that we will ever see again the same degree of social commitment to Shakespeare that went hand-in-hand with the Cold War in Europe, or the same level of public subsidy that supported it.

CHAPTER 5

The spectator as tourist

Tourism, despite derision and sleaze, is ever more important in global cultural life. All of us are tourists now and then, eagerly or reluctantly visiting the exotic, consuming the foreign, watching the great universal show. The past is particularly important: jet travel since about 1960 has become a form of time travel, allowing us glimpses of lost worlds, making us into historians of heritage and connoisseurs of the alien. This is why, as the sociologist Erik Cohen notes, 'tourism is a fuzzy concept'; his best definition emphasizes that tourists are people who travel 'in the expect- ation of pleasure from the novelty and change experienced' while away from the mundane rule of their lives (Cohen 2004: 22). Touristic experience takes many forms, from sun-and-seas escapes to participatory hard work like shovelling manure on a dude ranch, but is usually charac- terized by its extraordinary dimension, temporal limitation and the absence of responsibility. To be a tourist is above all to be a willing stranger.

Spectators at performances have much in common with tourists, at least on a superficial level. Whether in a theatre or a cinema, at a circus or parade, in front of a television or at live sport, spectators seek enter- tainment, refreshment and sometimes knowledge through entrance into or observation of an unusual event, extraordinary sight or fictive world. As travellers approach a touristic site, so spectators encounter a per- formance through the gaze, which implies a distance of subject to object. Both tourists and spectators are temporary visitors to another realm who expect to return to the quotidian. If they have psychological or other investment in the event, it is normally limited to a ludic complicity. They generally accept the commodification of the object and their own status as consumers unproblematically.

Much theatre discourse has assumed that what draws audiences to drama is the connection they make from the stage to their own selves; certainly this is the dominant view that operated in modernist thinking, whether based on ideas of identification or defamiliarization. Such a view elevates the moral status of the theatre, recovering some of the intellectual and spiritual power that it was presumed to have in ancient Athens, the premodern lending seriousness to the modern. A common theme in manifestos and commentary from Wagner on, especially in the condemnatory rhetoric of Bernard Shaw and the exasperated grievances of Gordon Craig, the insistence that the spectator should assume a virtuous union with the event strongly influenced subsequent thinking about the theatre. When compared to tourists, however, spectators may be seen less as participants in a moral venture and more as recreational travellers who construct themselves as outsiders for the sake of gaining playful entrance into another world.

The relationship of tourism to performance has begun to receive attention from an anthropological position (Kirshenblatt-Gimblet 1998; Balme 2007) and an economic one (Bennett 2005), but sociologists have been studying tourists for more than a generation and tend to be interested in other issues. The initiator of work in this line is usually taken to be Dean MacCannell's *The Tourist: a new theory of the leisure class* (1976), which asserts that tourism is a search for an 'authentic other'; leisure travel is prompted by a desire to experience that which is not us. Since the starting point for modernity is the alienation of the individual, tourists, lacking a sense of wholeness in their own lives, seek it in an alternative elsewhere. Tourists are modernity's paradoxical consumers who desire not merchandise but experience; the attractions of the world draw them with promises of sensation or renewal, inspiration or diversion. Experience can be marketed but is hard to commodify, not because it is immaterial but because it is eminently variable. If my experience is not your experience, how can an organizer know what punters will receive? Visits can be structured as in cruises and coach tours, and souvenir objects provided every step of the way, but the touristic site is only the occasion for the adventure. Extracting from MacCannell, we might say that seeing the Acropolis, touching its stones, is ultimately a prompt for an event that occurs in the mind of the visitor, just as, according to standard semiotic analysis, the meaning of a performance occurs in the mind of spectator.

THE TOURIST AS SPECTATOR

The high demands serious modernist theatre likes to place on spectators has been paralleled by a low demand by the tourism industry on its clients. Both tendencies may be rooted in simplistic notions about which leisure activities are appropriate to which social class. Traditionally rather harsh judgements have been made about the authenticity of touristic encounters by conservative cultural commentators (Boorstin 1964, Fussell 1980), who called into question the entire touristic enterprise. The argument goes like this: since the other is so difficult to know, and since the trade can so easily deceive unwary consumers about what is genuine, the tourist habitually succumbs to superficial sham. The search for authenticity may be real but the authentic, almost by definition, is not available in the touristic mode, and thus the tourist's moral status is highly questionable. MacCannell, not entirely free of this condemnatory rhetoric, holds that 'a mere experience may be mystified, but a touristic experience is always mystified' (1976: 102), tourists being satisfied by the 'staged authenticity' provided by the industry.

But MacCannell's hypothesis that all tourists are in search of an authentic other is troubling, since he does not sufficiently investigate what authenticity means. Especially challenging to his position are the numerous cases like the Disneylands where flagrantly inauthentic sites have nonetheless achieved large touristic success. Even at a genuine site the tourist tends to engage in a complex exchange, seeing not the authenticity but rather the metonym. Whatever its interest or distinction as a building, Westminster Abbey fascinates not only in itself but because it points to a sedimented history and culture, a connected otherness. Cohen's critiques and amplifications of MacCannell's structuralist premise are a useful antidote, particularly helpful in suggesting that authenticity is not a fixed state but 'a socially constructed concept' whose significance is not given; we should worry less about the authenticity of site and more about 'the manner of the negotiation of its meaning' (2004: 104).

Cohen recognizes that ethnographers and museum curators demand a high level of authenticity, which for them 'is principally a quality of pre-modern life' and highly difficult to find. For tourists, however, authenticity is mostly a personal bargain struck with the event. Since authenticity is not fixed, commodification does not in itself destroy the meaning of cultural products or represent fraud; in fact authenticity may gradually emerge, even in situations that are eminently counterfeit. We can witness the shifting ground of authentication in how the Disneylands, 'once seen as the supreme example of contrived popular entertainment, became over time a vital component of contemporary American culture'. They will in the future likely 'be perceived even by historians and ethnographers as an "authentic" American tradition' (110). The bogus nature of much tourist activity, therefore, need not destroy the pleasure of vacation travel. Maxine Feifer (1985: 259–68) goes further, identifying as 'post-tourists' those who revel in the inauthenticity of routine excursionary activities, taking fun in touristic games (see also Urry 2002: 11–13).

Spectators at a dramatic performance are similar, aware of the pretence of the event while normally comporting themselves as if it were not entirely pretence. But there is a further complication, because many spectators at cultural events actually are tourists. Cultural tourism, a form of recreation in which travellers spend leisure time and money on cultural activity, became important in modern Europe with the rise of the Grand Tour at the end of the seventeenth century, when the sons of aristocrats and gentlemen completed their education by observing the manners and art of other nations. Despite its widening to the bourgeoisie in the nineteenth, the Grand Tour was the property of an elite, like most high culture. A vast increase in domestic and international tourism occurred after 1960, fostered by paid holidays for workers, a generally expanding economy and the ease of jet transport. The World Tourism Organization calculates that between 1950 and 2006 international tourist arrivals rose from 25 million to 846 million per annum, a thirty-four-fold increase. The number is expected to exceed 1 billion arrivals in 2010 and 1.6 billion in 2020.[1] (World population in 2020 is projected to reach about 7.6 billion.) Tourism is now the world's largest industry, its gross annual receipts in 2005 in excess of one trillion (a million million) US dollars. A rising tide raises all boats; the general growth has enabled an increase in the number of cultural institutions offering themselves as likely material for the tourist's gaze.

While many tourists do not partake of cultural activities, or do so only incidentally, a significant number set out to entertain or instruct themselves with cultural practice, so much so that the European Union has frequently identified cultural tourism as a crucial element in the overall economy of its member nations (Richards 1996: 12). Many North Americans who go to Europe do so for underlying cultural and historical reasons, to gain what Pierre Bourdieu calls social and symbolic capital. Six of the top ten tourist destination states in the world in 2005 were the major nations of western Europe (in order, France, Spain, Italy, UK, Austria and Germany), all of them attractive to visitors for reasons of cultural heritage, though the good weather of Mediterranean areas is part of the appeal. Summer arts and theatre festivals have blossomed; fifty years after its founding the Edinburgh Festival offers almost a thousand events in three weeks and the Avignon Festival a hundred presentations a day for more than a month. In the heritage industry a maniacal growth occurred in the English-speaking countries during the Thatcher-Reagan years, commodifying a burgeoning concern with history and nostalgia (Lowenthal 1985): industrial age museums, themed historical parks, local history centres. In England alone more than a thousand new sightseeing attractions of various types opened in the fifteen years after 1979 (Herbert 1995: 8).

A large number of cultural institutions cannot survive on indigenous patrons, theatres included. Goodly portions of the audiences for Broadway are not residents of New York, in London overseas tourists make up more than one-third of the nightly houses for West End theatres, and the Royal Shakespeare Company in Stratford might close if it could not tap the stream of pilgrims to the Bard's Birthroom. Dramatic festivals from Wagner's Festspielhaus in Bayreuth to the numerous Shakespeare festivals in the US, by virtue of their isolated locations and temporal limits, have been founded on principles of cultural tourism, requiring their audiences to travel. The two largest theatre companies in North America, one named for Shakespeare, the other for Shaw, are in small towns in Ontario that have developed earnest tourist industries dependent on the festivals they host. The spectator's playgoing in festival environments is bracketed by a larger set of holiday commodities and practices – temporary accommodation, restaurants, bars, museum attendance, local transport, sightseeing, guides, shopping – which condition and affect the experience of the theatre. Speaking more generally, William Rees-Mogg, chairman of the Arts Council during part of Margaret Thatcher's premiership, proclaimed in 1985 that 'the arts are to British tourism what the sun is to Spain' (Hewison 1987: 107). Or as a European official put it, 'culture and tourism are destined once and for all to be together' (in Richards 1996: 12).

HISTORY AS THEME PARK

Richard Sennett holds that in the nineteenth century the nature of human exchange in expanding urban environments was significantly altered: no longer a verbally charged space of interaction between citizens, the members of the industrialized population became spectacle for one another. The individual, superseding the social group as the centre of human agency, 'fell silent in the city', he writes. 'The street, the café, the department store, the railroad, bus, and underground became places of gaze rather than scenes of discourse'; in the pub or café, a patron could construct the passing crowd into 'a theatre of one's private thoughts' (1994: 358, 346). In a similar vein Robert Hughes (1991: 12) notes that rapid train travel made for its riders a new theatre out of the passing landscape, and that the Eiffel Tower created a theatre out of the city.

Modernity and tourism are intertwined: as the technology of travel increased so more and more of the world became objectified as sights to wonder over or visit for private refreshment. Postmodernity has continued the trend with a vengeance; in keeping with economic globalization, an all-embracing tourism shapes much of social circulation. James Clifford (1997) argues that travel and the state of being between cultures most characterized the late twentieth century and its anthropological study. Concomitant with the expansion of tourism has been a substantial elevation of history and heritage. There is considerable controversy surrounding this movement, especially in Britain, with the opponents effectively divided into socialist and conservative views of the past. The 'end of history' has prompted a greater concern for history; *post-histoire* we are all the more obsessed with it. Conservation, as Raphael Samuel wrote a few years before he died, 'whatever the doubts about the notion of "heritage", is one of the major aesthetic and social movements of our time.' If tourism can make the voyager into a minor historian, the expansion of the matter considered suitable for the writing of history in turn creates new sites for touristic display. We live 'in an expanding historical culture, in which the work of inquiry and retrieval is being progressively extended in all kinds of spheres that would have been thought unworthy of notice in the past' (Samuel 1994: 25).

But one might take a gloomier approach to the growth market in history. Robert Hewison's *The Heritage Industry* (1987) saw the movement as a sign of Britain's decline under Thatcherite policies: 'instead of manufacturing goods, we are manufacturing *heritage*, a commodity which nobody seems able to define, but which everybody is eager to sell' (9). Industrial age museums, themed historical parks, local history centres, the list goes on: in Britain in the mid-1980s new museums opened at the rate of about one a day. Examples: the dental museum in London, the pencil museum in Keswick, the shoe museum in Street, to which we might add the leprosy museum in Bergen, the prisoner-of-war museum in Singapore and the Auschwitz museum. Baudrillard (1994a: 12, 22) ascribed apocalyptic overtones to this drift in international affairs. We are eminently busy,

reviewing everything, rewriting everything, restoring everything, face-lifting everything, to produce, as it seems, in a burst of paranoia a perfect set of accounts at the end of the century . . . Museums, jubilees, festivals, complete works, the publication of the tiniest of unpublished fragments – all this shows we are entering an active age of *ressentiment* and repentance.

It is easy to apply Baudrillard's notion to both popular and high culture, especially as the traditional distinctions between them continue to break down. Retro-fashion, cannibalizing itself with ever greater frequency; the intercultural culinary fads of the West, exploring Third World diets for new sensations and healthy-chic; intercultural art forms, looting the cultural storehouses of Asia and Africa; Hollywood movies of classic novels and remakes of classic films; the apparent end of communism, reprising in new areas the consumerist victories of plutocracy; and of course historical and heritage theme parks: these tendencies create what looks like a world made out of recycled objects and ideas, an impotent present, a mannerist savouring of residues. The past becomes a universal Disneyland.

But Disneyland is not just a convenient scapegoat, it is the logical model of the culture of pastness in a global economy. Despite their extreme merchandizing of culture, theme parks are popularly successful because they provide an accessible and diverting thoroughfare to an imagined history or mythical world. Like outdoor heritage museums, they are 'exercises in nostalgia, presenting a sanitised view of culture' (Shackley 1994: 396–7), but a view that clearly appeals to huge numbers of tourists having fun with commodity experience. In any case there is often an element of self-deception in tourist pleasure. Tourists may think they want authenticity, but most actually want 'some degree of negotiated experiences which provide a tourist "bubble" (a safe, controlled environment) out of which they can selectively step to "sample" predictable forms of experiences' (Craik 1997: 115).

And what about the complexities of art? Many people assume that high art activities, visits to the National Gallery or to Shakespeare plays, are more virtuous, yet corporations have also learned how to respond to the growing market in cultural leisure. The Disney Institute in Orlando hosts conferences in any field and holidaymakers who want to use their time profitably can enrol in a range of classes from cooking to film making. Visits from celebrities add lustre, including actors from the Royal Shakespeare Company. Disney executives call this 'edutainment' and also have a scientific word for the study of consumer behaviour in theme parks: 'guestology' (Var 1993). It's hard to avoid an ironic tone when pronouncing these terms, but they are simply reception theory gone retail.

No doubt you wish to escape commercialized environments on holiday and want me to distinguish between Shakespeare as art and the commodity art in Orlando, but anything can be merchandized if there is a market for it and everything is a potential heritage experience. The past is attractive to the tourist experience because it remains unapproachable yet tempts us with the illusion of the knowable. In a world of simulations we seek certified sites, verified objects, confirmed auras: this is Bach's clavier, this Marlowe's grave, this Agamemnon's bath. In the depths of a sceptical age we long for some one absolute, historic, veritable vision.

In a search for the unfeigned object you might wish to peer at the chasm of the distant past and visit the caves at Lascaux to see with your own eyes some of the oldest records of human culture. Sorry, you can't visit the caves at Lascaux, since they were closed in 1963 to prevent further deterioration of the wall paintings. Instead you will enter an enormous concrete bunker built twenty years later that copies in concrete every natural detail of the cave walls, a guidebook certifies; 'on this background painters have reproduced the figures and symbols as exactly as possible, using the same materials as the Magdalenians'. The replica 'gives visitors more detailed information and is more accessible than anything they could have gleaned by visiting the real cave at Lascaux' (Delluc 1990: 62). The original, though under lock and key, will decay and disappear, so the copy, *mise-en-abyme*, is better than the original.

CULTURAL CAPITAL AND CULTURAL TOURISM

But I must shake this ironic tone if I am to deal honestly with the topic, and I will attempt to do that by means of Shakespeare and with the help of Bourdieu. His argument that class is central to the establishment of taste has obvious applications to the appreciation of Shakespeare and the uses made of him. Briefly, Bourdieu's *Distinction: a social critique of the judgement of taste* (1984) holds that classes seek to distinguish themselves by taste attributes. Class establishes a plane or band which disciplines a person's cultural expectations or opportunities. This horizon of limitation is what Bourdieu calls *habitus*. 'A work of art has meaning and interest only for someone who possesses the cultural competence, that is, the code, into which it is encoded' (2). Education is a potential mechanism for acquiring the cultural capital needed to shift the horizon, but since schools naturalize the dominant culture the lower classes are always playing catch-up. It is possible to reject the 'classificatory struggle' but such a move merely acknowledges the power of the dominant taste, so that 'alternative' styles are always contained within greater rivalries over distinction. In the last chapter we saw how Shakespeare became entwined with the Cold War; now I hope to show how Shakespeare performance has become deeply enmeshed with cultural tourism.

Starting with Wagner at Bayreuth and Max Reinhardt at Salzburg, the modern arts festival has often evoked recovery of the past as a sanctified purpose. Like the restored Olympics in the first part of the twentieth century, the arts festivals laid claim to a connection with the quasi-religious festivals of ancient Greece, which for the theatre were idealized as arenas of political, social and spiritual integration. Two issues were crucial. First, performances in twentieth-century festivals tended to be placed in unusual designed or found spaces modelled on the circle that encouraged a sense of togetherness among spectators. Many modernist theatre directors believed that a renovated approach to performance could be achieved by returning to the ancient festival ideal of an enveloping audience, and Shakespeare was central to this movement. Second, the location of the festivals and their calendar limitations meant that a large portion of the audiences had to travel to reach them, encouraging a sense of pilgrimage to sacred locales, presenting themselves as edifying arenas for summer holidays.

The major English-speaking Shakespeare festivals fit the same pattern. The town of Stratford had been dependent on pilgrims since Garrick's Jubilee in 1769, though the Shakespeare Memorial Theatre, built about a century later, failed to become a significant cultural site until revitalized by Barry Jackson in that pivotal year of 1947. It grew enormously in cultural importance in the 1960s because of the founding of the Royal Shakespeare Company, but the town, difficult to reach by rail, could not have supported the greatly expanded seasons of the RSC without the growth in private car ownership and in coach tours from London. Between 1965 and 1985 passenger mileage in Britain grew by 60 per cent (Urry 1990: 6). Stratford Ontario, New York City and Stratford Connecticut opened Shakespeare festivals one after the other in the mid-1950s, and were followed by a number of festivals in North America yoked to touristic affairs. Though they did not share the same cultural attitudes or performance styles, they all claimed Shakespeare as central to contemporary theatre and assumed high-minded positions about his place in a historical continuity.

In fitting modernist fashion, the festivals saw Shakespeare as an acknowledged universal monument and attempted in production to realize his greatness. They continued enlightenment claims for high art: Shakespeare as transcendent inspiration, as political or moral force, and particularly in Britain and North America, as public heritage. Class was a central issue at many of the venues, usually in a progressive way;

Shakespeare festivals wished to widen their spectator base for both political and practical reasons. The most interesting case is that of the RSC under Peter Hall and Trevor Nunn in the period from 1962 to 1975, when its initial leftist leanings caused the company to reach out to students and the regions of Britain to the north of Stratford. Low-cost student tickets, group rates for schools, adult education endeavours, widespread touring, more contemporary styles like David Warner's déclassé Hamlet in 1965, a broadening of the repertory to include new plays and the creation of a permanent RSC venue in London (Beauman 1982) – most of these would now be called 'outreach' programmes meant to democratize the theatre. While some of them, especially those connected to education, eventually played into the hands of the Thatcherite heritage mongers of the 1980s, they initially succeeded in raising the cultural capital of people traditionally indifferent to Shakespeare and the theatre.

But attendance at the flagship house in Stratford still depended upon excursion; the barriers presented by the cost of the tickets, travel, meals and accommodation remained, as well as the unchanged notion in working-class culture that Shakespeare is highfalutin and boring. The apparent democratization of Shakespeare performance in the first fifteen years of the RSC, whatever widening of the British audience pool it may have achieved, did so by the usual method in the capitalist West, by *embourgeoisement*. In this process the 'new intellectuals', as Bourdieu calls them, moved up to become the new petite bourgeoisie.

Much more significant than any enlargement of the class base was the growth in audiences to Stratford brought by international travel, which tends to blur class lines. In the domain of the museum, for example, special interest collections like rock-'n'-roll museums and sports museums have flourished by drawing tourists from a range of social levels, constructing them as classless consumers in the manner of global capitalism. Amsterdam now offers the Sex Museum, the Pianola Museum and the Cannabis Museum; tourists, gazing at the exotic and unusual for the sake of refreshment, will often find those sites more interesting than Rembrandt or Van Gogh. Though some would still insist that viewing high art invites or at least permits a richer and more rewarding experience, as a touristic activity museum-going lumps all types of cultural production together. As occupier of the trekker's day, the Museum of the Cartoon in Brussels is equal to the Uffizi Gallery.

And why not? If we take Bourdieu's loose definition of class – which is slightly circular, in that personal elections like food, dress, housing and body demeanour are seen as defining rather than predetermined factors –

there is little doubt that in the West as a whole it is more difficult today to separate tourist attractions along strict class lines. Even many traditional art museums, accustomed in the past to an elite clientele, Richards holds, have abandoned 'the modernist project of universality, in favour of market segmentation and theming'. Far from destroying the idea of public collections this move has expanded the notion of what constitutes legitimate cultural production, compelled in part by a harsher era of public funding. As 'a single museum can no longer claim to contain the essence of European culture' (Richards 1996: 10–11), so no single plane or band of practice can afford to appeal only to its traditional patrons. Further, travel in itself is socially prestigious so that cultural tourism becomes an acknowledged means for gaining new cultural and symbolic capital, confusing the class issue all the more (Munt 1994; also Craik 1997).

And yet it is increasingly apparent that stable repeat audiences for high art products are limited and often remain stubbornly elitist. On the one hand we witness a dismantling of barriers between high and popular culture. The Three Tenors at the World Cup in 1990 made opera part of sport; advertising continues to unlock cultural storehouses for fresh commercial images; Baz Luhrmann's *William Shakespeare's Romeo + Juliet* and Richard Loncraine's *Richard III* made Shakespeare part of pop film. But on the other hand audiences for live theatre are not growing: the traffic goes one way. Statistical research shows that in the US as well as Europe education and class are more important determinants of museum attendance than twenty-five years ago (Richards 1996: 51). Most attempts to expand audiences through 'vertical equalization' of social classes and using market mechanisms to spread culture have not worked well; at the end of the twentieth century it appeared that development could occur only by widening the geographic market (13). In other words, bring in the tourists.

Under the conditions of postmodernity this cultural capital business is pretty complicated, more complicated than Bourdieu found in France in the 1960s when he conducted the statistical research for *Distinction*. (We should remember that he applied his results to that one nation only, and used evidence only from northern France.) Tourism, especially when it is international, is a different story altogether. Not that it flattens social class; the choices made by people about holidays and travel are important markers of class, manual and service workers tending to take one kind of holiday, the managerial sector another, and so on. The middle classes, students and new intellectuals more and more seek unusual activity holidays, educational trips or ecotours that reinforce classificatory difference, usually fostered by specialist operators whose brochures are based in exclusionary discourse (Munt 1994; Cohen 2004). But the globalized nature of travel means that audiences for cultural events that include tourists are highly mixed. It is not easy to analyse comparatively the cultural capital held by North Americans of assorted backgrounds on a ten-day tour of Europe, well-educated Germans on an annual bicycle tour around Britain and newly successful Koreans on their first trip to the West. Yet all three groups, and many more besides, are to be found at Shakespeare performances in Stratford. Complicating matters further are differences of age, gender and ethnicity that are magnified by travel and are not abolished by the global tourist enterprise.

MAKING A GLOBE

Shakespeare is many things in contemporary culture. He lives on splendidly in a number of contested sites, and even a few remaining uncontested ones. But whatever he is – even if he is the seventeenth Earl of Oxford – there can be no doubt that he is star-quality edutainment. And in the edutainment trade, the International Shakespeare Globe Centre in London is the most obvious example of heritage Shakespeare, predicated upon concepts of cultural tourism analogous to those of the Lascaux Simulation or Disney World. When the project was in planning and the building underway, considerable disagreement surfaced about the value and the purpose of the new Globe, centred mostly on the authenticity of the structure or of the playing, and occasionally on the social relevance of the concept. But as usual a different set of concerns comes to the fore when we consider the nature of the spectator's experience, and one of the chief results of the Globe experiment has been the large part that spectators play there, so different from public manners at most other Shakespeare performances in Britain. Whether audience at a performance or just sojourners to the Globe site, visitors seek an extraordinary realm. At the Globe they can define that realm in various ways – as art, heritage, history, education, recreation, amusement, frolic – but whatever meanings they ascribe, they are in the most straightforward sense cultural tourists.

The nineteenth- and twentieth-century movement to recreate the Elizabethan stage was an exercise in nostalgia operating as an invented tradition. It has historical justification, and valuable discoveries in the performance of Shakespeare and other early modern dramatists have been made through its influence. We could even say that the major developments in anglophone Shakespeare performance in the twentieth century derive from directors inspired by William Poel; not his anti-quarianism or historical costume re-enactment, which date from the 1880s, but his emphasis on speed of playing, thrust staging and elimin-ation of detailed realist settings. Granville Barker, Tyrone Guthrie, Peter Hall, John Barton, Peter Brook and Deborah Warner were affected in various degrees by Poel's discoveries and extended them into what became the standard approach to Shakespeare performance at the RSC and elsewhere.

Poel's strict Elizabethanism always solicited a set of material and performative circumstances that are unverifiable. Yet Sam Wanamaker, the American actor whose steadfast vision created the new Globe through a swamp of difficulties, accepted the premise that architectural recon-struction was intrinsically valuable. The new Globe is Wanamaker's dream but more importantly it is Poel's dream, a Victorian progressive dream of reaching through wood and plaster to the land of the dead. In this appeal the Globe seeks to become a touristic obligation, a must-see, based on a promoted connection to a constant called Shakespeare. And it has achieved that status, as witnessed by the crowds since its opening. In December 1996 an organization of travel journalists voted it the top tourist attraction in Europe, and it has operated at a profit without public subsidy since 1999, a difficult feat to achieve, especially considering that the theatre performs for about half the year. According to the Globe Trust's *Annual Review*, in the year ending October 2006 as many as 275,800 people attended its theatre productions; 261,000 took the guided tour; 80,000 participated in education programmes. Two-thirds of its income of over £10 million came from paid admissions and course fees, one-fifth from 'other trading receipts', and a very small portion from corporate or private donations.[2]

The Globe is willy-nilly in the edutainment business. What is its guestology? Whether or not you accept the analogy with Disneyland, it's undeniable that the Globe is a created heritage structure. Achieving sanctified status for an invented sight is a tricky matter: the promoters must first convince the public of its value and then guide them through markers that signal its distinctiveness. Since it is not the original like the Shakespeare Birthplace, nor located next to the surviving original like the Lascaux Simulation, nor built afresh on the very spot of the original like the new wooden horse in the ruins of Troy, the makers of the Globe assumed its credibility would be tied to accuracy of construction. The Globe cannot just 'be' like Chartres Cathedral or the Tower of London, since its meaning is bound up with a recalled past (a historiography), is hidden in the work of reconstruction and ultimately is a matter for mediation in performance. The Tower of London is also a heavily mediated touristic site, but its Norman stones are incontestable – at least some of them are – whereas the Globe can mean only through the intervention of its managers.

Thus the worry that the Globe might be just another theme park infected it from the start. When Wanamaker announced the project in 1973, his goals were carefully worded so that the first priority was 'to reclaim Southwark's Thames bank' and then to redevelop the area for 'culture, education and entertainment'. Rebuilding the Globe was ranked third on his list.[3] No doubt he intended these social and civic concerns to lend gravitas to the scheme; in reality they brought him even closer to Walt Disney, who also saw his parks as models for urban planning and even as experiments for the future, like the EPCOT Center in Orlando – EPCOT stands for 'Experimental Prototype Community of Tomorrow'. They also set Wanamaker on a long and expensive legal battle with Southwark Council that, despite his own leftist credentials, put him in bed with entrepreneurial property developers.

The Bankside anxiety over the serious and civic purpose of the Globe continued. At the time of the prologue season in summer 1996 London newspapers carried a flurry of articles emphasizing that the Globe is not a Disneyland, that its artistic director, the actor Mark Rylance, is a serious artist and will not let it become one, that 35,000 people have already enrolled in various classes and workshops through the education department. Meanwhile Michael Holden, then executive director of the Globe Centre, emphasized that a certain level of seriousness was required on the part of spectators as well: 'if anyone turns up in Elizabethan costume – as they have done in our workshop programme – we eject them from the premises'. The Globe wants to engage with Renaissance drama, he said, 'in the present tense, on stage and off' (*Observer*, 25 August 1996). No *Rocky Horror Picture Show* parties here. This seems a contradiction to the building, which itself is in fancy dress, and I wonder why spectators shouldn't be allowed to play the same game, but the real point is the continued concern that the Globe would be seen as a tourist trap.

Perhaps a solution to this problem could be found in another commentator on tourism, who has remarked that 'any authenticity claimed for a heritage structure' is a social construction of its creators 'rather than the intrinsic property of the object' (Ehrentrant 1993: 270). Thus the crucial issue for the visitor, to return to Cohen's phrase, is not the structure itself but 'the manner of the negotiation of its meaning'. If true for a legitimate heritage structure, how much more true must it be for an invented one. The energies that went into the building of the Globe – not to mention most of the money – were centred on the integrity of the edifice, something still emphasized in the exhibition and guided tours. But despite the controversies and historical research, the building was the easy part. How the visitors to the site and the spectators at performances relate to the enterprise, how its meaning is negotiated, are much more difficult.

From this standpoint Wanamaker was another structuralist: he believed that an appropriate way of playing Shakespeare is inscribed in the texts, and that an authentic building with no scenery would create an environment for studying these methods. This was always an impossible goal. While the building and its stage force a type of playing different from that in an indoor proscenium playhouse, the playing will be more affected by contemporary theatrical manners than the thoroughly unknown techniques of Shakespeare's company. No matter how well informed, attempts on the past take place only in bodies in the present. Just as the early music movement, despite accurate reproductions of antique instruments and research into styles of performance, can never escape the contemporary player or the contemporary audience, so any reconstructed performance at the Globe must inevitably be marked as historical conjecture.

In the larger project of the Globe little attention was paid to the gaps in Wanamaker's underlying theory and the meaning of the enterprise was poorly negotiated with its spectators. At first the managers approached the problem as one in contradictory capitalism: as a charitable institution the Globe wished to claim a serious (non-commercial) purpose, but without the security of state subsidy its overriding goal had to be attracting visitors. The building itself was allowed to carry the weight of authenticity, relieving the performances of that burden (though claims continued to be made for the laboratory nature of the work). This led to a marketing campaign in 1996 inviting spectators to throw tomatoes at the actors if they disliked the performance. Thoroughly ahistorical (there were no tomatoes in sixteenth-century England) the solicitation stands as an epitome of the Globe's frisky notions of its purpose. But would Rylance, like Marinetti, really want such disorder? I suspect that vegetable tossers, like anyone arriving in Elizabethan costume, would have been ejected.

So attending a performance at the Globe was framed from the start by a playful but contradictory discourse, and the few experiments Rylance took in recovery were eccentric at best, such as using reconstructed

Elizabethan undergarments in *Henry V* in 1997 or playing Cleopatra himself in 1999 on the foot of an unfounded theory that Shakespeare may have used mature men for older female roles. And those productions relied on modernist concepts of performance that can be seen in any number of Shakespeare productions elsewhere, using styles of acting, gesture and body posture notably contemporary in manner. In a fine analysis of these incongruities, W. B. Worthen (2003: 105–10) notes that the 'force of modern performance' at the Globe is more powerful than any sense of the antiquity of the text or the restored antiquity of the space. As Hamlet in 2000, Rylance played to the audience, subverting much of what is usually thought of as sombre content through a comic directness, probably influenced by his experience that comedy works better in the open air than tragedy. Our modernist expectation of controlled focus, a quiet and darkened house, directional stage lighting, guaranteed audibility, comfortable seating, protection from the weather – none of these are possible at the new Globe, and spectators tend to respond to the unusual environment as much as to the performance (illustration 7). Meanwhile reviewers for the press, who seem to want to be indoors, continue to have difficulties with the rowdiness of the audience, regularly complaining that noisy tourists (usually identified as American) distract from the effect of the play.

SHAX™

Most of these objections are not very important and the Globe has already found a surer path. A new artistic director, Dominic Dromgoole, was installed in 2005; his tenure up to 2008 suggests he understands the inherent problem of the enterprise. We must remember that no other playhouse in history has taken on the triple burden of historical accuracy in construction, performance of well-known classic texts under commercial conditions and a commitment to scholarship and education. It is eminently clear that, whatever the producers desire, spectators will assume charge in a way they cannot or do not in regular theatres. The open enjoyment the spectators take when standing in the yard before the stage might parallel that of their Elizabethan predecessors, but is that the result of the historically precise architecture of the building? The standees are having fun in the way they are accustomed to have fun at a football match or a rock concert or a panto, talking, drinking, eating, wandering around, shouting back at the actors. They laugh in the 'wrong' places in *The Maid's Tragedy*, or so the *TLS* reviewer insisted (5 September 1997: 19).

Illustration 7   The audience at the Globe Theatre for *Antony and Cleopatra*, London 1999

They regularly hiss the villain. In 1997 the villains were the French in *Henry V* and the hisses began on their every entrance, while for *Two Gentlemen of Verona* in 1996 the fact that one villain was Mark Rylance made the game all the more enjoyable. Worthen (2003: 100) heard a spectator say that booing the bad guy is 'what you come here for'. Audiences at the Globe quickly learned this behaviour: they are performing as groundlings. Queuing for tickets as at a cinema and paying cinema prices, standing close to the actors under the sky, subject to the vagaries of sun and shower, watching an informal performance mode and encouraged to throw tomatoes: the effect of the mix breaks down the rigid and solemn attitude that plagues so much Shakespeare performance. Visitors come in number because the Globe is more than a revived Elizabethan venue for Shakespeare. It has museum displays, gives tours, is interesting, diverting, educational, artistic, looks authentic, has a restaurant and bar and a great view, is close to the site of the original Globe and allows a certain amount of spectator play. Like an interactive museum, it invites an audience to join in the fun and gives them tales to tell about the experience when they get home.

Nonetheless the visitor is in a curious social position. The historical reference of the building and its project of producing Shakespeare suggest a high art appeal with all the attendant class implications. The issues of material and performative authenticity or accuracy underline that status. Yet in the Globe's institutional practice, history, Shakespeare and authenticity are wrapped up in a consumerist package that implies the abolition of class. Different types of touristic activity vary considerably in the amount of cultural capital they require; the romantic gaze upon an authentic historical site like Westminster Abbey demands much more knowledge and understanding than the collective gaze upon a modern and inauthentic site like Disneyland (Urry 1990: 104). Ancient sites are mediated through intellectual effort and imply that the visitor is obligated; theme parks build in whatever is needed and construct the visitor as already knowing. Even carefully manufactured historical parks like Plimouth Plantation in Massachusetts and Williamsburg in Virginia operate by subversion of knowledge, undermining or evading the large cultural capital that a historical site would otherwise require.

The Globe's exceptional nature is apparent here. Do the performances imply a prior knowledge, an educated eye and mind, as Shakespeare traditionally does? Yes, but also no. The Globe is both historical and modern: it looks like a late-Elizabethan structure, yet we know from the start it's a copy from the late age of the second Elizabeth. It is both authentic and inauthentic: it is carefully built using Tudor oak carpentry without nails and hair-and-lime plaster; yet it is as counterfeit and synthetic as any theme park. And it's part of London's newly extended cultural tourism district. Tate Modern in the former Bankside Power Station, next door to the theatre, has brought about four million people a year to the area since 2004. The attractions of a globalized metropolis abound: cafés and restaurants, a new underground station, the Millennium footbridge to St Paul's Cathedral, the walkway along the Thames filled with life from Southwark Bridge upstream to the National Theatre, BFI Southbank (formerly the National Film Theatre) and the Royal Festival Hall. It would be foolish to think of summers at the Globe as anything other than great fun. After Wanamaker's heroic struggle to create the thing, a struggle that recapitulates the plucky postwar festival spirit and that more than once seemed lost for reasons of finance or politics, a great irony has become part of its fruition. The Globe is gloriously successful because it has become the very thing Wanamaker said it was not. Though it arose through his modernist pledge to transmit humanist values, it can operate only inside a touristic postmodernity.

Many visitors to the Globe, I suspect, are recreational tourists, perfectly aware that the enterprise is not strictly genuine but willing to comport themselves as if it were. They might exercise a playful attitude to the building, closely allied to that of a theatre audience who are willing to give a part of themselves up to the performance. As playful tourist-spectators, they are out for a good time. Since the end of the Cold War most theatres in the world operate inside post-Fordist capitalism, and many have more or less abandoned the modernist testament at last. The heavily packaged megamusicals produced by Cameron Macintosh or Garth Drabinsky, which are cloned around the world in search of new audiences, demonstrate how live performance can be McDonaldized, so that the spectator is already constructed as a tourist.

'Shakespeare rocks', proclaimed the cover of *Newsweek* at Christmas 1996; 'A Bard for the '90s: Why He's Hot Now.' Shakespeare has made the big time (Bristol 1996) and he's big-time merchandise. *Newsweek* made it plain: 'He's gone Hollywood. He's on the Web. He's got theme parks and teenage fans.'[4] Whatever high art ideals, social agendas or traces of residual humanism might be entertained for the Globe, to the providers in the tourist trade it is simply a welcome addition to the universal cultural safari. In fact the Shakespeare boom of the 1990s was another example of the marketplace grabbing 'any pre-tested public domain property with instant name recognition' (O'Brien 1997), what we could call the Bardification of culture. As I sat near an open window at the unfinished Globe in 1996, I could hear an amplified narrative coming from tour boats on the Thames, describing the rising building as a 'fully accurate reconstruction' of Shakespeare's theatre where a 'fully accurate reconstruction' of performance was now taking place before an audience. Cultural tourism had completed its circle: as a tourist in the Globe I had become a touristic site.

But for the tourist the division between self and other cannot be absolute. We may seek the other but all too often we find the other has become like us, and meanwhile without knowing we have become like the other. Tourism is an exchange that thrives on difference becoming familiar, the distance of the foreign or the inapproachability of the past transformed into a package tour, Craik's 'safe, controlled environment' that permits us to experience the other on our own terms. Like Poel, Sam Wanamaker sought for Shakespeare's plays a reformed performance style in a radical architecture, a fundamentalist restoration to their Elizabethan state. There are big flaws in the idea, but it does have the virtue of highlighting Shakespeare's otherness, of chronicling the distance the texts have travelled across time and culture. Despite his commodification and ideological appropriation by conservative forces, much of the West continues to admire Shakespeare because he is at the heart of western culture and yet somehow remains mysterious, enigmatic, finally undecodable.

The paradox of the Globe enterprise, however, is that it has turned Shakespeare's distance and strangeness into one of the most familiar of touristic commodities, the easy delights of the heritage museum and historical theme park. The manufactured authenticity of the building sets the Globe firmly within the heritage industry and suggests that a spectator's cultural capital can be left outside the door. The groundlings are pretty middle class and socially the audience is less mixed than in 1599, but when watching a play from the yard there is a strong illusion that we're all in this together and class doesn't matter. It's fun, it's evocative, yippee, it's Bard Lite! The Globe has effectively broken down the distinction between the old modernist ideal of the committed spectator and the new pomo notion of the uncommitted tourist. Far from disdaining its reliance on cultural tourists, as modernist projects regularly did, the Globe welcomes them as central to its enterprise.

In a world where the individual is valued as shopper and difference another market obstacle for Coca-Cola to overcome, could we expect anything else? As Baudrillard (1994a: 118) says, the world has become 'a triumph for Walt Disney, that inspired precursor of a universe where all past or present forms meet in a playful promiscuity, where all cultures recur in a mosaic'. I am a tourist. I go to the Globe whenever I can. At first I was convinced that despite its claim to the contrary, the enterprise collapsed difference by glossing over the unknown, converting Shakespeare into a heritage property that justifies a self-satisfied present. But I have changed my mind after watching the spectators for more than a decade. They attend the Globe specifically so that they can assist at the spectacle. They refuse to take the heritage business solemnly, refuse to stand quietly and listen carefully; they are not bothered by the claims of authenticity and even manage to disregard the officious proscriptions of the ushers. In the midst of a commodified experience, they refuse to be commodified. 'Shakespeare's Globe is a field of dreams', Worthen (2003: 116) concludes of the reconstruction project, which was built on the proposition that 'if we build it, he will come'. So Wanamaker thought, and perhaps Rylance did too. But in a visual environment where carefully designed costumes are overwhelmed by the bright motley of tourist dress sharing the same light – the theatre will sell you a colourful mac in case of rain – spectators can see more than ever that they are the centre of the play, not the actors. Strangely, because of its touristic success the Globe now actually highlights the otherness of Shakespeare, who remains hidden by the very building meant to house him, the distant victim of the tourist gaze.

CHAPTER 6

Interculturalism and the global spectator

And if occasionally he'd ponder
What makes Shakespeare and Beethoven great.
Him I could love 'til I die.
Him I could love 'til I die! (Meredith Willson, *The Music Man*, 1957)

In the early twenty-first century cultural differences in the world again became marked by military aggression, international terrorism, political refugees and a discourse of fear. For the government of the United States of America these circumstances constituted a return to the moral condition of the Cold War, though without its political conveniences: absent are mandatory military induction for its citizens, the balanced threat of Mutual Assured Destruction with an identifiable enemy and massive financial investment in a new arms race. Yet that government nonetheless justified pre-emptive invasions, deadly wars on-going still in 2008 and well-publicized increases in domestic surveillance and defences. Significantly this new condition of the Tepid War has not yet been accompanied by the severe restrictions on personal liberty and travel that characterized the Cold War, despite an aggravating increase in security controls at airports. Indeed more people are travelling throughout the world than ever before. Though worries have rapidly grown over the price and availability of oil and the future of the environment, as I write the Tepid War has had remarkably little effect on the expansion and dispersion of international capital that has proceeded more or less unabated since the fall of the Soviet Union and its protectorates. Routine practices in many parts of the globe allow people to cross cultural barriers without care or knowledge, through inexpensive and (usually) safe travel, worldwide marketing, the mobile phone, the internet, satellite television, integration of banking and financial markets and legal economic migration. Large-scale international meetings and sporting events are common occurrences, hotels are stacked high with rooms for travellers and the atmosphere is degraded by the exhaust of airplanes.

As one of these events, the World Shakespeare Congress (where the last sections of this chapter were presented, in Brisbane in 2006) is directly parallel to the World Cup, socially, economically and perhaps politically: both require global travel, are dominated by the English language and derive from England, the home of Shakespeare and football. The rapidity of communications and the intermixing of people of different ethnicities over the past few decades have combined to suggest a world culture that has left certain traditional boundaries behind. Under these conditions it is not surprising that the theatre would become interested in the inter-cultural, nor that Shakespeare, already a multinational brand like Coca-Cola – or perhaps more like Starbucks – would further complicate the issue.

In this chapter I address the difficulties theatrical interculturalism poses for the spectator. I draw upon Shakespeare again because the inter-national status of the plays has prompted more frequent performance and appropriation than any other dramatist or set of dramatists. Inter-culturalism is a very broad topic, so for the sake of clarity I will define intercultural Shakespeare performance rather strictly, as cases in which a director or designer's interventions force into the mise-en-scène attributes from one or more cultures plainly foreign to a text ascribed to Shakespeare, or one based directly on his work. The stage thus reveals uncertainty or ambiguity about locale, backdrop, language, character, image or their relation to theme.

Intercultural performance, almost by definition, draws upon material that is not fully within the cultural competence of the attending audience. It might be designed for an audience familiar with Shakespeare but not familiar with the theatrical mode (usually derived from a different cul-ture), or it might be designed for an audience familiar with the mode but not familiar with Shakespeare. The spectator of interculturalism is both inside and outside the scene. Especially in examples made in the inter-national style for touring or for receiving tourist audiences in festivals, productions often are set in a beautiful no place, as if in an airplane, indicative of the cultural indeterminacy of the performance. Directors may believe that some form of cultural exchange takes place on stage through mixing of scenic or dramaturgical elements, but what happens in the mind of the spectator? Theoretically there is large opportunity for engagement with the other through the displacement that the inter-cultural brings, but does this happen?

The first major examples of intercultural work on Shakespeare occurred in the 1980s in productions in Paris by Peter Brook and Ariane

Mnouchkine and in Tokyo by Ninagawa Yukio. Their methods differed but they shared a tendency to dislocate the scene and pull away from a precise notion of what constituted the base text. Implicitly imagining a global spectator as consumer of global cultural product, these directors foregrounded the visual based on the freedom to mix and match: India, Africa, China, Japan and the West served as products on the universal shelf and were equally applicable to Shakespeare, Aeschylus or *The Mahabharata*. This move, parallel to the way that some multinational companies imagine a global consumer, seemed based on the idea that we all understand the same things about other cultures. In the examples originating in Europe, the establishing hypothesis for interculturalism was the same as the hypothesis of nineteenth-century colonialism or contemporary global merchandizing: that the principles and priorities of the West may procure and adapt the cultural products of the East with impunity.

In the act of using Shakespeare as material for cultural exchange, international theatre companies began to look a little like global corporations. I do not intend this metaphorically. The large, well-established troupes, even when not particularly rich, have been able to use classic texts as vehicles for a theatrical communication across cultures, relying on mise-en-scène rather than on the word. Shakespeare's case is doubly intriguing because from the eighteenth century onwards the traditions of his appreciation have been rooted in language. Since Shakespeare is performed in translation more frequently than any other playwright, there is a contradictory circumstance at work here: officially Shakespeare is valued because of his language, especially in the anglophone countries, but he's performed worldwide in translations of varying degrees of foreignness. His written words become a pretext for a new kind of sensibility, based on what Patrice Pavis (1992) calls the supermarket of cultures.

INTERCULTURALISM AND ECLECTICISM

'Eclecticism is the degree zero of contemporary general culture.' So Lyotard realized a generation ago. We're all familiar with its results: 'One listens to reggae, watches a western, eats McDonald's food for lunch and local cuisine for dinner, wears Paris perfume in Tokyo and "retro" clothes in Hong Kong; knowledge is a matter for TV games' (Lyotard 1984: 76). Circumstances have altered, perhaps forever, long-standing notions about human separateness, geographic isolation and nationhood. Vast new migrations, coupled with the marketing strategies of global capitalism, have created an environment where distinct, separate cultures blend into one another, through borrowing, appropriation and imposition. At the same time our proximity to the foreign has increased the likelihood of aggressive reaction. The immigration of peoples from the south and east into northern Europe and North America, and the continued racial and ethnic difficulties apparent in a depressing number of locations, demonstrate the political complexity of cultural issues that seem incapable of solution by liberal democratic methods.

The transfer of one cultural tradition to another is a fact of life for resettled peoples and for their host countries. These are actual problems of actual people, and are very different from playing with cultures for aesthetic effect. If I go to a Chinese restaurant in Beijing or New York and eat with chopsticks, or go to a Maharashtra shop in Mumbai or London and buy mirror-cloth and incense, I hardly become Asian. In fact as a consumer of 'the Asian' on one level I participate in a form of cultural defacement as an ancient civilization is further deprived of its rootedness and particularity. I become a purchaser of foreignness.

If you believe in rootedness and particularity, I'm not buying a culture, after all, but only a simulation of a culture or a detachable and usually excess artefact of a culture, as a tourist buys souvenirs. Cultures hold authenticity through the materials and practices that comprise them but also by belief, and all three are subject to change. Tourism over time can certainly force changes to a culture, just as Kathakali performances for tourists in Kerala force changes to the form so presented, but often such materials and practices were already undergoing change when touristic opportunities presented themselves.

Let's start with the three productions directed by Ariane Mnouchkine for the Théâtre du Soleil. Mnouchkine came to Shakespeare only when stuck in trying to write an original play on the tragedy of Southeast Asia in our time. Considering her own political commitment and the history of Shakespearean production during the Cold War, it is curious that she turned to Shakespeare because of what she called his ideological neutrality, turning her back on the methods of both Brecht and Jan Kott, who had dominated the theory of Shakespeare production since the 1950s. 'Shakespeare is not our contemporary and must not be treated as such', she said in an interview; 'he is distant from us, as distant as our own profoundest depths.' Conflating his distance with the timelessness of myth, Mnouchkine hoped to use Shakespeare 'to learn how to represent the world in a theatre' (in Bradby and Williams 1988: 100, 98).

To accomplish this, she thought, required an abstract style, one that evoked images rather than messages. So Mnouchkine manufactured an Asian exoticism to uncover the mythic dimensions she sensed in the text.

The first of her productions, *Richard II* in 1981, was a self-consciously mixed metaphor in which French actors borrowed elements from Asian performance to create a vision of the English medieval court for a French audience. Character was established by mask or mask-like makeup and by non-psychological patterns of gesture and movement, emotion established through formalized song and dance and chanting, the tragic dimension through ritual conjurations like those in Nō and Kabuki with some additions from Kathakali and Beijing opera (Jingju). To appropriate Shakespeare, Mnouchkine first appropriated assorted cultural details of eastern theatre. Like Yeats and Artaud and others before her, she explored Asian methods in a search for new ways of dealing with the body.

Powerful and innovative as this method was, from a political perspective it demonstrated the same western relationship with the Orient that Edward Said (1978: 4) identified as that of the colonizing dominator to the inferior other, eastern mysteries 'domesticated for local European use'. Orientalizing, whatever else it may be, is a process of commodifying, drawing out the other's riches while stipulating difference, a process of marginalizing or feminizing which maintains alterity for the sake of controlling it. It is strange to think that a feminist company like Théâtre du Soleil would participate in such a process, but Mnouchkine and her collaborator Hélène Cixous insist that 'the Orient is feminine'. That femininity, they hold, can be exercised without reducing it to an inferior position. 'I discovered in Asia such beauty in things, in gestures', Mnouchkine said, 'a simple ceremonial which seems to me indispensable in the theatre. In Asia every act is perpetually formalized. The everyday aggressiveness in the West, especially in France and above all in Paris, comes from a total loss of any formalisation of relationships' (in Kiernander 1993: 130–1). This essentializing of Asia, drawing sweeping cultural conclusions from uncritical and sketchy observations, deliberately ignores cultural particularity to grapple instead with the insecurity of difference.

Mnouchkine appropriated a series of separate styles and detached them from their origins: Kabuki, Kathakali, Jingju, Indian music and costumes mixed together. As Kiernander (118) notes, the Kabuki movements and the gestures of Kathakali were 'invented and not authentic'. Theatrically speaking, the practice was highly impressive: the athletic and virtuoso abilities of the actors created a sense of the marvellous, of the wondrous otherness of Shakespeare's fables. Of course it was not done with malevolence. There is nothing morally wrong with it, and I found Mnouchkine's productions highly appealing, even overwhelming, as I found *Les Atrides* (1990–2), which used the same methods, this time with an international group of actors. But however tasty the Oriental Shakespeare at Théâtre du Soleil might have been, it achieved its success through enormous cultural dislocation. Mnouchkine's use of superbly foreign modes in the history plays tended to detach them from any political and historical reference, Elizabethan or contemporary. She claims this was not her intent, that she was historicizing the present in a Brechtian manner, but the style dominated, eliminating the social for the sake of the aesthetic. It's not surprising to find Jan Kott objecting: 'fake Japanese and fake Shakespeare' (in Elsom 1989: 16). In that comment we see the battle line between Kott's Cold War Shakespeare, insisting on contemporary relevance, and apolitical interculturalism, not insisting on anything, beautifully, magnificently saying 'whatever' to the universal diaspora. Kott assumed there is such a thing as an authentic Japanese culture and such a thing as authentic Shakespeare, and that it's possible to know the first and stage the second. Mnouchkine's productions implied a theatre free to range over cultural artefacts and practices in order to 'to learn how to represent the world'.

UNIVERSALIST SHAKESPEARE

Mnouchkine had originally intended to produce a cycle of ten Shakespeare plays, but for company reasons was forced to abandon the project in 1984 after *Henry IV* and *Twelfth Night* and thereafter directed quite different work. Though the basic methods have not changed, it would be unfair to hold her to her 1980s approach to the intercultural, which marked an early stage in its development. Her later productions on Islamism (*Tartuffe*, 1995) and political and economic refugees (*Le Denier caravanserai*, 2003) took a much harder look at those issues, going beyond an easy acceptance of exoticism. The other two directors used different methods but achieved results similar to Mnouchkine's Shakespeare. From the standpoint of the spectator of interculturalism, the most interesting fact about Brook and Ninagawa is that within a few years of each other both chose to work on *The Tempest*. The colonial implications of the play make it an obvious choice to investigate intercultural issues. Prospero, immigrant and hegemon, is an ambiguous master of the island he exploits. Colonialism itself, a barely formed political project in England in 1612 when the play was written, is also presented ambiguously in the text; the conqueror's power, his magic and his assumed European superiority are full of perplexity. The rightful Duke of Milan, deposed from grace and reigning now on a barren rock that might be south of Malta in the Old World or just east of the Americas in the New, operates as an authoritarian patriarch and enslaver of the native population, even if a very small population. Prospero is the earliest representation in western drama of the doubled colonial subject, the governor who becomes defined by the governed, the conquistador who cannot escape his need for the indigene, troubling the issues of dominance and assimilation.

Characteristically, neither director was interested in the colonial theme; both glossed over political issues to find different meanings connected to international and intercultural positions. In Brook's case, all his work since the founding of his international centre in Paris in 1970 was informed by two conditions: the international make-up of the company and the experimental search for theatrical origins or essences that cut across cultures. Composed of actors from many lands, the company has defined itself by research into theatrical and paratheatrical conditions in non-western societies. Thus Brook's interculturalism was substantially different from Mnouchkine's. Whereas Mnouchkine reached across cultures by appropriating stylistic details from the East, Brook habitually worked through diversified actors who in Europe already incarnate the other. Mnouchkine's Shakespeare exoticized by importing foreign strategies onto European bodies, Brook staged the foreign directly through miscellaneous global bodies. The results of his exploration became highly visible in global tours of performances adapted from other cultures, especially with *The Mahabharata* (1985).

The actors in Brook's company, however, do not generally use traditional theatrical forms. While some have been trained from early ages in Nō, Indian and Balinese dance or African storytelling, for example, their skills tend to disappear in the melange of Brook's innovation. The repeated image is that of multiracial harmony, a United Nations of drama, where the native arts of Asian, African, European and Middle Eastern actors are not used for themselves but are drawn upon as source material for Brook's inquiry into a universal theatrical method. Indeed *The Mahabharata* was heavily criticized for cultural imperialism: written by a Frenchman, directed by an Englishman, designed by a Greek, this version of the Hindu sacred texts contained only one Indian in the cast of thirty-three actors and musicians. As Rustom Bharucha (1993: 80) wrote,

'Why assemble an international group of actors if the expressive possibilities of their culture are negated in the production?'

Brook might well be remembered as the most important director of Shakespeare in the twentieth century, as he staged numerous productions of great force in England from 1946 until his move to France. Though not the mainstay of his work in Paris, Shakespeare's work remained important to him personally and to the larger goals of his troupe. The first of his productions at Les Bouffes du Nord, the resurrected Paris theatre he operated, was *Timon of Athens* in 1974, which was followed in 1978 by *Measure for Measure*. In both cases Brook deliberately abandoned the modernist methods he had used for most of his work since the war at Stratford, including any notion of absolute fidelity to the text. He told his French translator, Jean-Claude Carrière (who later wrote the script for *The Mahabharata*), that the major danger was translationese, what Carrière refers to as a language of 'traduit de'. The ideal performance script for Paris, Brook said, would be one that appeared to be 'a new play, written in French, and written by Shakespeare'.[1]

The 1990 production of *The Tempest* struck a new note with clear resonances to *The Mahabharata*. Some of the distinguished international actors from that piece took major roles in *The Tempest*. Brook relied on the same multiracial casting and similar scenography: sand on the stage floor, African and Asian instrumentalists in full view, flowing robes, extreme visual simplicity. But whereas the overriding culture of *The Mahabharata* was Indian, that of *The Tempest* was African. Whether African or Indian, we might think that a company with a large number of actors from developing nations would be interested in the issue of colonialism, but Brook took trouble to upset this reading. The African Prospero had an African brother, an Indian Miranda, an African Ariel and a German Caliban, throwing off any easy view of European domination of the magic isle. Gonzalo was Japanese and even Antonio and Sebastian were racially mixed. Shakespeare's text, made foreign by translation, was further distanced by the speech of the actors, only a few of whom were native speakers of French.

The Paris intercultural movement of the 1980s put the spectator in an uncustomary and somewhat awkward position. Bombarding the audience with alien signs, the productions attempted to dislocate both the play and the spectator's theatrical grounding. Shakespeare was chosen because his status allowed foreign applications to adhere to the familiar, yet the exoticism spoke not of other times and places but of a brave new world of borderless culture. In the case of Mnouchkine, it was not necessary for the spectator to know the origin and meaning of imported forms like Kabuki or Kathakali, since the originals were irrelevant. What mattered was witnessing the spectacle of foreignness which attempted to uncover a universalism of the spirit. Brook, whose faith in Shakespeare remained limitless, followed a similar universalist approach in which the production became a speculation on the potential for global harmony. In their stylistic eclecticisms, both Paris directors conveyed an underlying humanist and liberal message that the world can be one, all people are basically the same, we can understand each other despite racial, ethnic and cultural divides: the very message of global capitalism.

Ninagawa's Shakespeare is a further challenge to customary approaches. In one sense Ninagawa is the ideal director for intercultural Shakespeare, since he is not western and has neither a life-long commitment to Shakespeare like Brook nor a belief that Shakespeare can revitalize the world of the theatre like Mnouchkine. Though he was raised in the highly politicized movement of the Tokyo avant-garde in the 1960s, his best-known productions have been commercial enterprises for large-scale Japanese entertainment companies. A number of his Shakespeare ventures since 1985 have had major impact when travelling to Britain, including *Macbeth*, *A Midsummer Night's Dream*, *Hamlet*, *King Lear* (in English), *Pericles* and *Titus Andronicus*.

For Ninagawa Shakespeare is a monument, but clearly a foreign one. He thinks of himself as a detached and silent observer, an outsider, a couple of removes from the western culture he stages. In a Japanese interview in 1987, conducted during rehearsals for *The Tempest*, he called himself a 'listener' to foreign culture. Visiting Italy, for example, he preferred to read about the Adriatic than swim in it. He had never seen a production of *The Tempest* and the play did not strike him as a masterpiece. He was intrigued by the possibility that it was Shakespeare's last work; otherwise his production was more influenced by *The Sacrifice*, Andrei Tarkovsky's last film (1984), which gave him basic ideas about music and tone.[2]

His starting point for *The Tempest* was to transform Prospero's isle of noises into Zeami's isle of Nō theatre. The programme gave the title as *The Tempest: a rehearsal on a Nō stage on Sado Island*, and the performance began with a recital of drumming in the well-known Sado style. The Japanese audience therefore had a clear idea of the setting and some idea of the overtones. They would know the history of Zeami (1363–1443), the Shogun's favourite Nō player and one of the founders of the art, who late in life had been exiled to Sado, some 150 years before Shakespeare was

born. A remote and rather desolate island, Sado is a powerful cultural
memory for the Japanese; today there are some thirty-five outdoor Nō
stages there, often used by amateur troupes of players. When Ninagawa
visited the place he was struck by how weather-beaten the Nō stages are –
he found them, he said, lovely and quite magical, 'as though the dead
were looking down at me from the sky'.

The Tempest began with a director rehearsing actors on a dilapidated
Nō stage with a thatched roof, surrounded by a thicket of trees, which
was constructed inside the proscenium arch of the Nissei Theatre in
Tokyo. The conceit was that amateur players were putting on a production of Shakespeare's play, under the direction of a man who was their
colleague, who became the exiled Prospero and who implied the exiled
Zeami all at once. The stage effects were spectacular but accomplished by
visible, black-clad stagehands in the tradition of Nō and Kabuki. Offstage
actors stood to the side and watched this 'rehearsal', as the Prospero-
director followed the book. According to one Japanese reviewer, 'rather
than being allowed to lose themselves in the beauty and fantasy of the
drama itself, the spectators are forced to observe the action of the play
carefully' (Senda 1997: 254). The noble characters performed in a style
suggestive of Nō, especially in moments like the disappearing banquet
scene, while Caliban and the servants used the devices of the comic
Kyōgen plays that are seen between Nō performances.

It would be wrong to suggest that Ninagawa's method is to adapt
Shakespeare to fit comfortably inside Japanese sensibilities, since his work
is a mixture of Japanese and western motifs that challenges his Japanese
spectators to question both codes. In the midst of native styles in *The
Tempest*, for instance, he introduced naturalistic acting, overtly emotional
moments, western instrumental music and a haunting soprano voice that
accompanied the Japanese formality of the wedding masque. He said that
'he is trying to break down the artificial barriers between different forms
of theatre by combining ritual, naturalism, Kabuki, Nō, Hollywood
musicals, and film westerns' (Barnes 1992: 389).

Ninagawa turns the tables on Mnouchkine, raiding western culture for
its tendency to hybrid art then forging a new eclecticism directed towards
eastern audiences. But what happened when *The Tempest* toured abroad?
For British audiences at Edinburgh (1988) and London (1992) the Zeami
framework on Sado Island was meaningless, as was the opening moment
of Sado drummers. To make the production comprehensible, both had to
be explained in a programme note, an artificial method which hopes to
force an intellectual shift in the spectators, if they bother to read it. In

Britain the precise use of Nō techniques was received as a generalized Orientalism. Out of some thirty reviews and articles on the British performances only one mentioned the crucial difference between the Nō style for the noble characters and the Kyōgen style used for the comic scenes.[3]

Ninagawa's interculturalism is more complicated than Brook's because his method is more miscellaneous. There was no one 'source culture' for his *Tempest* but rather a number of them: Japanese theatre and theatre history, a Russian-Swedish film, western music, Stanislavskian acting and of course 'Shakespeare', not so much the text of *The Tempest* and its English traditions but a speculative or symbolic Shakespeare which includes his place in world culture as well as his theatrical usefulness.

Ninagawa's Shakespeare placed the spectator, East or West, in a radically uncertain position because the performance refused to locate itself in any cultural tradition: to the Tokyo audience *The Tempest* appeared western, to the London audience it was Japanese. Like Brook and Mnouchkine, Ninagawa turned to Shakespeare because the work can evoke a global response, because it continues to appear as a stable referent in a shifting theatrical environment and shifting world. Under all the exotic foliage, as it were, spectators are comforted by the familiar sight of a tree trunk. As the *Independent on Sunday* put it, 'hearing Shakespeare in Japanese is like seeing a Technicolor X-ray: the bones stand out, but fuzzily' (6 December 1992). The condition of the global spectator, at least in theory, is unstable amazement, drawn to the exotic as a tourist is drawn to the display of the other. 'No tongue! all eyes! be silent.'

SHAKESPEARE, BEETHOVEN AND SUBSIDY

We have seen that a huge rise in state subsidy for the arts occurred in the period from 1946 to about 1985 on both sides of the Iron Curtain. Most of the governments in the Soviet sphere held firm to the socialist notion that 'the great nineteenth-century traditions of culture could be effectively democratized in a society free of class distinctions' (Botstein 2004: 60), while the market-based economies in the American sphere introduced or sustained public investment in the past on the basis that heritage cultural products represented and promoted the highest achievements of western civilization. From opposing political positions the two sides reached the same conclusion as Marian Madame Librarian in *The Music Man*: Shakespeare and Beethoven are great, deserve to be pondered, and performance of their works should be encouraged on humanistic grounds.

In the West artistic enterprises that had been unsupported or poorly supported gained significant public standing, and the anglophone countries at last joined the club of nations which provided or assisted large-scale theatre systems. Support implied the continuation of prewar bourgeois culture and the often unspoken social distinction associated with European high art: educated spectators were desirable, even if the rationale for funding asserted democratic and inclusivist ideals. The sustaining assumption was that high art is good for the people and should therefore receive the people's money.

The social agenda underlying this cultural policy is clearer if we look at classical music. As Leon Botstein has noted, the political economy of opera and concert music today remains centred on a nineteenth-century repertoire and the continuation of what we can call bourgeois tonality. Modernism had little effect on the mainstream concert repertoire in the West and certainly no advantageous political effect on public subsidy (though modernist composers were often well supported privately). Modernism's aggressive atonality was a critique of the aspects of nineteenth-century music that supported the contention that a large and well-rehearsed symphony orchestra was civically virtuous. Patronage, whether aristocratic, ecclesiastic or philanthropic, had long been an intimate part of the European high-art musical tradition. This is well-known for the eighteenth century, but it continued into the nineteenth and twentieth as well, with Wagner cared for by Ludwig II, and Mahler, Tchaikovsky, Debussy and even Schoenberg all supported by Nadezhda von Meck, the widow of the wealthy Russian railway industrialist, Karl von Meck. Subsidy from private individuals was obviously expensive for them, but not so much as now, especially for performance: the businessman 'Henry Lee Higginson required less money (in real value) to support the Boston Symphony by himself in the 1880s than his numerous counterparts did a century later' (Botstein 2004: 56–7). When the royal, noble and private funders would no longer beat the drum, the state tended to step in without changing the rhythm.

How does subsidy affect the audience for Beethoven? The economic limitations of concert music are the same as they were in the nineteenth century. It is not possible to create halls that seat more than two to three thousand listeners if auditors continue to expect non-amplified sound, and while salaries and other costs go up, the unit cost of live performance cannot be lowered through mechanized or technological means. It is not generally feasible to pay for the production of live orchestral music through ticket sales alone. Taking the year 2002 as the basis, 'if consumers were to pay for all the expenses, then each ticket in a sold-out 2,700-seat Avery Fisher Hall for a routine New York Philharmonic concert would cost over $150' (Botstein 56). In actuality a Beethoven concert in October 2006 by that orchestra was priced considerably lower, from $28 to $94 a ticket.

Thus subvention in the field of classical music, which sometimes props up recordings as well, necessarily grants a museum function to its performance. As Botstein puts it, 'The perception that the concert and opera tradition is not viable as a living art has itself contributed to its relegation as a museum' (49). I don't want to give the impression that I disapprove of museums, but they are the primary example of art institutions which require enormous financial support to be created and to continue. The British Museum is free to all, in 2008 the Louvre charged between €6 and €13 and was free to certain classes of people, but it would be desperate to contemplate the admission charge were their visitors to pay the entire costs of operation, not to mention pro-rated acquisition. Great national museums, usually built on royal collections or imperial appropriation, can admit the public at low cost only to the extent that states or private funders value the patrimonial status of such institutions as sites of cultural preservation.

How does subsidy affect the audience for the great Shakespeare? The story for theatre is not much different than for Beethoven. I do not have figures for the Royal Shakespeare Company if spectators were to pay the entire cost, but the charge for tickets for commercial productions on Broadway or in the West End, which for spoken plays in 2008 could easily exceed $100 and £60, demonstrates that only subsidy, whether state or corporate, keeps Shakespeare regularly on our stages at affordable prices. Whether of classical music or classical theatre, the spectator is normally enabled by a complex set of economic, social and political policies that sustain bourgeois tonality. Even when productions of Shakespeare align themselves with dissident positions, or radically challenge the dominant, or even when, as in the early days of the RSC, the direction of the company is avowedly leftwards, it has been the humanist and preservationist assumption that Shakespeare holds transcendent value that ultimately grants the grants. The museum function is inescapable. For the spectator, the result since 1946 has been unparalleled opportunity for watching Shakespeare. Obviously I cannot answer for everyone, but it seems reasonable to conclude that the fact of subvention – regularly proclaimed in programmes with the names and logos of the sponsors, whether governmental or corporate – affects the spectator with an oddly disorienting sense of watching a pre-approved event.

LANGUAGE AND THE SPECTATOR

A major change occurred in the sources of theatrical and musical subsidy during and after the Thatcher-Reagan reforms in the capitalist states and after the fall of the Soviet Union in the socialist ones. In brief, public or tax-based subvention declined substantially in real terms throughout much of the world. At the same time there was an increase in support from the corporate sector, a great deal of which went to the large and highly visible festivals whose audience demographics suited the marketing tactics of the sponsors. The festivals embarked on a course of attracting international spectator-tourists to festival sites by means of splendid productions that were scenographically luxurious. As an early example we can return to Brook's *The Mahabharata*, which opened in 1985 in Paris. It looked simple visually but with a large cast it cost $7.2 million to tour to the Brooklyn Academy of Music in 1987, including the renovations to the Majestic Theatre which Brook demanded. The case is instructive because it demonstrates how major productions became implicated with cultural tourism and global capital. Its three-month run at 97 per cent capacity brought in $1.5 million from the box office. The rest came from the City of New York, which owns the building, and sponsorship (D. Williams 1991: 289–93). Characteristic of the era, sponsorship was provided by the American Telephone and Telegraph Company and by the Ford, Philip Morris and Rockefeller foundations, money that derives from the communications industry, car manufacture, tobacco and oil.

The arts festivals encourage and engineer productions by celebrity directors such as Robert Wilson, Robert Lepage, Mnouchkine and Ninagawa, who tend to stress the visual over the verbal, a logical response to the international constituency of spectators at globalized events. It is true that today most shows are surtitled in the local language, an issue I'll return to shortly, but in a sense that strategy only further acknowledges that language has become less significant. The festivalization of theatre promotes a kind of performance that dislocates both itself and the audience.

The movement has gathered substantial force since the early 1990s, and Asian performance has not been exempt from the process; Ninagawa is only the most recognized brand. A few years ago in a version of *Twelfth Night* in Beijing, Malvolio, trying to construe the letters M, A, O, I in the message he picks up, concluded they must spell McDonald's. While this is chiefly a joke on globalization, a number of examples show that Shakespeare has frequently been used in Asia because his high name recognition helps to promote the productions internationally. This has been true for some time with Ninagawa. In a post-show discussion in Singapore in 2003, the Taiwanese actor Wu Hsing-Kuo acknowledged that it was Shakespeare's name that provided the opportunity to tour with his one-man adaptation of *King Lear* (*Li Er Cai Zi, King Lear Is Here*), even though his chief intention was to revivify Jingju (Beijing Opera), not Shakespeare. The Chinese director Lin Zhaohua admitted that he selected *Richard III* in 2001 because it increased the prospect of moving on to the Asia Pacific Cultural Festival in Berlin; the seventeen days of its run in Beijing drew empty houses and made a considerable loss, so that local origin was chiefly a platform for international attention (Li 2003: 228).

Central to the move in Asia was the Shakespeare trilogy of the Singaporean Ong Keng Sen, which was spread over the years 1997 to 2002. The first instalment, an adaptation called simply *Lear*, began in Tokyo in 1997 and subsequently travelled to theatres and festivals in Hong Kong, Singapore, Jakarta, Perth, Berlin and Copenhagen. This was a complicated project but briefly Ong's goal was to counter Eurocentric interculturalism by presenting a performance led by Asian artists with Asian funding and Asian premises. While his purpose was admirable and his procedures clever, his solutions were curiously literal: he used actors from a number of different Asian countries speaking the text in their own languages and performing in characteristic national modes: the (Japanese) King in Nō style, the (Chinese) Goneril-Regan figure in Jingju style, Cordelia a Thai Khon dancer who didn't speak, a court attendant a Malaysian martial arts expert and so on. In contrast to Mnouchkine's invented Orientalism, the stage thus displayed the 'authentic' with regard to its formal characteristics – Asian performers and reasonably accurate Asian performance modes – but at the same time the amalgam of styles was deliberately disjointed, inauthentic in purpose and effect. This was interculturalism with a vengeance, in keeping with a century's tradition of European avant-gardism, elevating the aesthetic intentions of the producers above reception by an audience. The director's note said as much, insisting that 'No one culture should be able to understand *Lear* in its entirety' (see Kennedy 2001: 332–3).

That was true on one level, yet another practice ran counter to it, since the multilingual set pieces and dialogues were projected in surtitles in the language of the locality of the performance. Not only did this deny Ong's expressed statement, making the piece linguistically accessible anywhere, it added a further reception conundrum to the already multi-modal condition of performance. In fact the greatest development towards

internationalism and festivalization in the theatre has been the technological advance of computerized surtitles. Surtitling (or supertitling)
began rather slowly for opera in the West in the 1980s but by 2000 was
standard practice in many opera houses because it is democratic and,
crucially, now easy to accomplish.

The translation of drama is a deeply complex enterprise but with
surtitles a further burden is placed on the translator by the need for
instant communication with the spectator. One of the most stringent
criteria is length. At two lines of about forty characters for each title, space
is at a premium, forcing the translator to look for a highly concise means
of expression. Antiquated or bombastic language, such as Wagner's,
presents a special challenge, because it looks much worse in type than it
sounds when sung in another language. With Shakespeare an additional
problematic arises when a play performed in a foreign language is seen in
an anglophone country, an event now happening with regularity. Should
the titles be a heavily edited version of the original English text, with its
familiarity and antiquated diction, or should they reflect the much more
contemporary speech used on stage by the translation into German or
Polish or Japanese? Shakespeare's words or a translation of a translation?
To put this another way, what is the original text for? In Ninagawa's
productions in England, such as when his Japanese *Pericles* travelled to
London in 2003, the original text was used in the English titles as if in
support for the authority of the Japanese speech on stage: this may look
and sound exotic to you English, the production seemed to imply, but
just read the titles and you will be located in your usual Shakespearean
world. In Ong's *Lear*, on the other hand, the surtitles were a straightforward and colloquial translation of the onstage speech, but that already
was a radical adaptation so that the audience was further distanced from
the original. A long time ago there was a play called *King Lear*, the
production implied, but that was in another country and besides the
writer is dead.

In allowing productions to cross borders with greater ease of understanding, titles create a form of double sight for the spectator, occasioned
by the constant switch from reading to watching. To understand the
spoken words it will be necessary for most of us to read the titles, but
reading the titles forces us to attend less to the stage action. Even if the
titles present a highly condensed version of the text, we will be caught in a
dilemma between two modes of perceptual experience. Of course reading
surtitles is optional for a spectator and can be occasional, but nonetheless
titles foreground the text as a literary object in a way that actors' speech

does not. By presenting the text outside the mouths of actors, by de-corporalizing the lines, a surtitled performance adds an extra-dramatic awareness that increases the theoretical difficulties of interculturalism. Titles defamiliarize the text while at the same time familiarizing the stage adaptation.[4]

THE INTERCULTURAL SPECTATOR

I have sketched how the aesthetic side of theatrical interculturalism might affect the social side. I am not trying to speak for the variety of spectators or imply that I know how individuals actually respond. As usual, I am moving toward the main philosophic issues and the major one involves spectator understanding. The tentative model that Patrice Pavis proposed in 1992 for interculturalism assumed that the meaning or effect of an intercultural performance was primarily a matter of reception: spectators, drawing on their more-or-less imperfect understanding of the foreign aspects of the mise-en-scène, would receive them the way one receives strangeness, attempting to incorporate the onstage signifiers into their own expectations and understandings. With regard to Shakespeare this means that the destabilizing quality of the presentation – the coupling of the classic English playwright with unexpected visual and performative fashions deriving from some alien domain, Asian or African – would in theory permit a renewed or refreshed understanding of the text or a reinvented meaning. Spectators would thus be able to receive the alien in light of the familiar, judging the distance between them as a space for interpretive pleasure, a kind of exoticized transference of signifiers.

But the interpretive issue of interculturalism raises further troubles. In their individual minds spectators will construe the implication or force of the cultural other in different ways, perhaps vastly different ways, depending on their own cultural and political positions, even when the audience is reasonably coherent socially.[5] Thus the intercultural can never claim a singular value, no matter what the director intends. It exists 'inter', not 'trans': it lies between cultures and their meanings, in a space that is always a becoming. If the intercultural is self-consciously the opposite of rootedness, it nonetheless assumes the existence of rootedness (and often implies that rootedness is Asian and premodern). Though the director may operate on a semiotic assumption, the intercultural is finally a psychological condition, loosed from cultural substance. Thus the alterity of intercultural theatre is not just a fiction, it is a caprice, and cannot maintain relevance outside the mise-en-scène. What starts out as a social or political move about the other ends trapped in its own aestheticism.

The real difficulty in theorizing interculturalism is this: does a spectator shift cultural ground by watching interculturalism at work? Does a western diner become Chinese by eating pork fried rice? Despite the frivolous question in both cases something might be happening to the recipient in the space where the intellectual meets the corporeal, where mental knowledge meets embodied knowledge. But we are no more what we see than we are what we eat: both pass through: we shit cultural product as easily as digested rice. In fact the intercultural spectator in the theatre replicates the condition of the global tourist. It is perfectly possible for us as tourists in a foreign clime to remain unaffected by the culture we are visiting; this is the usual high-toned critique of sun-drenched tourism. But it is also possible for tourists to engage the challenges of the foreign, as they see the other now in its own location and are forced to recognize their foreignness to it. In either case, however, tourists almost certainly remain outside the cultural and mental landscape of the visited locale, while at the same time they are physically inside it.

Remember that tourism is the world's largest industry. Perhaps we should recognize festivalized and globalized theatre as part of that industry. Just as the huge expansion of international tourism since 1950 was enabled and driven by the generally rising economy in the West, so intercultural performance has depended on the relative ease of travel and its metaphoric extension, the desire of spectator-tourists to witness the performance of the foreign. None of this is meant to disparage tourism, only to recognize it. Whatever else it does, whether we think of an audience watching a performance at its place of origin or outside it, with or without the linguistic competence to understand it, with or without surtitles, intercultural theatre, and especially intercultural Shakespeare, implicates spectators in the anxieties brought by the globalization of cultural identities.

CHAPTER 7

The body of the spectator

Any space we occupy deeply affects how we perceive events inside it. We are bodies which occupy space and metaphorically are occupied by it. Especially when we are present in a space marked off from the mundane, like a sacred temple or a chamber for the exercise of power, we are likely to alter not only our behaviour but our frame of mental reference. Theatres, which are spaces separate from ordinary life by definition, affect us not only by their architecture and decor but also by the spatial relationship established between actor and spectator. From the hillside amphitheatres of Athens in the fifth century BC to the concrete cinema bunkers of contemporary shopping malls, a theatre space is inscribed with ideas about the position of drama within the culture that built it.

For Shakespeare the issue of space has assumed particular importance, and in the modern era has been highly contested, partly because the status of Shakespeare's plays has focussed attention on where they can be seen to best advantage. While most of us imagine James Burbage's The Theatre or the Globe when we think of the original productions, the plays were performed in their own time in a variety of public, private and royal spaces, a fact that should make us question the common notion that they were written for the public theatre or were somehow contained by it. Yet the Elizabethanist movement of the end of the nineteenth century, associated with William Poel in London and Jocza Savits in Munich, made that proposition the basis for much subsequent worry over the right space for Shakespeare. Taking the radical inference that the performance space was inscribed in the text itself, Poel and Savits, and their more successful heirs like Granville Barker, Tyrone Guthrie and Sam Wanamaker, vastly affected how Shakespeare relates to the spectator in the physical environment of the stage (Kennedy 2001: 34–42, 152–64; also Wiles 2003 and Carlson 1989).

Though Poel and Savits sought spatial authenticity, the spaces they established were conscious compromises with practicality and unconscious compromises with their ingrained theatrical biases. The right space for Shakespeare, regardless of any claims its architect might make about fidelity to a lost epitome, is always going to be the right space for a specific culture. The reified proscenium productions of Charles Kean at the Princess's Theatre were as right for mid-nineteenth-century London as Tyrone Guthrie's open-stage productions at the Ontario Festival Theatre were for mid-twentieth-century North America. Yet the intensity of the search, causing considerable expense in building and remodelling, was motivated by two ambitions specific to modernity: to get Shakespeare out of the boxed-in stages of proscenium theatres and (thereby) to create a rejuvenated or urgent sense of intimacy between the actor and spectator. Especially since the Second World War, producers of Shakespeare repeatedly appealed to the need for connection, hoping for a revitalized mode of performance that would affect audiences directly and capture (or recapture) the intensity presumed to be present in the texts.

For my purposes the crucial aspect of this story is that most theatres playing Shakespeare in the modern era, whether pre-existing or purpose-built, have been large. Of course 'large' is a relative term: the Theatre of Dionysos in Athens sat at least 13,000 bodies, the first Globe in London (1599) upwards of 3,000 and the second Shakespeare Memorial Theatre (SMT) in Stratford-upon-Avon (1932) a mere 1,500. But all of them seem large by the standards of the early twenty-first century, with substantial distance between the ludic space and farthest spectator. In some cases even to the closest spectator: at the SMT the scenic system in operation for many years discouraged the use of the forestage, so that the action was often over nine metres away from the front row. Guthrie's Festival Stage in Ontario (1956 and variously remodelled), designed for Shakespearean 'intimacy', sat 2,258 people, 858 of them in a balcony; though no spectator is more than twenty metres from the stage, that is nonetheless a big audience for contemporary theatrical performance.

All proscenium theatres coercively discipline the gaze, but large auditoria amplify the separation between audience and performer by sheer force of distance. As Guthrie (1964: 37) himself put it, spectator and actor in a proscenium arrangement are separated by two barriers, 'a barrier of fire, which is the footlights, then a barrier of space called the orchestra'. The bodies of actors on stage are therefore made to look smaller than the body of the viewer, more like puppets or imagined creatures in an autonomous and visually consistent world, and the farther away from the stage a spectator sits the more dream-like the actors will appear. The phenomenon is well suited to the affection of power the audience can assume over the players by virtue of the ocular relationship between silent watcher and speaking doer. As I noted in chapter 1, this idea reverses the usual semiotic assumption that the actor, as generator of signs, controls the spectator's reception. It's useful to recall that the perspective pro-scenium stage was developed to display the expensive and scenographically complex court musical entertainments that eventually led to seventeenth-century opera, a form historically associated with the prince as prime spectator. In a standard proscenium theatre the best seats for viewing, which are not necessarily the closest seats, are by custom the most expensive, and a clear downward grading is established for those with progressively inferior sightlines. Thus inscribed in the seating plan of large theatres – even those with open stages – is a scopic hierarchy that unconsciously replicates an antiquated social hierarchy. Especially in a theatre designed between about 1860 and 1914, with stalls, boxes, circle, pit and galleries built to distinguish the classes by space and to rank their regard of the stage, audiences today still form an ordered opticon of reception.

At about the same time that Poel and Savits were reacting against Shakespeare in the wrong spaces, a similar reaction occurred in Europe against the general habits of performance in large spaces. Early theatrical modernists, working against the grain of the established or commercial theatre, began to experiment with small and unconventional venues as part of their oppositional project. Unable to secure a regular theatre for the first production of the Théâtre Libre in 1887, André Antoine was forced to use a hastily arranged performance space that sat only 349. What was at first a necessity soon became a mark of distinction for others, and small spaces and small audiences were taken to signal a seriousness of artistic purpose and sometimes a disdain for bourgeois values. The Studio Theatre of the Moscow Art Theatre (MAT), which Stanislavsky created for Meyerhold's experiments with symbolism in 1905, became the model (even though it never performed for the public): the MAT opened a series of Studios later, Max Reinhardt started both the Schall und Rauch cabaret (1901) and the Kammerspiele (1906) in Berlin, Strindberg formed the Intimate Theatre (1907) in Stockholm for his own chamber plays, Georg Fuchs made the Künstlertheater (1908) in Munich a centre of analysis and reform. A studio, of course, is a place for study, a laboratory; the names of the other small theatres implied a similar emphasis on marginality or artist-audience process.

Most of these institutions did not survive the First World War. Though their aesthetic customs were sometimes kept alive by amateur players, it was the self-conscious revival of avant-garde attitudes in the 1960s and early 1970s that found renewed profit from the tradition. In the Off-Off-Broadway movement in New York, in the fringe movement in London, in left-bank theatres in Paris, in basement theatres in Rome and in university and alternative theatres from Moscow to Tokyo, theatrical marginality was exemplified and cherished. Indeed it was in this environment, usually associated with leftist political inclinations, that some of the most exciting theatre work of the time was hatched in small or unconventional spaces: the Théâtre du Soleil, the Living Theatre and the Open Theatre, the Taganka, and directors like Konrad Swinarski, Jerzy Grotowski, Richard Foreman, the early Robert Wilson, Joanne Akalaitis, Suzuki Tadashi, to name only a few, investigated the relationship between actor and spectator, trying to break down or lessen the separation between them, literally and metaphorically.

Prior to the 1970s Shakespeare was infrequently connected to the studio movement. The size of the casts, the length of the plays, the expense of production and the continued appropriation of Shakespeare as genteel high art, all colluded to discourage the radical experimentation and small purses associated with the fringe. In 1974, however, the British branch of the socially committed, marginalized theatre suddenly appeared in the centre of Shakespeareland, when under the leadership of Buzz Goodbody a corrugated metal storage shed up the street from the Royal Shakespeare Theatre in Stratford was converted to a playing space. Seating about 140 people in a rough environment with a temporary feel, it was consciously constructed as an alternative to mainstream traditions of the large theatre. Even its name, The Other Place, suggested its eccentricity (see Chambers 1980 and Kennedy 2001: 250–7). Since then small-scale or chamber performance became an important part of the RSC's work, and some of its most gripping and innovative productions were staged for the intimate surroundings of The Other Place or its London variants, the Donmar Warehouse (opened in 1977) and its replacement, a small flexible theatre in the Barbican called the Pit (1982). The Swan Theatre in Stratford (1986) continued the tradition, though in a much larger non-proscenium configuration. Meanwhile the chamber movement for Shakespeare had spread around the world.

Chamber performances place a burden on the finances of theatrical organizations because it is normally impossible for audiences of 200 or less to cover enough of the costs to make professional production feasible, even when expenses have been drastically reduced; some form of subsidy is necessary, whether external or internal, which means the producers must be firmly committed to the project to maintain it. Yet it's clear that many performers as well as many spectators are attracted to Shakespeare in reduced environments, preferring the intimacy achieved to the grander gestures and more detailed images in larger spaces. As Peter Holland (1982: 206) wrote about the Stratford of that period, 'the myth has grown up, however hard the company may try to rebut it – that the productions at the Royal Shakespeare Theatre itself are for tourists and school parties, while the productions at The Other Place are the justification for a long and miserable drive or an impossible confrontation with British Rail'. Myth or no, the importance of chamber Shakespeare is undeniable. Though Robert Wilson, Robert Lepage and some other highly successful directors have sought the coolness and spectacle of proscenium staging, at the same time we can note a movement in western theatre away from large-scale production and toward psychological intimacies familiar from film and television. In this chapter I investigate the reasons for the success of small Shakespeare through three speculations about the body, drawing on the productions of Trevor Nunn.

PERFORMER'S BODY AND SPECTATOR'S BODY

Erika Fischer-Lichte (1992: 101), looking at the theatre event in a strictly semiotic way, points out that traditional performance occurs when an actor (A) represents a character (X) while a spectator (S) looks on. Within this frame the triadic relationship A-X-S is irreducible. Because the actor is a three-dimensional body and always needs room, 'the stage space also represents an irreducible element of the theatrical code'; it is '(1) the space in which A acts, and (2) the space in which X is found.' But this formula omits a crucial element, the requirement of space for spectation, since S is also a three-dimensional body, and usually a number of three-dimensional bodies, taking up room. So actually – and staying within the semiotic code – there are two necessary spaces: the ludic space for A, and the watching space for S. The boundary of where X can be found is at the line where the two spaces meet. Though that boundary can be violated, it still adheres to the respective bodies of actor and spectator. In these terms the distance between X and S in large theatres reduces the apparent size of A, making it difficult and often impossible for much of the audience to read facial and gestural details and encouraging, as I noted above, a sense of S's superiority over A. This tendency is so much a part of the experience of the theatre in history that little attention has been paid to its psychological and physiological effects, though a number of theatrical moments have been forced to deal with it. There seems little doubt, for example, that the outsized masks of Greek actors were designed in part to make emblematic facial postures visible to spectators far up the hillside. Opera glasses, introduced as early as the 1730s but gaining significantly in popularity as playhouses expanded in size in the nineteenth century, were optical compensations with a similar purpose, adding an element of spying to the theatrical experience. Indeed the scopophilic reception model developed for film studies by Mulvey (1975), Oudart (1977–8) and others could be extended back in the theatre at least to the development of the perspective stage. The spatial distance between A and S has trad-itionally been offset by makeup, large gestures and loud voices; for Shakespeare that has meant a routine of acting variously called 'classical', 'big' or 'inflated'. To compensate for a reduced physical impression, the actor in a large space performs in a larger-than-life manner.

Thus when a performance occurs in a small theatre, especially one where the ludic space is not architecturally divided from the watching space, the proximity of A's body is the dominant physical impression made upon S. While distant views of a proscenium performance normally affect only the eyes and ears, keeping the danger of A's body at bay, the corporeal contiguity of small space performance can affect the range of senses. The results are not necessarily pleasant – especially when touch and smell are involved – but they provoke the audience to recognize that the actor is not merely a walking shadow. As an undeniable presence, as a space-occupying creature distinctly like the watcher in size, vitality and desire, the actor in a studio becomes both more human and more threatening. This is one of the chief reasons why a strictly semiotic view of the spectator's condition is insufficient, since the intimate and adjacent presence of the actor conveys so clearly the paradox of the theatrical double: the actor's otherness is both aesthetic object and human inci-dence, both signifier and corpus. For Shakespeare the proximity of A to S, and the less rigorous distinctions between ludic and watching spaces, can be more powerful than in other types of presentation. The transgressive opportunities of performance, particularly those violating common notions of where Shakespeare belongs and how he should be represented, can dominate normal fictive issues like story and character and theme. The space in which *Hamlet* is played, in other words, can be more important than *Hamlet* itself.

At the same time the spoken text becomes more emphatic. Most of the renovations in Shakespeare stage space since Poel have attempted to recentre the word, recognizing that the actor on a bare stage, especially when partly surrounded by spectators and untrammelled by decorations, is chiefly perceived as a body speaking text. In a small theatre the spoken word becomes as intimate as the environment, insidious, urgent and intrusive. Because the vocal qualities are close to those of everyday life, the stage events seem domestic in scale, a condition that cuts both ways: the performance can show violent or hilarious upheavals of that domesticity, or show mere banalities. By the simple fact of their proximity A and S become familiar. Sighs, whispers, ironic inflections, the electricity of sudden outbursts, these appear direct and genuine to the contemporary spectator, whereas large-scale Shakespearean acting may appear stagy or artificial. Why contemporary spectators might prefer one over the other is a question I will address shortly. First I hope to establish through an example some of the ways that audiences are affected by chamber Shakespeare.

There have been many notable successes on small stages but one of the most influential in English was Trevor Nunn's *Macbeth* at The Other Place in 1976. The production is doubly interesting to us because Nunn had staged the play in the main house in Stratford in 1974 then restaged it for the Aldwych Theatre in London the following year; dissatisfied both times by a lack of intensity, he mounted a chamber version using two of the company's stars, Ian McKellen and Judi Dench, to experiment with a big play in a small space. Nunn, who was at the time the artistic director of the RSC, had been a strong supporter of Buzz Goodbody's work at The Other Place. He had supervised the final dress rehearsals of her 'village hall' production of *Hamlet* in 1975 after her suicide in April, and the experience convinced him of the distinctive opportunities of studio performance. His *Macbeth* has particular weight as an historical example because it was one of the earliest of the RSC chamber productions; the comments of reviewers may be accorded more consequence than usual because they were not habituated to the rewards and hazards of such a Shakespearean enterprise.

Nunn and the designer John Napier notably set out to limit size and spectacle. The ludic space was a circle of about six metres in diameter, outlined by a black line painted on bare floorboards. The watching space consisted of a few rows of seats on the floor on three sides of the circle and few more rows on raised scaffolding, all with a quality of impermanence. The spatial relationship created the sense that spectators were staring at an intimate ritual of evil, helpless to act, even though it was close enough to touch (illustration 8). A circle of wooden beer crates was set at the

Illustration 8 The audience at The Other Place surrounds the magic circle for *Macbeth*, Stratford 1976

boundary of the ludic space, just outside the magic circle; seated on them, actors not involved in a scene watched the action, mediating between the positions of A/X and S. The crates were also used as props inside the circle, along with an extremely limited number of other items: a richly decorated coronation robe, a bell, a thunder sheet.

In such a minimized visual field, the smallest movements and the smallest voices were severely focussed. Almost all commentators recorded some reaction to how the cramped space heightened their discomfort over witnessing a dark intimacy, and many spoke of their sense of voyeurism at perverse acts. 'Everything is cribbed, cabined and confined', said the *Birmingham Post*, 'lit by sulphurous gleams.' Maurice Daniels, a long-time lighting designer at Stratford (though not connected with this production), reported that he felt 'like a voyeur watching with horror and fascination as Lady Macbeth and Macbeth became aroused, really unable to keep their hands off each other, as they planned Duncan's murder'. The theatre is often voyeuristic, or at least can be, and the proscenium stage lends itself especially well to the spirit of peering through a keyhole. The voyeurism of this *Macbeth*, however, struck many viewers as distinctly disturbing. Gareth Lloyd Evans related his 'sense of almost unbearable proximity to, and identification with, the world of the play: terror, apprehension, pity counterpointing with revulsion'. And Robert Cushman said that 'we are brought so close to Macbeth, and to evil itself (we are practically locked up with them), that we cannot disown them'.[1]

I suggest that the source of critics' disturbance lay in the condition of studio playing adopted at The Other Place: the actors publicly performed actions that in life should be hidden, as they do whenever *Macbeth* is staged, but in this case they did so almost unframed, tangibly close, yet *as if the spectators were not present*. They performed inside the conventions of psychological realism, overtly ignoring the presence of the audience, maintaining fourth-wall illusion though the fourth wall of a proscenium did not divide ludic space from watching space and was most plainly not implied. The performance created a disjunction between two attitudes to corporeality: spectators acknowledged the actors' bodies, indeed could not resist their carnal closeness, while actors appeared to deny the spectators' bodies and concentrated on their own.

The spectators' inescapable awareness of the actors' bodies in a closed space can be suggested by the frequency with which commentators reported physical details and movements, often noting unusually small matters. Some samples:

Jaggedness of movement and gesture...characterised the whole production.
[On first seeing the witches, Macbeth and Banquo] twirled rapidly around, with
daggers drawn, to face them. This 'twirl' became a feature of the playing and was
sometimes continued until the actor's body had passed through 360 degrees in a
complete pirouette.

The meeting between them was orgasmic in movement, and we later remembered the pushing movements of her hips and thighs when she gently but
insidiously pulled Duncan into her castle.

At Macbeth's return to court there is an instant outburst of cheers and embraces,
abruptly cut off as soon as the point has been made. For the coronation, Macbeth
performs a stately walk round the perimeter of the acting area clad in Duncan's
robe...If [the Macbeths] are sure of one thing it is that nothing can drive them
apart, a process that begins with the murder and is ruthlessly articulated up to the
moment of Ian McKellen lugging Judi Dench off like a carcass.[2]

This kind of characterized movement and gesture, which reveals inner
state as well as conveys emotional attitudes about the story, is familiar to
us from the cinema, where a raised eyebrow or an impassive face in close-
up can be used to enunciate enterprises of great pith and moment.
'There's no art / To find the mind's construction in the face', Duncan
holds, but in filmed performances audiences find it automatically. By the
1970s all audiences in the West were well habituated to psychological-
realist acting, the micro-acting associated with films and television, a
familiarity which made the production more accessible. Certainly the
acting used techniques of gesture and voice to create emotional closeness,
as Holland (1982: 214) noted:

All the incisive detail of McKellen's performance was aimed to make Macbeth
recognisable, to encourage us to empathise in the most complex way possible.
His presentation of the part had nothing to do with sympathy – indeed this was
the least sympathetic Macbeth I have ever seen – but the evil was explicable
rather than terrifying, closer to malice than an abstracted principle of negativity.

Reading the face became the central interpretive task, and when a
spectator's line of sight was obscured the production was in danger of
losing its hold. Roger Warren felt he missed a number of important
moments because of his seat location: 'I should dearly have liked to see
Judi Dench's face, for instance, as she greeted Duncan.'[3]
    Other features of the production also replicated filmic patterns.
Though it's already the shortest of the tragedies, Nunn cut *Macbeth* down
to two and a quarter hours and played it without interval, like a film; and
some of its visuals were clearly cinematic, like the line of red blood on

Lady Macduff's neck when a murderer cut her throat as the lights faded. Yet the moment remained highly theatrical, since Macduff himself (or his doubled actor), impassive and helpless, was watching the murder of his wife and children from a crate outside the circle. And the general feel of the production was theatrical as well, its best instances deriving from simple images of actors' bodies in space, like the magnificent moment after Lady Macbeth's death when McKellen stood frozen under a bare light bulb which hung from a cord. He set it swinging in a long arc, his face alternately in shadow and light, precisely indicating the rhythm of elation and despair he had traced in the play:

> I 'gin to be aweary of the sun,
> And wish th'estate o'th'world were now undone.

But overt theatricality only worked to a point. It was not able to include Ian McDiarmid's Porter, for example, which was almost universally condemned; McDiarmid played the role as a music hall turn, addressing the audience directly and forcing the obscenities and jokes. Not only did his performance seem too big for the small space, it violated the basic assumption of the production by admitting the spectators' presence. Even more telling, prior to its run at the Warehouse Nunn briefly mounted the production in the main theatre at Stratford in 1977, where its cinematic details and theatrical intimacy were hopelessly lost in the large space.

ABSENT BODIES, MAGNIFIED GESTURES

Actors in film and video, emerging as simulacra of light and shadow or as pixels in rapidly displayed optical lines, obviously cannot acknowledge a spectator's presence, though those simulations can be acknowledged by spectators in turn. Traditionally it has been assumed that since Shakespeare's work was intended to be seen in the theatre, the absence of the performer's body is the most significant phenomenological difference in Shakespeare on film and television. Before the revival of big-screen Shakespeare in the 1990s, many theatre scholars held this distinction as primary. 'Film occurs in a kind of virtual space', William Flesch noted about Shakespeare cinema (1987: 277). 'Lacking a dimension it lacks a basic presence in the world we live in. Nothing in film can touch or be touched.' The 'loss of the actor', as W. B. Worthen (1984: 197–201) called it, was at the time usually assumed to be a severe detriment. 'Although the camera simulates intimacy with the characters, it also keeps us safe from them' so that we are permitted 'to watch without risk'; denied the public dimension of Shakespeare's work, we are prevented 'from playing our part'. But how often does a spectator touch an actor in the theatre? Many spectators, perhaps most, recoil from the possibility that actors might touch them. In truth it's not actual touching of or by spectators that is notable about live performance, but only the possibility that it can occur.

Most commentators now recognize that in a media-saturated world the issue no longer appears so simple. The importance of physicality has been substantially reduced by varieties of screen presence, as Auslander (2008) and Causey (2006) reveal. At the same time the simulation of intimacy in film and television can be very powerful. What causes it, and why do spectators feel it? Prior to the invention of motion pictures, when the term 'live performance' was a tautology, dramatic representation was an uncommon experience, whereas film, radio and especially TV have made drama in postmodernity all-pervasive and practically universal. In much of the world it is difficult to get through an ordinary day without some exposure to electronic enactments, and many people spend an inordinate amount of time engaged by the various dramatic, pseudo-dramatic and speciously dramatic representations on TV. Despite their recent arrival, film and television and the internet are now part of us, and our cultural habituation to them has deeply affected the way we perceive the world – and how we behave in live performance.

These McLuhanesque commonplaces become important here because most films and television shows, whether delivering the news as drama or drama as the news, tend to present themselves as realist texts, as transparent windows on the world. We watch images of people engaged in ordinary or tenable actions, usually dressed and speaking like us, inviting us to accept them as given if not figure them out. If intimacy in live performance comes from the actors' presence, the simulation of intimacy in film and video, emphasized by close-ups and by amplified but unstressed voices, comes from their absence. Paradoxically, it is metaphoric distance which appears to make the actors closer, since the human images can be much larger than life without becoming a physical threat, the voices sinuous and alluring or enhanced and coercive without becoming abusive. The intrusive intervention of the actor's face, glowing from a screen that might be a metonym of the spectator's desire, invites psychological speculation and infinite fantasias of meaning. The actors' magnified absence encourages individualized readings of their images, creating an intense sensation of veracity.

The Trevor Nunn *Macbeth* on stage was already in psychological close-up. When it was shot for Thames Television in 1978, using the same sixteen actors and the same cut-down version of the text, it fit quite naturally into the new medium. The video director, Philip Casson, had simply to accent its imbedded mode of performance and bring the camera in close. This he did with great and almost tedious regularity, so that the dominant impression is of faces in turmoil. Television, of course, normally compensates for the small screen by replacing the panoramas of film with full-screen images of faces. (Though video monitors have become much larger than the standard in 1978, so that faces filling the TV screen can now be larger than life.) TV is thus – by convention, if not inherently – suited to a drama of psychologizing, a characteristic that works well in the domestic environment where we normally see it. Since we are in a space resonant with the ordinary, we are less likely to accept representations of the extraordinary on the screen.

'Your face, my thane, is as a book where men / May read strange matters' became the theme of the Thames production, and the camera provided ample opportunity to read faces. Filmed in a studio, there are no long shots and few shots of groups. Actors appear as if from a misty darkness and are immediately subjected to the camera's scrutiny. Even the prologue, replayed from the stage version, in which all the actors entered and sat on the crates at the circle's edge, focusses on individual faces as the camera pans from one to the next. For 'Is this a dagger I see before me', only McKellen's face and hands were lit, his black costume invisible; at the end of the soliloquy he rolled back his sleeve in preparation for stabbing Duncan, and the length of his white arm in all that darkness is terrifying. After the regicide his arm was streaked with bright blood. Similarly, on discovering the King's murder Macduff reveals horror in his face rather than in his words. The acoustic effects are directly parallel to the visuals; like the camera, the microphone amplifies extreme intimacies while maintaining the illusion of the typical. Sighs, intakes of breath, whispers and softly uttered cries are as much a part of the TV version as the enlarged faces.

Macbeth was successful on TV because on stage the production had domesticated the supernatural. Witchcraft and murder were arranged to fit inside the homey environment of the theatre-within-the-box by relying on faces to convey inner states rather than on external effects, and by making those faces indisputable. Speaking of Shakespeare video acting in a slightly different context, Robert Lindsay (who played Benedick in the BBC *Much Ado about Nothing* of 1984) said that 'the subtleties, the subtext, which are difficult to project on stage, you can do on television. Just the fact that you can stand next to someone and say one thing, while your eyes are saying something else, is wonderful' (in Willis 1991: 220–1). In *Macbeth* subtext was also conveyed by non-facial gestures and actions in the same close-up manner. Holding two daggers after Duncan's murder, Macbeth's hands were shaking: the blades lightly but insistently clicked against each other. At the end Macbeth's head on a pole would have been out of keeping with the extreme psychological realism, on stage and on TV; instead an actor brought the crown to Macduff's hands, which were holding two similar daggers still smeared with the tyrant's blood. For the video version the camera tightly focussed on this final image, searing it in the spectator's mind in a still frame that made the final moment darker and considerably more pessimistic than on stage.

THE REVISED BODY

Much recent scholarship has emphasized that the way the body is represented and perceived is historically determined, and our most 'natural' corporeal attributes are conditioned, shaped and controlled by culture. The actor's body is probably more subject to historical forces than the bodies of non-performers; regardless of its size, shape or beauty, the actor's body is almost inevitably read as exemplary because it is the object of the most intense and profound gaze in a culture. Indeed it seems fair to say that accepting the culture's gaze is a condition of acting. As Joseph Roach (1993: 11) notes, 'the complex values of a culture' become concentrated in the performing body as observed by the spectator. Fischer-Lichte (1989) goes even further, holding that the performer's body is representative of the whole of culture. When notions of the body undergo change, the actor's body becomes a site where that cultural crisis is represented.

Since about 1975 we have undergone a major transformation in the way Shakespeare is perceived on stage. As I have been suggesting, this change has been informed by the prevalence of film and TV in the culture at large, and their increasing bias to psychic revelation through close-ups and through small but precise signifiers. The actor's animate body on stage is now seen with eyes thoroughly accustomed to the actor's inanimate body on film, eyes that in many cases may prefer the distance of the screen. Further, there are substantially more films and videos of Shakespeare's plays available now than even in 1990, and because DVD recorders are common and cheap it is at least possible for the general public to see performances of the plays on demand. The successes of the films by Kenneth Branagh, Franco Zeffirelli, Baz Luhrmann and Michael Almereyda, relying on the old Hollywood formula for Shakespeare of spectacle and stars, demonstrate that the market is reasonably large. In their video versions those films join a burgeoning cinematic industry: for the first time in history, you can hire a Shakespeare production and at very little expense.

A large number of people have now been introduced to Shakespeare performance through video in the classroom. This form of Shakespearean spectation, because it fits with culturally accustomed habits of viewing, strikes many young people as less foreign or intimidating than watching Shakespeare in the theatre, but it comes with a cost: it tends to suggest that the plays are essentially about psychological states. Further, we are permitted to atomize video performances, and to investigate very small details in them, by means of the pause, rewind and slow-motion buttons. The technology of video encourages us to treat performances as if they were printed scripts, searching back and forth in them as we do in a written text, replaying moments, taking them out of their performative context, realigning them according to our own choices. With a remote control in hand, any viewer is a textual editor and perhaps a film director.

I don't mean to suggest that spectators who have grown up with video Shakespeare are inclined to stop live performances and ask for an instant replay. But it is likely that the electronic reification of the actor's body has affected the way those spectators watch in the theatre. They are more likely to look for psychological explanations of action, more likely to heed small intense moments that clarify inner states, unlikely to listen for rhetorical structure or be patient with self-conscious theatricality. These spectators are more likely attracted to the underplaying characteristic of studio theatres and to imperial themes treated as intimate occasions. It's intriguing to notice that from the start the most successful productions at The Other Place were tragedies or dark comedies rooted in family matters. Goodbody's *King Lear* (1974) and *Hamlet*, Nunn's *Macbeth*, John Barton's *The Merchant of Venice* (1978), John Caird's *Romeo and Juliet* (1984), Sam Mendes's *Richard III* (1992), all worked by using micro-acting and homespun theatrical virtues to underline the domestic situations of the plays. The lighter comedies or the more public histories were tried less often there, perhaps because they rely on broader styles which are difficult to play up close.

The domesticating effect of film and television on chamber work can be seen through Nunn's *Othello* of 1989 at The Other Place, some thirteen years after *Macbeth*. The cast was assembled specially for the occasion, and played for limited runs in Stratford and at the Young Vic in London. Unlike *Macbeth*, cut to the length of a film, this *Othello* used a nearly complete text and lasted over four hours. While magnificently theatrical, the performance nonetheless refined the micro-characteristics of its predecessors, especially in the acting of Ian McKellen as Iago. McKellen was a military iceman, obsessive about orderliness and under notable control: he was often brushing his uniform, straightening a carpet or pedagogically explaining to Roderigo exactly how to accomplish his aims. His face could show dedication to his general and perfidy to the audience at the same moment, yet be psychologically in tune with a nineteenth-century martial code assumed by the setting. 'The stiff military back, the fastidiously groomed moustache and the clipped northern accent persuades them all', said the *Spectator* (2 September 1989); 'only we seem to see how cold are his blue eyes.' The 'microscopic scrutiny' of Iago's character 'repeatedly puts you in mind of Strindberg. The locations may ostensibly be Venice and Cyprus, but spiritually we are inside the four walls of bourgeois naturalist drama.' Othello, on the other hand, was played by Willard White, a Jamaican opera singer acting Shakespeare for the first time – and acting in a large, operatic, indulgent style, allowing his voice to range in pitch and volume and his gestures to become grand and contrived. His passion was readily apparent, but it cast doubt on his mental state. McKellen was on TV, as it were, and White at Covent Garden, so I, strangely, trusted Iago and was suspicious of Othello.

The visuals of the production, designed by Bob Crowley, specifically elicited a cinematic reference. The Senate scene in act 1, for example, sat Othello at a small table to recount the story of his love: the council took place 'in a haze of cigar smoke around a table on which the maps jostled with the brandy decanter and glasses under a green-shaded lamp – a gentlemen's-club atmosphere'. It was a powerful image of a familiar world where decisions about women are made by men with the same brusque presumption that drives them to occupy and defend a distant island. That world was evoked in part by the numerous small hand props that allowed actors characterized tasks. McKellen rolled his own cigarettes, for example, as quickly and neatly as he misled Othello; Imogen Stubbs as Desdemona dropped her handkerchief after trying to cool her husband's troubled brow with it. McKellen mixed wine punch in a white enamel wash basin in the barracks scene, and later the drunken Cassio vomited into it. Stanley Wells noted that the physical details and psychological acting lent an 'almost Ibsenite social realism'; indeed 'a fully written account of this production would read like a Victorian novel'.[4]

In Cyprus it gradually became apparent that the costumes and props were derived from the American Civil War: blue Union tunics with brass and leather accessories, folding camp cots, wooden washstands. Because Willard White is black, this raised intriguing questions about slavery that might have been developed further, but Crowley said that he was not after a political statement: 'I tried rather to elicit key objects from the period that would have a huge resonance in a small space. This was Shakespeare under the microscope' (in Kennedy 2001: 255–6). With a few deft strokes the designer had evoked a major cultural quotation, not to the Civil War but to movies about the Civil War. Collective images of the past have always come from popular sources; they are now defined by Hollywood films more than by ballads or books or plays. Crowley explained he wanted to give spectators swift access to the situation of men travelling to a remote outpost for war, a few women tagging along, out of place in a male world. 'It's hard to do that with doublets and hose', he said, but military uniforms from more recent and visually accessible periods can quickly establish ranks, emotional dispositions and character displacements.

Cinema and video were important to Nunn's stage *Othello* in two ways, then: through the range of visual references that drew on period movies, and through a psychological acting that stressed intimate facial gesture and quiet vocal practice. The production's power derived not from its imitation of film and video but from the selective reconditioning of their methods, including the naturalistic habit of defining character through environment and objects. At the end of the piece McKellen stood unrepentant and unbowed in a fading spotlight, coldly staring at spectators only a few feet away, his face revealing nothing – Iago's 'Demand me nothing' fixed in a physical gesture – which meant spectators were free to read his face with impunity. It was intimate Shakespeare, all right: chillingly intense, psychologically convincing and thoroughly alien.

The production was made into a BBC film for television (1990), directed by Nunn himself. Unlike the TV-studio atmosphere of *Macbeth*, this version was a film of the stage production with multiple moving cameras, some cinematic techniques, a much slower pace and at three hours forty minutes almost as long as the original. Because the play is thoroughly domestic in its concerns, using habitual realist techniques for television had less effect than domesticating the supernatural did in the *Macbeth* film. The performances remained subtle and psychologically intense, with much use of isolated film noir lighting, close-ups of faces and anti-rhetorical speech, but ironically the camera tended to reduce the intimacy that characterized the theatrical version.

Actors' bodies, existent and incontestable before spectators' bodies in a studio theatre, will never be mistaken for the luminant phantasms of TV and film. But by drawing on the kind of acting and scenography familiar from the recorded media, Nunn's productions, and chamber theatre in general, have profited from contemporary cultural habituations while aggressively reapplying them to live performance. Caught in a three-way competition among modes of representation – the premodern (the theatre), the modern (the cinema) and the 'more-than-modern' (video) – spectators in the playhouse can still be surprised by the antique pleasure of corporeal presence. Confronting the theatrical other in a claustrophobic space, we sense the familiar performative modes of film and television and at the same time the inescapable danger of other bodies occupying a shared present.

PART III

Subjectivity and the spectator

CHAPTER 8

Society, spectacle and sport

The final part of the book concerns the relationship of spectation to subjectivity, taking examples from sport, gambling, game shows, performance memory and religious ritual. I begin by turning back to 1967, to Guy Debord's *The Society of the Spectacle*. In that iconoclastic work, and in a follow-on book twenty-one years later, Debord applied a revised Marxist analysis to the condition of the individual in society, a method he and his colleagues called situationism, based on the theory that the attitudes and behaviour of an individual are determined more by the false representations of surrounding circumstances than by personal attributes or qualities. Debord's importance goes well beyond the situationist programme, especially in his consideration of the world as spectacle. He defined 'the spectacle' as 'the autocratic reign of the market economy which had acceded to an irresponsible sovereignty, and the totality of new techniques of government which accompanied this reign' (1994: 29). Citizens have become passive and reticent spectators at the great show of the world, while global business and complicit government – the doers, the actors – have created a culture of acquiescent consumers. To be a western consumer is to be a spectator.

For Debord the spectacle, which overrides everything and intrudes everywhere through the 'spectacular industries' of film, television, radio, newspapers and magazines, involves 'the elimination of the limits between the self and world'. We are swallowed up by the spectacle; there is no room outside it. 'There is no place left where people can discuss the realities which concern them', he insists, 'because they can never lastingly free themselves from the crushing presence of media discourse and the various forces organized to relay it' (Debord 1990: 19). Monopoly capitalism constructs the world and its contents as spectacular commodity. Jameson (1990) famously noted that the most significant feature of postmodernity is the commodification of almost all aspects of life, including politics, charity, religion and sport. As Debord puts it:

The spectacle corresponds to the historical moment at which the commodity completes its colonization of social life. It is not just that the relationship to commodities is now plain to see – commodities are now all there is to see; the world we see is the world of the commodity (1994: 29).

In T. J. Clark's view, this colonization 'points to a massive internal extension of the capitalist market – the invasion and restructuring of whole areas of free time, private life, leisure, and personal expression' (1984: 9).

Jean Baudrillard's idea of simulacra (1994b), though more nuanced and less politicized than Debord's spectacle, follows in the same tradition. If the phantom simulations that surround us are more present than the concrete realities they supposedly replicate, then authenticity is dead, the 'real' object (the object with reality-in-the-world) is obsolete, since it is no longer possible to distinguish sufficiently between an event and its simulacra, perfect copies of a non-existent original. Not only has society become dramatized, it has also become conditioned and controlled by the mass media, what we might call the simulation industry. Without television contemporary politics and the global economy are impossible. Both driving and responding to the triumph of consumerism, the media create an hysterical culture of celebrity where power and status are granted by face recognition and where, in turn, recognized faces are readily commodified.

Inside a world so circumscribed, it is tempting for a performance historian to propose that the spectator as living witness of a live presentation is a special case, an archaic survivor perhaps, but an envoy nonetheless of the desire for community and sentience. In the midst of the deceits of spectacular culture, conducting oneself as a living witness offers the chance to certify actuality and collective existence. Cybernetics and the mass media may confuse our sense of reality-in-the-world, and perhaps will eventually erase the distinction between that and the non-real, but for now when the original actually exists we usually know, or want to know, the difference between it and its copies. As performance through bodily presence gets rarer, what we gain from it becomes more precious; shared or communal witnessing in a physically gathered audience becomes an escape from the culture of commodity we see on television.

It is getting harder to maintain that position with social conviction. Compared to TV and the internet, theatre in the twenty-first century looks like a cul-de-sac off the Infobahn. We are already in an era of post-theatre, where much of it is either touristic or uncommon, with the quaint charm of a ride in a horse-drawn carriage as SUVs roar by. And most of us are now completely immunized to the theatricalized social performance and the para-dramatic performance which surround us. With the ceaseless flow of images on TV – especially through satellite on-the-spot reporting, reality television and other transmissions that mimic the live – we are justified in being a little confused over the nature of embodiment and presence. We are all constructed all day, every day, as spectators.

Meanwhile theatre calls upon the new technologies. The heavily commodified megamusicals rely on hi-tech light and sound systems, and at the other end of the market innovative theatre and live art troupes have created work that investigates cybernetics and the hyperreal, or what Romeo Castellucci calls the 'dis-real', or that challenges the centrality of liveness: the Wooster Group, Robert Lepage, Castellucci's Socìetas Raffaello Sanzio, among others. The body may still be crucial to live performance but there is now considerable doubt about what constitutes the body, or what the body means, or if the body can be essentialized and distinguished from the machines that connect to it: and this is sometimes true about the bodies of actor and spectator alike, what Causey (2006) calls 'postorganic performance'.

SPORT AS SPECTACLE

Theatre audiences are not free beings: they give up part of their agency when they agree to assist at the spectacle. The approbative and disapprobative audience gestures conventionally available in theatre are limited and they confine spectators to predetermined and relatively compliant roles. The physical and vocal passivity of the spectator, frequently condemned in the avant-garde tradition of the twentieth century, is partly necessary if the performance is to proceed: audience participation is workable on a continuing basis only when it occurs inside the producers' plan.

I have said before that one of the most consistent features of theatrical modernism was a desire to organize and control perception, conditioning or requiring the spectator to assume a set of gestural, postural, visual and perceptual attitudes: sitting upright, attentive and quiet in the dark, trapped between armrests and the knees of other spectators, freeing the mind of preconceptions, open to the command of the work, staring at the light. Nineteenth-century habits of response were often anarchic, with spectators assuming the right to disrupt the occasion, talk, move about, eat and drink, but modernism found this both anti-naturalistic and antagonistic to the mood of the performance. In the new century it would be the producers who would lead the consumers, not the other way round.

This audience movement was reinforced by the invention of cinema, which absconded with most of the popular audience for theatre fairly quickly and permanently. While spectator habits in the first years of cinema remained boisterous, that resulted from the brevity of the films and their exhibition as part of a live variety show. Once full-length narrative films were the norm, the darkened auditorium and the bright screen image made the audience substantially more quiescent. The introduction of spoken dialogue in 1927 insured that audiences for film were at least as compliant as for live performance. Meanwhile the *embourgeoisement* of theatre in the West had become almost complete, and the rowdy mode of reception associated with the male working class transferred to music halls, vaudevilles, burlesques and strip shows.

It transferred even more notably to sport. The rise of professional spectator sports in the second half of the nineteenth century, beginning in England and spreading throughout the world, brought one of the most significant changes in history to the manners and entitlement of the spectator. In obvious distinction to the restrained behaviour at films and bourgeois theatres, sport fans from the start were encouraged to display emotions, approbation and partisanship in an open and free-playing manner. In most sports it is beneficial for athletes to have vocal assistance and of course this behaviour is not disruptive as it is in dramatic ventures in the modernist tradition, whether live or recorded; the sport contest would seem deadened without the noise of communal support. While endorsing the team, sport spectators are also invited to connect their own fantasies to the ordeal on the pitch. Their vociferous responses indicate the degree of investment fans can assume with the match, and further suggest the liberating and recreative spirit available for live witnesses.

Compared to a theatre spectator the sport spectator assumes a playful freedom. I have three suggestions about what that means. First, it is the freedom to negotiate a relationship to other unknown spectators, something that rarely occurs in theatre or film. In the stadium fans assume wide options about their fellow spectators, ranging from ignoring them to creating a bond over mutual regard to vilifying or striking them for rooting for the opposing side. In a newspaper article written in 1926, Brecht claimed that fans know exactly why they attend a sporting match and what will take place there; they thus relate to the event and each other in a straightforward way (we might say in a Brechtian way). In drama, on the other hand, 'the demoralization of our theatre audiences springs from the fact that neither theatre nor audience has any idea what is supposed to go on there' (Willett 1964: 6).

Much of this particular spirit derives from the spectator making a civic or tribal investment in the team. Sport spectators can have a range of investment, from the casual TV viewer to the season-ticket holder to the gambler with a lot of money on a football match. Sporting events are of course overt contests and are teleological or outcome-oriented; they easily lend themselves to an engaged spectatorship of fanatics intimately interested in both the details of athletic performance and the final result of the game. Around the world sport teams are most frequently identified with a specific city or region. Despite the fact that players and their coaches infrequently come from the sponsoring city or even the same country, and in some sports are bought and sold with distressing regularity, spectators often look to the team as a representative of the *polis* and take civic or national pride in their 'ownership' of it (Jackson 1988). In the psychological sense, sports spectators seek, through a process of identification, a refuge from urban anonymity: an imagined return to an imagined small community. When the team wins, the city or the country wins and thus the invested spectator shares the lustre, becomes ritually distinguished from non-invested persons and especially from the losers.

The relationship of one fan to another is quite extraordinary in sport, especially for males, and follows from this engagement. Openly emotional behaviour is sanctioned as the level of excitement gathers force. 'It is not uncommon, in any sport, to see spectators behaving in a way that would be uncharacteristic of them in any other context: embracing, shouting, swearing, kissing, dancing in jubilation' (Buford 1991: 166). Even male weeping is accepted. Emotional behaviour is particularly notable in that most male and most working-class of all British sports, Association Football (or soccer, its nickname from the 1890s, derived from the abbreviation Assoc.). The infamous British terraces, where groups consisting almost entirely of men stood in extreme proximity, concentrated the experience of communal excitement through unavoidable and constant physical proximity. 'Physical contact to this extent is unusual in any culture', Bill Buford (168) notes about the terraces. 'In England, where touch is not a social custom and where even a handshake can be regarded as intrusive, contact of this kind is exceptionable.'

The second free-play characteristic for sports spectators is the freedom to condemn the performance's outcome and reject the manner of play.

Fans can know better than the coach, demand more of the team, see more than the referee. If the result displeases them, they may well express their dissatisfaction publicly. It is true that any theatre spectator can do this, but since the investment of theatregoers is substantially less ardent their disappointment is also less and they rarely express it openly, except by staying away in the future. Further, sport fans can indicate dissatisfaction on a continuing basis, communally and with statistically supported knowledge. In dramaturgical terms a sporting season or tournament is like a serial TV show, with the same players meeting challenges each day or each week that are both new and not new. The character identification that some TV viewers assume with actors in soap operas, sitcoms or series dramas is parallel to the heroicizing of sports stars, and little like it is possible in the theatre.

Third, sports spectators have freedom to vary or alter the purpose of their presence. Theatregoers technically participate in this condition and in the past often attended a play as a pretext for other public behaviour, from flirting to conducting business. In the twentieth century, however, most of this ancillary activity was abandoned for both theatre and film. Under the rigours of theatre architecture and the modernist revisions to the actor-audience association, theatre spectators have been deprived of much of the privilege to write themselves into the event. The sports spectator, meanwhile, has elaborated the Victorian working-class patterns of public behaviour as a method of owning the experience.

SPECTATORS AND VIOLENCE

In addition to class issues, fan deportment is significantly connected to gender. Sport has become a male preserve because it is one of the few areas of life where aggressive male behaviour is sanctioned. This is more complicated than first appears, since many women enjoy watching sport and more and more women engage in both solo and team sports. On the whole, however, it is reasonable to say that men still dominate sport and sport culture. As Allen Guttmann (1986: 170–1) summarizes, the modernization and industrialization of traditional societies has left games like boxing and football of all types (including rugby and American football) as legitimate enclaves of violence for the fans as well as the players. Sport may not be the most important factor in 'the production and reproduction of masculine identity' but it plays a crucial role in reinforcing macho aggressiveness 'in a society where only a few occupational roles, such as those in the military and the police, offer regular opportunities for fighting, and where the whole direction of technological development has been for a long time to reduce the need for physical strength' (Elias and Dunning 1986: 283).

In the post-industrial world male strength has been transformed in purpose, away from work and war and into symbolic power and sexual allure. This is a movement away from use value to exchange value, or away from the need for the masculine to the performance of the masculine. Male strength becomes male display. Clearly sports are crucial to this development, since they require both strength and its display. In this light spectator violence is an extension of the same traffic: finding few legitimate outlets and almost no social need for ferocity and destructiveness, some spectators in some sport environments have channelled male strength into a public display of fighting. Spectator violence is a form of audience involvement that indicates a most serious commitment to the show. Riots in the theatre and riots outside it caused by theatrical events were probably never as common as the laws attempting to control them imply; it was usually the extreme fear of riotous conduct, rather than numerous actual incidents, that led to state constraints. But however frequently they occurred in the past in the theatre, we almost never hear of them now.

In sport, however, the curve of spectator violence increased after the Second World War. During the Thatcher years the British tabloid press found regular material for overblown stories in what was dubbed at an early stage 'football hooliganism'. The conventional view was that perpetrators of soccer violence off the pitch were examples of the feared other inside British culture. In the 1970s and 1980s the press and government policy treated them as sociopathic ruffians born out of recent economic and cultural change; it is true that for a while hooliganism seemed an extension of the punk movement with right-wing allegiances. This popular view, however, has been challenged by a number of sociologists and psychologists.

The dominant sociological position was led by Eric Dunning and his colleagues at Leicester University. Dunning was heavily influenced by his German colleague Norbert Elias, whose well-known work on the civilizing process (Elias 1978, originally 1939) proposed an evolutionary model of human behaviour. Far from being a new development violence at football is ancient, having arisen at the very foundation of the folk game in the Middle Ages, an anarchic territorial competition in ludic form. As Cashmore (2005: 285) notes, folk football was described as early as 1514 as 'nothing but beastlie furie and extreme violence'. Even the destruction of property by non-players outside the pitch that became common in the

1980s had its parallels in the folk game, prompting prohibitions as far back as the reign of Edward II in 1314 (Dunning 1999: 84). Elias and Dunning's joint book *Quest for Excitement* (1986) argues that civilized societies more and more look down upon highly excitable behaviour in public: 'Great fear and great joy, great hatred and great love have to be whittled away in outward appearance.' Spectator sports provide a carnivalesque outlet for emotional conduct otherwise unavailable. 'In advanced industrial societies', they write, 'leisure activities form an enclave for the socially approved arousal of moderate excitement behaviour in public' (64–5). From this angle violent fan behaviour results from the mixing of an existing macho working-class culture with alcohol and the emotional enthusiasm authorized by sporting matches.

There has been serious criticism of the Leicester approach, even accusations that it has enabled repressive police action and the policy of spectator containment that led to the Hillsborough disaster of 15 April 1989. On that sad day Liverpool and Nottingham Forest played an FA Cup semi-final at the Hillsborough stadium in Sheffield. The authorities followed the common policy of containing fans in the terraces. Worried that fans excluded from entry would create a violent protest outside, the police allowed far too many of them inside. Once in the terrace there was no way out, as the cages were locked. In a surging movement of the crowd, ninety-five Liverpool fans were crushed to death. As one commentator puts it, the deaths were the direct result of a false interpretation by South Yorkshire police that the problem was 'a violent crowd pitch invasion, rather than a problem of safety and over-crowding, itself created by allowing thousands of Liverpool fans to mill around outside the Leppings Lane end of the ground' (Redhead 1997: 11–12).

While there is no need to enter the debate about the Leicester approach here, it is clear that hooliganism is a complex issue. Though it has not gone away, British football violence declined significantly after Hillsborough. The lessons took a while to sink in, but more enlightened stadium construction, the elimination of many of the terraces, better seating arrangements, more expensive and more fairly apportioned tickets, arrangements for travel and visitors' accommodation and preventive policing have had positive effects. Some traditional fans regret these changes, which are part of the movement toward globalization in football, and a few commentators have suggested that football hooliganism in the 1980s was a reaction against the commodifying trend.

Sociologists concerned with British football violence often wonder why a similar problem does not exist in the United States, one of the most violent societies in the world. Distance is one reason: the great distances between rival professional American football teams have worked to keep down fan violence, whereas in Britain hooliganism increased in the late 1950s when fans could travel readily and cheaply to rival cities, often in special trains. This factor does not apply to local rivalries in America, especially in high school football and basketball; some clashes have been so extreme, and so implicated in racial turmoil, that spectators have been barred from games entirely. But on the professional level there is no equivalent in the USA to British hooliganism, just as there was no equivalent to the crowded terraces. At an American football game, even in the 1970s, every spectator had an assigned and usually expensive seat. (Dunning (1999) provides a comparison of crowd violence in the two sporting cultures.)

Most importantly, violence-prone young men, like those in street gangs, have not found sport an appropriate locale for confrontation in North America, whereas in Britain expressing hostility to the rival team is part of spectatorship. Young men involved in serious violence in Britain tend to think of fighting and encounters with rival fans 'as an integral part of attending a football match'. The songs and chants of inter-fan rivalry support this; 'during a match the rival groups direct their attention as much and sometimes more to one another as they do to the match itself, singing, chanting, and gesticulating *en masse* and in what one might call spontaneously orchestrated uniformity as expressions of their opposition' (Elias and Dunning 1986: 249). In the USA fan opposition tends to be 'civilized' or ritualized through cheerleaders, bands and manipulative stadium displays. In the 1980s in Britain much of hooliganism was in fact organized violence, prompted by groups of dedicated supporters who called themselves 'firms' and who travelled to matches with the express purpose of starting brawls with rival fans. The main purpose was not watching the match but using the match as opportunity for an analogous arousal. For the members of the firms, causing harm to others was the direct expression of their engagement, a pleasurable effect of spectator commitment. Nick Hornby's *Fever Pitch* (1992) brought extreme football obsession to wide attention, followed by a number of insider treatments about working-class culture and the firms that have clarified the nature of violent fandom (such as King 1996 and Cowens 2001; Cashmore 2005: 288–93 summarizes alternative explanations of crowd violence).

The hooligan problem returns us to the main theme through the issue of live witnessing. Both violent and peaceable fans will go to extraordinary lengths to be physically present for an important match, even when they have no hope of entering the stadium, a sign of how powerful gathering and witnessing has become in an age of electronic simulations. We are all mediatized spectators now; surrounded daily by televisual enactments and luminant fantasies, we have achieved a new relationship to the live event. The social overtones and high-art associations of theatre have made it a rarity in most peoples' lives, but it has thereby assumed a value it could not have prior to the twentieth century. Just as the living witness in a court of law is a throwback to a time when travel and communication were difficult, so the spectator at a live performance has a status that is technologically unjustified. In theatre, where the unreproducibility of the experience is the point, the spectator is assumed to desire the archaic status of witness – it is a choice, made to achieve a condition of observation and audition unattainable through television. The case with sport is more complicated in that sporting events are one of the very few remaining examples of live television transmission, and thus fans who attend in person underline even more their status as specialists in witnessing, while at the same time authenticating the liveness of the contest for those at home. Like tourists photographed in front of famous monuments, live sport spectators wish to claim a trace of originary authenticity in a world of manufactured experience.

From this angle hooliganism is a form of being there, and despite its destructive and antisocial results is a method of taking ownership. It is helpful to note that the football riot, which we associate with the decadent capitalist world, 'was always part of the Soviet sports scene' as well. The composer Dimitri Shostakovich, 'a rabid and knowledgeable soccer fan', wrote a letter to a national sports daily in 1946 complaining of rowdy and ill-behaved crowds in stadiums, where he felt his young son was threatened and intimidated (Edelman 1993: 3). The official Soviet view was that violence did not occur in sport but as late as the 1980s 'visitors to Moscow and Leningrad', Guttmann writes (1986: 162), were 'warned by their Intourist guides not to attend soccer matches, where high spirits are often sent higher by vodka'. Today, whether in Russia or Britain or the USA or Japan, the tribal cohesion provided by inter-civic and international sports contests, which appears to be so forceful, may be just another illusion of postmodernity. In many cases in professional sports the community of spectators, whether in the stadium or watching the box, is a thoroughly commodified cohesion, packaged and sold with great marketing skill, sometimes with the borrowed power of the state adding to its presumed communality. The state or commercial sponsors managing the major sports events, and the complicit media broadcasting them, frequently and cynically prey upon the very lack of cohesion or lack of community that spectators otherwise feel in their everyday lives. Football hooligans seem rather sad in this regard, Little Englanders fighting in the streets of France or Italy for a national identity that no longer exists.

POLITICS AND SPORT

Sport has been of major interest to a number of sociologists and political thinkers because it presents one of most difficult social uncertainties in modernity. Organized socialism and modern spectator sports both arose in the late nineteenth century, both the product of industrialization and urbanization, even though they were rarely connected in discourse. Socialists generally took the view that spectator sports 'undermined prospects for social change and revolution' (Edelman 1993: 3). The left considered the Victorian attitude to sport 'an aristocratic desire to keep the working class out of the fun and games... the early Bolsheviks wanted no part of the Olympic movement's elitist version of amateurism' and boycotted the Games in the 1920s and 1930s to organize their own workers' sports pageants instead (5). The official USSR view developed thereafter: mass sport was to strengthen the population for work and war, and spectators had no official standing. Thus the spectator sports that did exist, mostly notably soccer, were effectively fostering behaviour that was 'destabilizing, even counter-hegemonic'. The Soviet state sports system, which eventually emphasized Olympic success for its international propaganda value, was a correlative to 'the huge steel mills, dams, and turbine factories long favored under Communism, while spectator sports can be viewed as yet another element of the long-neglected consumer sector' (15). 'Capitalist mass culture tailored its messages to win an audience, while Soviet mass culture tailored its messages to teach its audience' (23).

The Soviet dislike of spectator sports was anticipated in politically conservative thought at the turn of the twentieth century, which reacted against the professionalization of sport, insisting that its value was in the playing, not the winning. The cultural historian Johan Huizinga, for example, did not approve of the professional leagues first established in Britain in the late nineteenth century. Pierre de Coubertin and José Ortega y Gasset preferred the gentlemanly amateurism of England to masses of passive spectators, as is apparent in Coubertin's aristocratic credo for the modern Olympics, which he established in 1896: 'It is not if you win or lose, but how you play the game.' The gentlemanly code of conduct fostered by English public schools passed into the US as well. Walter Camp of Yale wrote in 1893 regarding spectators, 'It is not a courtesy upon a ballfield to cheer an error of the opponents. If it is on your grounds, it is the worst kind of boorishness. Moreover, if there are remarkable plays made by your rivals you yourselves should cheer' (in Guttmann 1986: 88). The gentlemanly code was perfected by the All-England Croquet and Lawn Tennis Club at Wimbledon, with the players all in white, symbolizing 'their distance from dirty work', while 'spectators sat in complete and utter silence' (Guttmann 1986: 97). In the USA games of tennis and golf became centred in exclusive country clubs which kept the working classes out, ensuring that spectators maintained the same manners as players.

But the gentlemanly code was frequently put under pressure by *Realpolitik*. The Olympics, started as a celebration of amateurism and to foster international understanding, have been notably altered by dissension. The Nazi party attempted to control them for propaganda purposes in Berlin in 1936, and during the Cold War they became a site for ideological confrontation between the superpowers. The practice of adding up the scores by nation, entirely antagonistic to the Coubertin ideal, was the chief way that the Soviet Union, the Eastern European states and the United States made political profit. In 1980 the games were boycotted by sixty-two nations because they took place in Moscow, and four years later most Soviet-bloc countries boycotted them because they were in Los Angeles. If the Olympic festival now seems depoliticized, it is for the usual reason: it has become a saleable product, a global brand.

A protective attitude to sport was adopted in Fascist Italy and Nazi Germany, in that those governments were less interested in the personal triumphs of athletes than in the display of mass bodies moving in military rhythm, revealing a perfect social machine working together in all its parts. For this reason mid-century theorists of the left continued to worry about spectators. The Frankfurt School critique of mass culture condemned spectator sports along with jazz and other popular amusements 'as harmful compensations for capitalism's distortions of the human spirit' (Edelman 1993: 8; see Horkheimer and Adorno's *The Dialectic of Enlightenment*, written 1944). But it is important to remember that the Frankfurt School contempt for mass culture was driven by its members' experience of Fascist control of it. Sport was too close to militarism, they thought; Horkheimer and Adorno were reacting to Fascism's cult of the body and the theatricalizing of sport with classic Marxist asceticism. Later leftists were able to counteract this move. Stuart Hall, for example, rejected the Frankfurt notion on the grounds that it assumed that the 'public uncritically accepted the messages of popular culture . . . society can reject products placed before it or transform their meanings' (Edelman 9–21).

The idea of a public transforming the purpose of the products that capitalism manufactures is central to Certeau's escape from Debord's concept of the all-encompassing spectacle. If consumption gives ordinary citizens a right of resistance and a power to deflect the dominant order, it becomes another form of production set against 'centralized, clamorous, and spectacular production' of capitalism (Certeau 1984: xii–xiii). The ways of using the products of the dominant economic order 'thus lend dimension to everyday practices'. From this standpoint, football hooliganism is an acute example of spectators taking control of the sport, wresting it from the hands of the owners and from the increasingly commodified features of the modern game. A number of political ideologies in the twentieth century, right and left, attempted to control sport and appropriate it for their cause. But 'if any political ideology can advertise itself through sport . . . sport functions as an undifferentiated vehicle of self-assertion by the state' and 'is relatively autonomous and cannot be completely controlled'. It may support the dominant power but 'in a less than fully efficient manner' (Hoberman 1984: 1). Its spectators may choose its ultimate significance or appropriate it to personal use.

SPORT AND THE SPECTACULAR SOCIETY

Bear in mind Abercrombie and Longhurst's assertion that in the spectacular society the audience has become 'diffused'. Since we are surrounded by media and performance, and since through a version of narcissism we are always performing ourselves, 'everyone becomes an audience all the time'. Their proposition is that 'the world, and everything in it, is increasingly treated as *something to be attended to*', resulting from the ever-growing commodification of the material and spiritual elements of life. As the boundary between tourism and everyday life has been blurred and 'people are much of the time "tourists" whether they like it or not' (Urry 1990: 82), so narcissism, which should be seen as a cultural condition rather than a personality disorder, has had a parallel effect. It enables us to

gaze upon the world, as a world of spectacles, *as if* it were owned or could be potentially owned. It is not that the perceived world and its contents *is* owned or even that it realistically *could* be owned. It is that it is gazed upon by people who are owners in other respects and see everything in that light (Abercrombie and Longhurst 1998: 83).

Thus a football match, a straightforward affair in which corporeal contestants play in front of corporeal spectators present at the same site (a 'simple audience'), might go through a series of commodity changes until it reaches the level in which an individual viewer, most likely a man, invents an imaginary circumstance in which he owns the event, perhaps in fantasy placing himself on the pitch, scoring the winning goal, making a final save, watching in slow motion, replaying a crucial moment, or any number of inventive activities that can be conducted in private space.

Slow motion, whether produced by the broadcast company or through recorded replay at home, is particularly connected to this fantasy. In televised sports the pace of time is again and again retarded during moments of intense action. Slo-mo is used 'to celebrate and display the male body in action, to produce a sense of awe by making the physical performance appear beautiful. The male body in televised sport does not consist merely of brutish muscularity, but is aestheticized', since 'speed and violent impact' (Whannel 1998: 228) are transformed into moments of balletic grace. In sports coverage as well as in action films, slo-mo works 'to eroticize power, to extend the moment of climax' (Fiske 1987: 219; also Guttmann 1996: 82).

From this standpoint it is hard to see how the spectator of major sports can escape the confines of Debord's society of the spectacle. The rules of soccer and rugby have not been bent to accommodate commercial breaks, but American football, basketball, baseball and ice hockey, with their regular interruptions for strategic timeouts, quarter breaks or intermissions between innings, seem designed for exploitation. Advertising proceeds as if commerce were the ultimate purpose of any match. Around the world the salaries and bonuses of players are reported with gleeful incredulity, TV rights make important clubs extremely rich, and stars like David Beckham become exceptionally saleable commodities. At the height of his fame Michael Jordan was highly popular in Britain and many other countries where US basketball was not seen; he was the first choice of school students in Brighton asked to pick which celebrities most influenced their values. Jordan was known because he appeared in globally broadcast advertisements, and he willingly abandoned all political implication in the process, since the sponsors in sport 'demand the kind of brand allegiance which has traditionally been the preserve of the nation state' (J. Williams 1993: 247).

The spectacular tendency reaches its absurd point with the National Football League's annual Super Bowl, with about a 150 million viewers in the US (approximately half of the population of all ages) and untold numbers worldwide. The ten most watched programmes in American TV history have all been Super Bowls, a fact directly reflected in the price of advertising. In 1998 the average cost for a 30-second commercial slot was $1.3 million. Ten years later the number of viewers remained flat but the top price had doubled to $2.6 million, far above the rate of general inflation. This huge audience gathers despite the fact that in a Super Bowl broadcast lasting three and a half hours the ball is actually in play about ten per cent of the time. Further, most major sport is contextualized by meta-television commentary from former players who attempt to establish and police the meaning of the game, a movement towards hegemony of understanding that is congenial to passive acceptance of the messages of big business.

The same spectacularization is now common for live spectators. The invasion of the stadium by commodity culture is everywhere apparent: blatant Vodafone or AIG logos on the red Manchester United jerseys, rebranding of teams and stadiums with corporate names, giant video screens that replay slo-mo moments, overloud music and announcements that leave less room for reflection, upmarket food and drink concessionaires. It is obvious that TV has altered the nature of big-time sport, both its rules and its display. It has been doing so since the 1960s (Rader 1984), and live fans in the stadium have become part of the show. Fans-in-presence are needed to create the necessary atmosphere for TV fans-in-absence. In 1989 the executive producer of 'The Match' in Britain said that it is no use broadcasting even First Division games of the lesser-supported clubs because they will not draw a full stadium, and without the atmosphere of a full house the match does not look right on TV (J. Williams and Wagg 1991: 224). We may watch at home in a diffused audience condition, but apparently we want the secure knowledge that the ritual is proceeding correctly for the simple audience at Old Trafford.

Many spectators turn to amateur sports to escape the worst aspects of the reign of commerce. In Ireland, where I have lived for some years, most sport is officially amateur. Even the great national pastimes of hurling and Gaelic football, whose championships are played at Croke Park in Dublin before 82,000 fans, are county sports with part-time players, capable of inducing all the more fan dedication by their relative lack of commodification. As with many issues in Ireland, part of the enthusiasm for Gaelic games has been historically anti-colonial, adding a further degree of dedication. In the past sports with identifiable English origins were regularly referred to as 'garrison games', and until 1971 members of the Gaelic Athletic Association were prohibited from playing or even attending non-GAA sports. Only in 2005 was the ban on playing such games at Croke Park lifted. (The change is temporary, to accommodate matches of the Football Association of Ireland and the Irish Rugby Football Union while the other major Dublin stadium, Lansdowne Road, is undergoing reconstruction.)

While exceptions similar to the Irish case certainly exist, the audience for most big-time sport around the world is willy-nilly constrained by global commodity culture. Hamil (1999: 23) notes that until the early 1980s many British football clubs were locally owned by 'wealthy and indulgent benefactors' who were prepared to lose money for the sake of the game, whereas by the end of the century football had been incorporated into the larger leisure industry. Now clubs are commonly owned by corporations, listed on the stock exchange, involved in complicated transactions over highly paid international players and expected by investors to offer a range of leisure activities from family-day outings to sporting goods shops. English and Scottish football, historically a diversion for working-class spectators on Saturday afternoons, has been utterly transformed by television and celebrity players into a major force of general entertainment. The rise in the number of international club tournaments has also made fans more sophisticated about the larger world. Without an extra sports package, I can watch on cable TV in Dublin matches and highlights of all the first-rank European leagues from Spain to Turkey – and will often see English players working for teams located far from England.

The deterritorializing movement engendered by television and the corporate outlook has significantly affected the make-up of fans. No longer is a club's spectator base primarily local. The geographical distribution of season-ticket holders for the Chelsea Football Club in 1998–9 revealed that only 4.35 per cent were from Fulham and Chelsea, 28.61 from the rest of London and fully 66.73 per cent from the UK outside of London (Sandvoss 2003: 88). Fans now seem to choose their favourite team based on emotional reasons and imagined connections, just as they admire certain players regardless of national origin. But fervent and biased involvement has by no means disappeared. In a survey of the popularity of the Premier League among Chelsea fans of the same period, the researcher discovered intense dislike of other sides. With 5.0 as the top value, fans averaged only a 1.9 degree of liking for the next rated club, Charlton Athletic, much distaste for Tottenham Hotspur (−2.9) and extreme aversion to Manchester United (−4.2). In the German Bundesliga, a similar statistical distribution was discovered among Bayer

Leverkusen fans, who hate i.FC Köln as intensely as Chelsea fans hate Man U (Sandvoss 94–5).

But while corporate ownership and commercial television constrain the production of sport, they do not entirely constrain consumption. TV audiences do not sit supinely watching the box in a semi-drugged state, as many critics in the past would have it. They often take an active stance regarding programmes, watching them with family or friends, discussing them while in progress, arguing over the remote control. The classic study by Collett and Lamb (1986), which installed video cameras in living rooms in Britain to observe the uses made of TV, discovered that some people watch with attention some of the time, but occasionally no one is watching at all and the set becomes a droning companion or default activity while supposed viewers iron, read, sleep or make love. The Super Bowl parties in the US are a good example of repossessive exploitation. Large numbers of fans watch what is an over-hyped and often under-exciting game because they gather in groups to drink beer, eat, chat, cheer and agonize with their favourite team, hardly attending to the aggravating commercial interruptions and timeouts: they are not passive watchers but procedural accomplices who celebrate solidarity, masculinity or any number of socially beneficial attributes. Even though the Super Bowl is one of the principal opportunities for American capitalism to promote itself, the selective watching strategies of its television audience offer substantial resistance to the spectacular culture on display.

Watching sport is distinct from experiences with the rest of television. Among all types of programmes in Britain only sport and soap operas 'show a marked gender preference, with more men for sport and more women for soap operas', though the gender difference is 'rarely much more than 60 to 40' (Whannel 1998: 222). Those two forms, along with game shows (discussed in the next chapter), have a relatively low social status, which in part derives from their disdainful treatment by print journalists and critics and in part from a false belief that they are watched by audiences of low intelligence and low initiative. Yet they are the three TV forms that are most likely to prompt an active engagement from viewers. Some sports are clearer and more engaging when watched on the box, especially those which are won by measurements too fine to be perceived by the spectator at the contest, like photo-finish sprinting, swimming or total times in skiing.

Of course there are spectators for TV sport who are couch potatoes but the issue of audience passivity is more complicated than it seems. Even in the theatre the issue must be treated with caution. Whatever passivity

means, it does not mean that theatre is a low-involvement activity. As
Susan Bennett notes (1997: 206): 'Spectators are thus trained to be passive
in their demonstrated behaviour during theatrical performance, but to be
active in their decoding of the sign systems made available.' Sport spectators, whether in the stadium, at a big-screen sports bar or at home, are
likely to be the most active audience of all, able to resist, ignore or
diminish the effects of the powerful messages of the spectacular society for
the sake of the excitement and enjoyment of the game.

On television the excitement level of sport is most importantly connected to the tradition of live broadcast. Very few television shows are
transmitted live, meaning in real time and as they happen; even the news
is partly recorded; quiz and game shows enacted before live audiences are
subject to considerable scrutiny before they are finally aired. But because
the outcome of a sporting match is in doubt, often until the very end, live
broadcast conveys the teleological excitement experienced by stadium
spectators and the players themselves. The final try, the penalty shoot-out,
the final game of the final set, all offer opportunity for ardour and
engagement that no filmed or live drama can provide. 'Sports events
offer a liminal moment between certainty and uncertainty', Whannel
notes (229); 'unlike fictional narrative, they are not predetermined by
authorship, nor can they be predicted by cultural code or even specialized
knowledge. They offer the rare opportunity to experience genuine
uncertainty. This is part of the unique fascination of genuinely live events
as opposed to those that merely offer the appearance of liveness.' And
unlike most other television, this aspect of sport transfers through
broadcast with something of nostalgic purity, probably because sport is
ultimately tied less to commodification and more to carnival. Raymond
Williams (1989: 95) held that TV sports, despite control and commodification by government or commerce, normally escape complete appropriation, maintaining a strong sense of their independence. The chief
distinction of sport is the freedom fans assume to create, in a public
forum and communally, a meaning and experience directly out of
spectation, separate from the text of the game or the meanings assigned to
it by the media or official agencies. Sport is part of spectacular culture,
but at the same time provides a chance for spectators to escape it.

CHAPTER 9

The aroused spectator

Of all the questions raised by the study of audiences, spectator arousal is the most difficult to assess. I use the term *arousal* in the psychological sense, to include conditions that range from excitement, exhilaration and fright to frenzy, ecstasy and anguish, regardless of their prompting. Prompting may occur by strong emotional connections to an event, the hope of financial gain, the distress of loss, danger or fear of harm, threats, physical or psychic aggression, crowd panic, sexual pleasure or a number of other provocations that can render the human organism in an animated or agitated state. Occasionally in theatre history we come across reports of fear or terror in the audience caused by the action on stage, miscarriages brought on by the sight of the Furies in *Eumenides* or panic triggered by the devils in *Doctor Faustus*. In modernity, however, most of the time the issue of aroused spectators in public performance is actually a predicament of taste, as it was with *Hernani* in 1830 and the Italian futurists in 1913. With few exceptions audience members who are over-excited, intoxicated or in proto-violent states have been considered a threat to conventional manners, civic order, other observers or themselves. Spectators in an openly aroused condition have traditionally been identified not with respectable traditions of theatregoing but with lower-class, indecent or scandalous forms of entertainment.

We see this as early as Terence's preface to the *Hecyra* (before 160 BC), which complains that the audience abandoned the first performance for the distractions of boxers and a tightrope dancer, while a gladiatorial contest emptied the theatre at the second performance. Such grumbles were common in the early modern period, especially from classically inclined playwrights like Ben Jonson. At a time when the same London venue was used for bear-baiting on Tuesday and Jonson's *Bartholomew Fair* on Wednesday (the Hope in Bankside, built by Philip Henslowe in 1614 for this dual purpose), the tension in the spectator, located between popular traditions of entertainment and the refined work of the 'renaissance', could be acute. In playwriting the sophisticated or literary side won out, and was heavily reinforced by the principles of neoclassicism in the seventeenth and eighteenth centuries under French influence throughout Europe.

The inclination was exacerbated by theatrical modernism, which developed a persistent concern about audience behaviour. Modernism promoted elite or specialized audiences who were intellectually and emotionally committed but sufficiently quiescent so as not to disturb the show. Behaviour considered unwelcome in most playhouses, opera houses and concert halls in the twentieth century included interruptive applause, the institution of the claque, ambulatory spectators, eating and drinking in the auditorium and audience gestures of any type that interfered with the dominance of the work. For the avant-garde the problem was even more severe, as we saw in chapter 3.

What caused the modernist reaction is well known: in the mid-nineteenth century in Britain and America working-class audiences expected a boisterous good time in the theatre. The theatre was the major source of legal entertainment readily available for the urban lower classes created by the industrial revolution, and spectators, especially male spectators stimulated by drink, often considered a jolly disruption or a good fight part of the evening out. In London prior to the 1843 Theatre Regulation Act, an out-of-the-way playhouse like Sadler's Wells, which specialized in melodrama and extravagant aquatic shows, would regularly draw rough trade. Dickens said the audience made Sadler's Wells into a 'beargarden... resounding with foul language, oaths, cat-call shrieks, yells, blasphemy, obscenity – a truly diabolical clamour. Fights took place anywhere, at any period of the performance.' When after 1843 Samuel Phelps attempted to turn this chaos into a respectable theatre for Shakespeare, he had to face the opposition of spectators used to shouting down what they did not like; he sometimes stopped the play, protected his costume by a long cloak and stepped down into the auditorium to direct the police to troublemakers. Less than a decade and a thousand nights of Shakespeare later, Phelps had succeeded in taming his audience, as *Blackwood's Magazine* noted with amazement in 1852: 'Are they the same people, or the same class of people, who roared and rioted in the pit in the days of the real water? Exactly the same.'[1] The *embourgeoisement* of audience that Phelps, Charles Kean and others worked for could be accomplished only by eliminating most of the overt arousal from the house.

Ironically the orderliness thus achieved ultimately led to objections in the twentieth century that culinary theatre, as Brecht called it, had created passive audiences insufficiently engaged with the work or open to its meaning. This is a complex matter. Abercrombie and Longhurst (1998: 206) note that whatever passivity means 'it does not necessarily imply that the theatre is a low-attention/low-involvement medium. Quite the reverse: theatre audiences are giving high attention to the spectacle and, partly as a consequence, are closely involved.' I have already quoted Bennett's (1997: 206) concise semiotic appraisal: 'Spectators are thus trained to be passive in their demonstrated behaviour during theatrical performance, but to be active in their decoding of the sign systems made available.' Emotional involvement is good, blatant displays of emotion are bad. The confusion about active/passive audiences, and the place of propriety in the auditorium, underlines how the spectator presented theatrical modernism with one of its most persistent problems; in wishing to control perception it was working against its own best interests.

Plainly this changes in sport and other teleologically ordered events. When the outcome of a presentation or feat is in doubt, partisanship is a plausible result. Of course a spectator may witness a competition objectively or neutrally, interested only in the quality of play or its virtuosic displays, but it is much more common to support one side, or one horse or one racing driver. Partisanship encourages spectator investment, so that winning and losing have implications beyond the confines of the venue, and the uncertainty of the result promotes arousal. In this chapter I look at two activities parallel to sport that elicit spectator stimulation through financial involvement: wagering and game shows. Many of my comments are speculative, as so little evidence exists on spectator arousal.

PLAYING FOR KEEPS: THE SPECTATOR AS GAMBLER

If football violence demonstrates the thorny side of audience involvement, gambling by spectators on sporting competitions introduces the sphere of sublimated rivalry. Staking a bet commits a spectator to the chosen side in a material as well as emotional way, and thus the degree of arousal available, while less than that created by punching opposing supporters, is nonetheless heightened beyond the usual condition of the observer. Clearly there are degrees and types of spectator arousal. A Roman gladiatorial combat was the occasion of considerable wagering, and the often mortal outcome in the arena perhaps supports the theory that gambling is a sublimated death wish. In our own time the contest which most obviously reveals repressed spectator aggression is prize fighting, where two men thump away at each other in front of witnesses encouraging them to hit harder. In contrast one hundred euro on a horse race is a relatively objective bet, probably determined more by knowledge of racing than by emotional connections to the horse. Punters will cheer on their favourites but their arousal is created by the joy and thrill of the race combined with the money staked.

A similar bet on a football match between local rivals might engender a different type of commitment from the spectator, whose wager is less objective, more the result of an already existing allegiance. Well before the introduction of football pools in Britain in the 1920s, wagering on fixed odds with bookmakers on individual matches was common; a large number of bets were made on the first FA Cup final in 1872 (Munting 1996: 127–9). Spectators bet on sport, Guttmann holds (1986: 179–80), because they want to feel closer to one side, and then feel even closer because they have bet. Money may not be the primary reason for the bet, however, for betting allows spectators to take a special stake in the match: 'Sports have always provided the spectators with a chance to play a metagame of their own in which they test their abilities to back a winner in whatever game the metagame is based on.' But in all cases the gambling spectator articulates a connection between wealth and winning, and both tend to foster a high degree of passion.

In a useful treatment of the topic, Jan McMillen (1996b: 6) notes that 'Gambling is one of the few social activities that occurs in nearly all cultures and in every period of time.' Though its nature differs considerably over time and place, shifting from a quasi-religious position in antiquity to a category of leisure in modernity, it carries risk as its central component. The ancient Hebrews used the casting of lots as a way of resolving questions incapable of human solution, believing this evoked divine intervention, a practice still present in the New Testament when, by drawing straws, Matthias was chosen among the apostolic candidates to replace Judas (Acts 1.26; see Brenner 1990: 2–3). Many modern societies have replaced god with chance as a controlling aspect of life, seeing in the randomness of lotteries an echo of the randomness of the universe. But whether you think the seven is brought up by divinity or probability, gambling is always already subject to 'fluctuating conceptions of morality', themselves reflecting prevailing social and economic conditions. The negative view of gambling was heavily influenced by the 'strength of Protestantism in western capitalist societies', based on the conviction that gambling was 'a denial of the work ethic and a threat to production', since it fostered the idea that one could make easy money without the requisite labour or disrupt family and social structures through compulsive gaming (McMillen 1996b: 7, 13). Historically many gambling laws were enacted because authorities concluded that the poor were not working to competence.

Thomas Jefferson was a supporter of state-sponsored gambling – a lottery, he said, is 'a wonderful thing: It lays taxation only on the willing'. But most policy since the eighteenth century has assumed gaming is a vice, comparable to pornography, prostitution, drugs (and, until recently, abortion and homosexuality) and must be controlled. For these six 'traditional vices', as Dombrink (1996) calls them, the question for authority has been threefold: how to regulate their spread to the lower classes, how to limit the social disruption associated with them and how to capitalize upon them. The heavy duty imposed on tobacco is exemplary. The logic is syllogistic:

A. Tobacco is bad for public health.
B. But smokers do not worry about health.
C. Therefore the state should impose levies on smokers.

By taxing tobacco the state simultaneously indicates disapproval and reaps financial reward. As to gambling, a general liberalizing and democratization of formal postures has occurred in many western countries since 1950, part of a process that Dombrink calls 'the legalisation of vice'.

The switch in official thinking has led to the extensive spread in the West of two monitored forms of gambling: casinos and state lotteries. The aristocratic casinos of Europe (Monte Carlo, Biarritz, Wiesbaden) provided evening entertainment to the affluent at existing resorts; their expensive locations and strict dress codes prevented unwelcome incursion by ordinary folk. They were part of the tourism trade but at the highest end, the baccarat end, the James Bond end. In contrast the 'people's casinos' of the past half-century are sites of destination tourism, welcoming all comers, eliminating dress restrictions and offering less sophisticated or more user-friendly games, including the mechanical games that dominate Las Vegas that are less threatening for the inexperienced gamer. Gambling legally returned to some of the former communist states of Eastern Europe soon after 1990; as Munting (1996: 144) puts it, capitalist ideology now includes 'the freedom to lose money'. The people's casinos have nonetheless been ordered into special locales, set off from ordinary life – whether individual clubs as in Britain (until September 2007 strict membership rules prevented walk-in players), specialized river boats, municipalities such as Atlantic City, Native American reservations or the entire state of Nevada – and thus carry the overtones of festival and fairground, a type of what Foucault called heterotopias. Other forms of legitimate gambling which involve spectatorship are also normally restricted to licensed premises: race courses and dog tracks, betting shops in Britain and Ireland, jai alai courts in Mexico. The method of regulation chosen by the modern western state is to police the borders of gaming locations to limit range, and this explains the concern of the US federal government about the spread of internet gambling, which, like internet pornography, is extremely difficult to patrol.

A very large amount of sociological and psychological research has been conducted on gambling, though little of it I have encountered addresses the emotions of the player or the player-as-spectator. Yet some studies are revealing about the extent of gaming, its gender inflexions and its appeal to different classes and groups, and these have implications for my topic. For example, a comprehensive review of gambling behaviour in Britain published in 2000 found that betting was extremely prevalent, with 72% of those interviewed having gambled at least once in the past year. This figure did not vary significantly when isolated by sex (76% men, 68% women), age, marital status, economic activity, household income or social class.[2] When we turn to the type of gaming activity, however, we discover large differences among the social categories. By far the greatest number of respondents were wagering chiefly on the national lottery, with scratch cards the second ranking activity, neither of which are usually considered spectator games (though the lottery draw has become a glitzy TV show), and no difference in participation between men and women was noted. Twice as many women as men played bingo, but otherwise men dominated traditional gambling, especially in male-ordered spaces like pubs, sports stadiums, betting shops and the track. The breakdown figures from this study are revealing:

type of gambling	men	women
fruit machines	20%	8%
football pools	13%	5%
horse and dog races	24%	11%

Other wagers with a bookmaker, casino table games and private bets were even more male in activity (totalled, 26% men to 8% women).

A parallel but smaller study in the US found similar data, with 82% of respondents having gambled in the past year. The lottery was by far the most commonly played game, though casino wagering accounted for the greatest personal involvement. While men and women were equally likely to make bets, men did so more frequently and had larger wins and losses, particularly on sports and games of skill.[3] Other studies, especially those conducted by psychologists with an interest in addictive gambling, tend to conclude a deep relationship between gaming and risk-taking or impulsivity in life in general.[4]

The differences between the gambling patterns of men and women, which parallel certain gender stereotypes, tentatively suggest that men, especially young men, seek the thrill of uncertainty and risk more than women. But that inference seems less significant than the overall conclusion that gambling is widespread across the social spectrum in Britain and America. For most people it is not so much a vice as a leisure activity with the possibility of financial reward. More and more the state has enabled and profited from this circumstance, as it does with alcohol and tobacco. Of course problem gamblers exist, just as problem drinkers exist, but the great majority of gamblers set aside relatively small amounts of money for steady-state gaming. They are aware that the odds of winning lotteries are infinitesimally small, but take the risk because the cost is not so high as the hope. And, crucially, the result will be rapidly known. Wagering on a game or race while watching it increases the excitement and expectation; even if depression sets in as the effect of loss, there is always next week's match to renew the chance.

Regrettably the poorer segments of populations in the West spend a higher portion of their income on gambling than their better-off citizens, and from a Marxist perspective one can object that widespread gaming, especially state-sponsored lottery, provides exactly the kind of worthless aspiration that keeps the less fortunate in their place. It's often been pointed out that the lottery is a perfect model of contemporary capitalism, as well as its social justification, since the lottery suggests that inequalities are due not to personal insufficiencies but solely to chance. And there is no question that gambling is now a large-scale globalized business, often designed to simulate excitement through mechanized casinos, the trappings of luxury and big-time shows. The large choices that gambling in postmodernity offers, when uncovered a bit, too often turn out to be versions of ordinary consumerism. In Britain the major bookmaking company Ladbrokes will give you odds on just about any event with an uncertain outcome, from election results in France to the Academy Awards in Hollywood. And all of this is reflected in Las Vegas with the vengeance that only monopoly capitalism can rally. Currently the city averages thirty-six million visitors annually, and the taxable revenues from gambling in the state of Nevada in 2005 were above $11 billion.

Again it is sport that offers the prospect of wagering unaffected by corporate intrusion. One can bet directly with a friend on a football match, a baseball or basketball game, even a school hockey contest, and be reasonably assured that those competitions have not been fixed, their outcomes untainted by elements outside the sporting occasion. The stake brings added commitment and is likely to increase the degree of arousal.

Laws controlling gambling, like those licensing theatres or classifying and censoring films, remind us of the ways in which the state recognizes its citizens as prospectively aroused spectators with the capacity to disrupt. Theatre is not considered dangerous in the West these days, but it was so quite recently in the Soviet Union and its protectorates and still seems a threat to public order in China and some other areas of the world. It is the gathering together of large groups of spectators that can cause trouble, and the more excited they become the more likely their arousal will, like the riotous soccer fan, spill over into the street. The betting spectator at the race track poses no such threat; the legal constraints on gaming concern themselves more with the potential for financial abuse than with regulating aroused participants. Nonetheless the excitement or despair inspired by wagering create for us a separate category of spectator whose investment can easily, if temporarily, cause emotional and physical excitement far beyond that experienced in other realms of public performance, an excitement almost irresistible if one is present and has a vested interest. Even the rambunctious audience activity at rock concerts seems cultivated and conventional by comparison. The final elation or desolation felt by a spectator who has gambled on a sporting event may be closer to what Aristotle meant by catharsis than the experience of watching tragedy or comedy in a contemporary theatre. We might recall in this regard that the ancient Athenian dramatic festivals were actually contests for the best production and best actor, perfect opportunities for a wager.

GAME SHOWS: THE SPECTATOR AS CHARACTER

Taste is not the only concern on the topic of spectator excitement, but usually is central to its discussion, if often recessive or unacknowledged. Part of the reason, as I mentioned before, is the class-inflected expectation that high art in the European tradition, art that is good for you, whether sacred or secular, requires a quiescent reception, while popular art and popular entertainments allow and sometimes encourage a boisterous one. We sit in silence and listen attentively at a Philip Glass concert, but move, shout, jump, dance and sing along at a Rolling Stones gig. The price of the tickets has not determined how we behave, since we paid a lot more for the Stones than the Glass. To phrase this from the standpoint of the *Hochkulturbetrieb* – the high culture business – the long-established assumption is that excessive emotional or physical involvement in an audience renders it less competent to recognize the value and sophistication of a work of delicate or deeply significant art. A sign of the elitist aspirations of most theatrical modernisms was their tendency to approve of respectful audiences and disapprove of interfering ones. As Bourdieu shows, the clearest marker of distinction is the disgust one social group feels for the taste of a different (usually 'lower') group.

I have also mentioned that this remained a concern for the Frankfurt School, who associated mass culture with the political demagoguery of Nazism and worried about irrational crowd reaction. Horkheimer and Adorno insisted that the diversions provided by the entertainment industry are not based in populist desires but are anaesthetics manufactured for the sake of profit: organized, as it were, not by Big Brother but for Big Mac. Whether contemporary mass culture encourages spectator passivity, however, is a bit more complicated. Even if commercial television constructs spectators as consumers of its advertisers' products, globalized marketing has realized that active consumers spend more and promotes goods that cater to or enable activity, choice and the appearance of personal control. This is a leaking life raft, of course. Certeau may be right in asserting that the tactics of everyday life can subvert the logic of commodity capitalism, but those tactics also confirm the logic they upset.

There may not be a way in industrial and post-industrial societies to escape entirely the conditions so wrought. Wordsworth's sonnet 'The world is too much with us' (1807) described the negative psychological effects of modernity very early in the era, brought about 'late and soon' by our 'getting and spending', a potent anticipation of Debord. Certeau's somewhat prayerful alternative is not very convincing when we look at the contemporary prevalence of shopping, late and soon, which now encompasses even the most local occasions and minor sporting events that once existed in a non-commodity or 'purer' state. Fans as well as tourists want to bring home the emblazoned T-shirt. Are we ever able to restate or refuse the commodity status of watching a spectacle? I want to worry this in the dog pen of the spectacular society by looking at the spectator as consumer expert, in the television game show.

Considering the preposterous pecuniary motives of the genre and the social orientation of media studies, it is surprising how little serious commentary exists on game shows, or their first cousins, quiz shows. (In game shows participants perform activities for rewards based on chance or physical agility, in quiz shows they answer questions based on knowledge. Some programmes join the two forms.) The few extended studies emphasize the obvious and are often condemnatory. We have Holbrook (1993: 11): 'I can imagine no artefacts of popular culture more apparently worthless and more seemingly unredeemed by any vestige of intellectual, esthetic, or moral value than those that constitute the daily spectacle paraded before the public in the form of television game shows.' Rapping (1987: 61) calls game shows 'the dregs of American culture and American life itself . . . public displays of greed, misery, emotional excess and freakishness.' A more historical book by Hoerschelmann (2006), while interested in the implications of the popularity of the genre, still repeats the same distaste over the vicarious commodity experience of the media audience.

I do not intend to argue that quiz and game shows are high-class entertainment, but in light of their long-standing popularity the censure they receive reveals an uncertainty about their spectatorial status. The objections raised by academic and journalistic critics usually focus on the display of avarice on the part of participants, magnified by their aroused behaviour. Fiske and Hartley (2003: 120) note that American game shows deliberately

exploit the emotional yo-yo between the elation of winning and the despair of losing: cameras dwell in long close-up upon the faces of contestants and their emotions – one contestant who wanted a car in *The Price Is Right* was reduced to gibbering with greed, the camera closed up on him, the compère taunted him; drawing out his anticipation.

Contestants are usually aroused by the act of their appearance, but unorthodox behaviour is encouraged for most studio audiences as well and often accentuated for broadcast. Holbrook (75) summarizes audience reaction to the announcer's evocation of products on the same show: 'screams, whistles, cheers, shouts, clapping, stomping, shrieks, and a general din of truly volcanic proportions': the approbative audience gestures mostly discouraged in polite performance.

Given the overtly participatory nature of these programmes, it will be useful to review what distinguishes spectator behaviour from that in other performances. I will concentrate on American examples but since many shows have crossed the Atlantic, the Rio Grande and even the Pacific, a number of issues apply to other countries in one form or another. (In the case of 'reality' game shows produced after the year 2000, the movement has been reversed, most of them originating in Europe and spreading to North America.)

First, as with all programmes recorded before a studio audience, game shows contain two levels of spectatorship. The general theory of broadcasters has been that the display of reactions in the studio audience will guide those of the home audience: laughter, applause, boos and shouts at the transmitting end will suggest that similar gestures, or at least similar internal responses, should occur at the receiving end, thereby bringing the media witness closer to the disembodied event. But unlike televised sport, shows that exist only for TV must manufacture the studio response by inviting on-site spectators and guiding their responses. The falsity of this procedure was most obvious in the use of pre-recorded laugh tracks for some sitcoms, but all studio audiences are fabricated, their commitment established by a selection procedure, advance ticketing or hours of queuing. In the case of quiz and game shows, spectators in attendance are even more dedicated since they hope to be chosen as participants (*The Price Is Right*) or have accompanied previously selected contestants (*Who Wants to Be a Millionaire?*). Thus the programmes are premised on a manipulated spectatorship, which opens the possibility that the game itself might be fixed.

The second distinction is that the arousal of participants and observers appears to have acquisitive motives: excitement is engendered by the opportunity of winning large cash or material prizes. Since American culture in general approves of personal wealth and individualist competition, and locates economic growth inside commodity culture, winning prizes could be seen as a model of the social process. But like gambling, quiz and game shows offer the chance of easy money, rewards not worked for (except for the work of appearing on them), and thus potentially subvert the class and labour principles on which capitalism has traditionally been based. Clearly the old Puritan work ethic has been slipping in America and Britain, as witnessed by lotteries and other state-approved gaming. And it's impossible to determine how deep the psychological bias against easy money may run. Nonetheless the televised display of contestants battling each other for valuable goods and services seems to disturb commentators from the right and the left. Perhaps it's simply an issue of public propriety: dog may eat dog on Wall Street but not on daytime TV.

Third, the aroused behaviour is often tasteless by the usual standards of bourgeois society in the West, even when compared to sporting events. (And in Japan it can be even worse; extremities of the game show like *Takeshi's Castle* appear as deliberate violations of a rigorously polite culture, involving the public humiliation of contestants which would be meticulously avoided in normal life.) In this sense game-show audiences are parallel to those at confessional appearance shows (*Ricki Lake, Jerry Springer, Maury*), where previously selected applicants, usually from lower economic and social strata and often angry, are confronted by their sins, indiscretions, criminal actions or personal betrayals before a raucously critical studio audience. In fact the confessional show and the reality courtroom show (*The People's Court, Judge Judy*) follow the dramaturgical pattern of the quiz show: emotional exposure of the participant, response from the participant, judgement. For the TV viewer the most intriguing element might be the sight of Jerry Springer or Maury Povich remaining cool and calm while provoking guests to further verbal or physical outbursts. A good deal of language is bleeped out for transmission, adding to the sense of violated norms.

Fourth, the arousal exhibited often seems disproportionate, for the etiquette of spectators at game shows like *The Price Is Right* is exaggerated in relation to the reward of being in the audience. It is easy to understand why a punter screams and shouts at the horse he's bet on. Members of game-show audiences act in a parallel way, even though we can assume they have not bet on the outcome.

The fifth characteristic is related: the arousal of spectators is often biased and partial, the result of a prior commitment to certain players, since some shows encourage the attendance of family and friends and seat them in designated areas. *American Gladiators*, a sport-derived game show in which athletic contestants compete with each other while large, muscular, attractive professionals try to prevent them from scoring points, replicates the condition of a sports stadium, with bands of supporters shouting encouragement under banners that identify their favourites.

The most significant characteristic, however, is not directly related to taste: the opportunity for members of the audience to become contestants. The transformation from spectator to character is highly unusual in any performance circumstance. Its most familiar figure is the volunteer from the audience who assists a conjuror's trick. In the mass media its historical form is the 'vox pop' or man-in-the-street interview of random passers-by, thrusting those who are normally the audience onto centre stage, a tactic that dates from the early days of radio. The goal of the producers of participation programmes has been to create the impression of a deep connection between the show and its wider audience by presenting on the air individuals who can be taken as representative of its viewers or listeners. This is a crucial matter for TV games and quizzes. Without the effect of banality, contestants could be understood as planted, the show taken as fraud. Hoerschelmann (2006: 6) makes this point well: 'Instead of reproducing a clear separation of performer and spectator, of text and audience, quiz shows provide a space in which broadcasters attempt to redefine the relation between programs and their audiences . . . the genre enables the development and articulation of social fantasies of interactivity and immediacy in mass communication.'

Fantasies surely, but fantasies with power. What are often called 'people shows' on television are premised upon the idea that ordinary persons are of interest to a media audience because of their ordinariness. Of course once on the show they are no longer ordinary; for a short time they become TV personalities. But in sympathetic terms the most successful are those who retain familiar qualities. Reality television, especially programmes that promise stardom or other forms of fame to the victor (*Pop Idol, American Idol, Survivor*), has succeeded in creating celebrities out of just plain folk, suggesting that eminence and notoriety are within the grasp of the common person who is the presumed viewer, just as lotteries promise uncountable riches to the lucky winner. In an age when distinction can be achieved without much talent or accomplishment, few qualifications are required for the transformation of the not-famous to the famous: winning on *Big Brother* is enough, and if the subsequent celebrity game is played well, fame may even last more than fifteen minutes.

Scandals in quiz shows, which date back to the infamous rigging of *Twenty One* on NBC in 1956, directly attack the integrity of the audience-performance relationship because they destroy the presumption that the game is clean and the contestant trustworthy. Broadcaster misdeeds have continued into the present, most recently with phone-in irregularities on the BBC and other British channels in 2007, when game and talent shows built upon the selection of winners by popular vote were discovered to have chosen their champions before the lines were closed. Not only did these shows violate the trust of the home audience on which they depended, they fraudulently collected telephone charges assessed to belated callers. Such obvious disdain for the spectator, excused by the producers for reasons of time and programming, has again awakened citizens and government to how easily we are manipulated in front of the TV.

COME ON DOWN!

The Price Is Right is a different class of programme from the talent search or a game requiring athletic proficiency, and as far as I know has never been accused of fraud. The knowledge and skills it rewards are commonplace, yet it is one of the most popular of the people shows and remains resistant to substantial change. The American version is the longest running television programme in history, having been broadcast from 1956 to 1965 (hosted by Bill Cullen) and in a revised format from 1972 to the present (hosted until 2007 by Bob Barker). Licensed versions have been created in over thirty countries and on every continent. In the US the show has made occasional forays into primetime but has remained anchored around midday, traditionally appealing to housewives who are engaged in the practice of buying commodities similar to those offered on screen (Holbrook 1993). While most commentators condemn this aspect, Fiske (1987: 276–7; also 1990) suggests the show foregrounds the expertise of women: 'translating the womanly skills and knowledge out of the private sphere into the public gives them a status normally reserved for the masculine', just as the excessive studio effects, 'exaggerated expressions of elation or despair from competitors and audience . . . separates the game off from "normal" shopping and shifts it towards the carnivalesque'.

I doubt that in contemporary America the terms 'housewife' or 'homemaker' mean what they did when Bob Barker took over. In the last decades of his regime a retro quality dominated the show, celebrating a notion of womanliness more mythical than actual, just as his two decades hosting the Miss USA and Miss Universe pageants (1967–87) participated in a parallel myth of female desirability. Perhaps the 1950s form of beneficial consumerism, which was in effect a war-recovery strategy and was the basis of the original version of the show, is inscribed in its administration. Whether or not considered woman-centred, the gamesmanship *The Price Is Right* demands is a parody of commodity capitalism, the object being to win material prizes by bidding on them accurately. Though the show uses a variety of bidding games, in most cases the winning player has estimated the retail cost of an item or group of items more closely than other competitors, *without going over the official price*. Its message is clear: a good consumer is rewarded by never paying even a penny too much. And certainly the show implies that good consumerism is difficult, for in its gala and indiscriminate advance of merchandise a player might be required to price 'a can of beans, hair shampoo, pain medicine, a waffle iron, an alarm clock, and a cordless phone to win a

$15,000 truck' (Hoerschelmann 2006: 108). The items are evoked with 'a fetishistic splendor' (Fiske 1987: 266) that exalts the mercantile, offering a promised land of possession in which the trifling (tin openers, tool sets) are stepping stones to refrigerators, home cinemas, jet skis, living rooms, cars and first-class tours to Japan. From this standpoint the extreme display of cupidity in the audience is indeed repulsive.

But while the products on display are essential to the game, I suggest the spectator arousal and carnival atmosphere of *The Price Is Right* are not the results of greed. Though the prizes are certainly desired, what provokes extreme excitement in contestants and studio witnesses is the simple opportunity to appear on the show, to take part in a ceremony that has over time authorized aroused behaviour. 'Judy Miller, come on down!' The mantra of the programme, the invitation to an unsuspecting ticket-holder to run on stage as a contestant, neatly announces the aspiration of the studio audience. And Judy does come down, in every case, often wearing a T-shirt reading 'I ♡ Bob'. Just as football fans in the stadium act in specific customary ways, so the audience of *The Price Is Right* is performing the audience of *The Price Is Right*. One of the least recognized qualities of television is how it grants to the media audience the knowledge of how to act on television. In an era when citizens in developed countries gain much of their information through television, spend many leisure hours in front of it, and in which television has intruded into great areas of daily life once free of its influence, appearing on screen is a recognizable and legitimate aspiration, in sports stadiums, on the news, on the street. The studio spectators of *The Price Is Right* already know how to behave because they have been watching the show at home for years, and tell us so.

If we believe what we are shown, above all else studio audiences are having a good time, whether they are shouting down misbehaviour on *Jerry Springer* or shouting out bidding advice on *The Price Is Right*. In general producers capitalize on the popularity of a show by showing the degree of commitment of its studio audience. Much camerawork is designed to exploit complicity with the event, providing frequent shots of the live audience and shooting from its point of view. Cinematically *The Price Is Right* 'almost completely collapses home viewer, host, studio audience, and contestants' (Hoerschelmann 2006: 108), thereby brilliantly achieving the chief goal of a people show, the suggestion that the spectator at home is identical to the spectator in the studio. And since the studio spectator could become a character-contestant at any moment, the show expands that possibility to the home viewer, and in a closing voice-over invites applications for admission to the taping of a future episode. Producers mask the fact that shows are recorded, sometimes in groups of four or five in a single day, offering a version of liveness to the home audience borrowed from televised sport, projecting a sense of immediacy and uncertainty of outcome.

At first glance it must seem odd to look to *The Price Is Right* for a way out of the dilemma of the spectator in commodity culture. To do this without invoking Certeau's idea of consumers 'poaching' products for their own purposes, or Fiske's similar ahistorical optimism that television is ultimately a democratic tool at the service of the viewer, it is necessary to recognize the significance of spectator arousal. There can be no doubt that the show is a raucous festival of merchandise. For its producers and the manufacturers of its prize-products it is a temple of consumerism. The 'showcase' of commodities, the grand prize of each episode, speaks only the language of acquisition. You desire me, it says to the contestant, how much do you desire me? Calm down and translate desire into a cash figure. Listen to the roar of counsel from the audience, but don't go over the retail value because you then lose the consumer's game. If the sign can be priced, it has reality-in-the-world. In the main gesture of *The Price Is Right*, Baudrillard's sign-as-sign becomes an actual car (it is automotive), a sign of a car (it is new and shiny) and a car as sign (it confers distinction on the owner).

But for the studio spectator, who is the contestant manqué, the showcase is not a sign at all but a behavioural trigger, a pretext for revels, like dressing up for a midnight showing of *The Rocky Horror Picture Show*, like hissing the villain in a Christmas panto, like celebrating a winning goal, like waving the flag of England and singing 'Land of Hope and Glory' on the last night of the proms. Whatever the producers may think, the studio witnesses of *The Price Is Right* are more important to the home viewer than the prizes or the contestants. As non-playing participants, studio witnesses maintain a non-commodity status in the darkest heart of commodity culture. That status is achieved because their aroused behaviour, even if expressed in a partisan fashion, fuses disparate selves into an audience that is essential to the game. The condition of assisting at the spectacle overpowers the meaning of the spectacle itself. It is not to everyone's taste, this use of the commodity fetish for the purpose of revelry. It is antithetical to the modernist idea of appropriate audience manners. I suspect that some of my readers find the show's manufactured passion repulsive. But whatever else one might think of *The Price Is Right*, it is an astonishing display of spectator agency, reminding us that spectators can be forged into an audience by agitated behaviour as well as by acquiescent or reflective aesthetic experience.

There are numerous counterparts to gambling and game shows that can similarly agitate spectator behaviour: music gigs, weddings and funerals, political and religious rallies, even courtroom trials. The major question they raise is analogous, how does emotional arousal affect spectation and what are the physical and social results? For example, was the display of feeling at Princess Diana's funeral in 1997 an expression of deep public grief or a simulated and self-congratulatory sign of televised egoism – performed grief? Does the active spectation at the new Bankside Globe diminish the authority of a performance of Shakespeare? Is the acceptance of topless bars and lap-dance clubs a sign of the decadent morality of the West or another example of the civilizing process, whereby risky or dubious activities are circumscribed and the threat of spectator disorder contained?

These questions beg a larger one: how might we distinguish between 'authentic arousal', which we assume to be instinctive and natural, and 'performed arousal', the learned behaviour of spectators that has been authorized by convention and is playful and ironic? Is one opposed to the other? Can an observer tell the difference? The problem of sexual stimulation is a case in point, and the liberal western democracies are uncertain about how the state should manage the sensitive arena of sex performance precisely because of this difficulty. Since sexual desire is typically acted out in private, sex shows, which explicitly seek to arouse their (usually male) spectators, rattle the gates of laws which forbid sex for sale or sex in public. The main rule at most strip joints is that the female performer can do anything but the spectator cannot touch her, endorsing uninhibited public titillation without the possibility of public fornication.

But the point I wish to make requires distinguishing between more-or-less private provocation (a porno film viewed alone on the internet) and male group response to an exotic dancer or female group response to a Chippendale male stripper. While the private experience might lead to some form of sexual satisfaction – no need to go into detail – the public performance tends to provoke a frolicsome response in both men and women, shouts of 'take it off' and 'wouldn't mind a bit of that', joking remarks about the performer's body, parody miming of sexual gestures, all of which are tongue-in-cheek, knowing or mischievous and usually light-hearted. Performed sexual arousal is quite distinct from authentic sexual arousal. Performed arousal is directed outwards to companions and other spectators, while actual sexual arousal tends to be directed inward, is not boisterous, and is teleological. Of course the display of eroticized bodies might lead to actual arousal and to antisocial behaviour or illegal acts. Because of the possibility of spectator misconduct, the state assumes a regulatory duty over sex shows, as it does with gambling and sometimes with cinema and theatre. But when producers and performers in a platform presentation seek to stimulate spectators sexually, yet without the opportunity of sexual gratification, they are likely to meet with performed rejoinders, a studied or playful response. Such arousal is less about sex and more about the camaraderie of assembly, recalling once again the significance of live spectation.

The complications of arousal also remind us of how little we know about spectator response outside our personal experiences. Despite the history of work on spectator subjectivity and audience theory, we know almost nothing about the psychology and emotions of spectators, individually or in groups. We hesitate to speak on this elusive topic because we understand that audiences are pluralistic, that gender, class, ethnicity, sexuality, education, health and age all condition reaction. We understand that when grouped as an audience spectators do not make up a unitary psyche but respond to the same event in highly individual and sometimes idiosyncratic ways. Given the difficulty of analysing actual responses, we are not likely to solve the conundrum soon or with the methods currently available. But we might learn a little more by turning the problem around slightly, to ask questions about how the emotions of spectators are constructed or manipulated by different types of performance, and especially how arousal is encouraged, discouraged or tolerated.

CHAPTER 10

Memory, performance and the idea of the museum

Memory, entwined so much in human life and our awareness of death, is one of the most prevalent concerns of observers of culture. However we think of memory – as historical, psychological or pathological – it must enter on some level and at some time into serious considerations of our relationship to the planet, to each other, to ourselves. The operations of memory in the self and in the world remain in part a mystery, though a mystery with a vast amount of scientific and cultural explication attached. As Susan Crane notes (2000: 1–2), 'The mental process of memory takes on corporeal form in the brain, but this physical form is invisible to the naked eye: memory becomes sensible and visual through imaginative recollection and representation.' Memory is an act of 'thinking of things in their absence'. When we turn to art production, memory's call is particularly insistent, since art is inevitably caught in the bend that lies between time and attempts to stop it: who are these coming to the sacrifice? For Keats, the still travellers on his dislocated Grecian urn were beautiful because their frozen gestures complicated memory's place in the nature of art. In performance the tension between time and memory becomes acute. Performance is one of memory's greatest tests, precisely because performance does not elude time, because it decays before our eyes, and thus in the moment of its accomplishment escapes into memory. Its remnants and residues are the stuff of theatre histories. Performance is the opposite of memory yet is impossible without memory. As Blau (1987), Roach (1996) and many others have observed, the theatre is always busy reviving (i.e. remembering) ghosts. For Carlson (2001) theatre is a 'memory machine'. From Aeschylus and Sophocles to Ibsen and Beckett, plays great and small open the passage to the underworld of memory. The two tragedies that most haunt western culture, *Oedipus the King* and *Hamlet*, do their haunting through ghosts who walk when the minds of the living wake them.

Memory is significant to producers in less philosophical ways, from the playwright's memory to the actors' memory of lines, from the work of the prompter to inherited stage business and Stanislavsky's 'emotion memory'. Once begun, there is no necessary end to considerations of memory, in or out of performance, as the material on the topic suggests. Reviewing that commentary is not my goal. I am interested in an issue not much discussed: how performance is remembered by spectators.

THE RUSE OF HISTORY

Think for a moment of Shakespeare in history. Since the seventeenth century a tension has existed between the book and the body, the text and actor, the silence of reading versus the publicity of performing. The monumentalizing aspect of remembering Shakespeare, the cultural significance of the English national poet and world icon, usually likes the book. The book is memory materialized, solidified, made historical and referable, while performance always escapes it, leaving behind its remembered shadow. But who is doing the remembering? Do we speak here about a spectator's memory, which is the self, or about cultural memory, which is the other disguised as the self? I must begin by making distinctions regarding the memorializing impulse, and I call briefly on two cultural historians.

First Michel Foucault, whose well-known essay on heterotopias (1986) draws a line between the accumulative and the transitory analysis of time. Unlike utopias, which by definition are no places, heterotopias are real places in the world which attempt through material means to represent or propose a utopian vision. When they are linked to 'slices of time' they are of two types. The first are 'heterotopias of indefinitely accumulating time, for example museums and libraries', which since the rise of modernity have become places 'in which time never stops building up and topping its own summit'. Museums and libraries are based on the nineteenth-century utopian dream of enclosing 'all epochs, all forms' within one place 'that is itself outside of time and inaccessible to its ravages'. In direct opposition are heterotopias linked 'to time in its most fleeting, transitory, precarious aspect, to time in the mode of the festival', such as fairgrounds and vacation villages, places which exist specifically to enclose the 'absolutely temporal'. It is clear that performances normally participate in the second type of heterotopia.

Next Michel de Certeau, whose essay on the history of psychoanalysis (1986) summarizes the opposing ways that memory operates in psychoanalysis and historiography. He reminds us that psychoanalysis is based on Freud's most central discovery, 'the return of the repressed'. Through this 'mechanism', as Freud calls it, memory is central to consciousness. If the past, in the form of something which took place during a significant or traumatic event, is repressed, 'it *returns* in the present from which it was excluded, but does so surreptitiously'. This 'detour-return' is for Freud the inescapable way that memory controls the present. Accordingly, memory is the basis of the talking cure: the psychoanalyst guides the patient towards exposing repressed memory and uncovering its significance. We should recall that one of Freud's favourite examples comes from *Hamlet*: the son, as a child with Oedipal desires unconsciously wishing to remove the father as rival claimant to the mother's affection, is faced as an adult with the old man's actual elimination. The suppressed then arrives in apparitional state to awaken consciousness. As Certeau puts it, 'Hamlet's father returns after his murder, but in the form of a phantom, in another scene, and it is only then that he becomes the law his son obeys.' The detour-return in Shakespeare's drama is the working model for memory's rule. For Freud the process is 'uncanny', in that the present tries to expel the past but 'the dead haunt the living', the past 're-bites', secretly and repeatedly. History is 'cannibalistic', and memory

becomes the arena of conflict between two contradictory operations: forgetting, which is not something passive, a loss, but an action directed against the past; and the mnemic trace, the return of what was forgotten, in other words, an action by a past that is now forced to disguise itself. More generally speaking, any autonomous order is founded upon what it eliminates; it produces a 'residue' condemned to be forgotten. But what was excluded re-infiltrates the place of its origin . . . and, behind the back of the owner (the *ego*), or over its objections, it inscribes there the law of the other (Certeau 1986: 3–4).

Despite our efforts the repressed past invades the present, returning as a ghost of itself to occupy the region of the mind it had been exiled from, the personal counterpart to what Hegel called 'the ruse of history'.

In contradiction to the discourse of psychoanalysis, the historical method 'is based on a clean break between the past and the present'. The past and present are two distinct domains: the present is the place where the work of writing history takes place, relying on the 'apparatus of *inquiry* and interpretation'; while the past is understood as 'set off in time', incapable of direct cognition. As Certeau continues,

Psychoanalysis and historiography thus have two different ways of distributing the *space of memory*. They conceive of the relation between the past and the present differently. Psychoanalysis recognizes the past *in* the present; historiography places them one *beside* the other.

By implication, then, the self apprehends its accumulated recollection as a partial refutation of time, while the historian (whose own self is theoretically placed aside for the sake of the work) insists on the absolute distinction between past and present.

It is a bit surprising that Certeau would see historiography as so conclusively separate from the present. It is now well acknowledged that 'history in reality refers to present needs and present situations wherein those [past] events vibrate', as Benedetto Croce wrote in 1938 (1941). E. H. Carr and Hayden White have elaborated the ways that the writing of history is itself part of history and thus always an elision of the past and present. Yet despite Certeau's overstatement, it will be useful to consider how the discourse of psychoanalysis operates in a different cognitive field than historiography.

FESTIVALS AND MEMORY

As we saw in chapter 5, the revival of the ancient festival was one of the most persistent aspirations of theatrical modernism. A number of thinkers and artists from the mid-nineteenth century on saw in early festivals what they thought modernity had lost, a deep relationship between performance and the life of the spirit. Especially in the festivals of Greece, they saw an engagement of ordinary time with extraordinary or divine time, so that the ancient festival, by definition a special place, also represented a flight from chronological instance. The modern epoch, ruled by the Taylorian stopwatch, stood in direct opposition to the formulas of premodern performance: the Dionysia and the Olympiad were wrapped by modernists in a fervent longing for the primitive, a hope of escaping the mundane, a substitution of art for religion. In the most influential early instance, Richard Wagner sought to activate his dream of the relationship of the German past to the German present by creating a festival in Bayreuth that would reorder the space of memory. The psychological and the historical would merge. The spectator would be overwhelmed (the self encased in private emotion) but also be taught valuable lessons (the self in relation to the other of history). The 1876 Festspielhaus suggested through a semicircular auditorium the union of its spectators with each other and with the *Ring* cycle, which progresses with melancholic longing.

In Foucault's terms, Wagner's festival was (and remains) a heterotopia of the second type, a location for performance that seeks to revisit a moment of past significance by abrogating time. But as it has always been a high-art festival rather than an anarchic folk event, it also called upon the first type, the heterotopia of accumulation of the library or museum, since it evoked a sedimented past and demanded the spectator bring significant cultural capital to the show. Because Wagner endorsed nineteenth-century theatrical historicism, he also created a memory image on stage imbued with an unquestioned belief in the value of archaeological reconstruction. The first theatre in history to be dedicated to the work of a single person, who happened to be its founder, the Bayreuth Festival embraced the contemporary as what Nietzsche would call the eternally recurring.

Not so its immediate imitator, the Shakespeare Memorial Theatre in Stratford, which opened on Shakespeare's birthday three years later in 1879, the first theatre in history dedicated to a single playwright. Bearing his memory in its name, this time the festival concept was already dominated by the idea of accumulating time, since the purpose of the SMT was to cherish Shakespeare as the English national poet and to celebrate his birth with a few provincial productions whose quality was less significant than the act of their performance. Other European festivals before the Second World War included the Salzburg Festival, founded in 1920 by the director Max Reinhardt and the composer Richard Strauss, and the Glyndebourne Festival Opera in Sussex, founded in 1934 and managed by the Viennese impresario Rudolf Bing until 1947. Both sought to package for a growing summer audience the exhilaration of place with a concentrated experience of music and theatre. Whatever their original intentions, they became havens for the upper and aspiring classes, with high ticket prices, high social cachet and a repertory of high art. All my examples were organized along German or Austrian models, part of the *Hochkulturbetrieb* or high culture business.

The significant rise of festivals occurred after the war, as we saw in chapter 4. In the summer of 1947, with much of Europe still in ruins, both the Edinburgh and the Avignon festivals were established specifically to assist in cultural reconstruction. Bing, one of the founders of the Edinburgh Festival and its first director, brought the same conservative attitude to high culture he had displayed at Glyndebourne and would continue at the Metropolitan Opera in New York, which he managed from 1950 until 1972. The purpose of the Edinburgh Festival was the same as Jean Vilar's at Avignon, to use the arts to recover from the austerities of the war by producing music and drama that evoked the glories of European civilization.

Surprisingly even the Shakespeare Memorial Theatre caught the fever and immediately after the war hired as artistic director Barry Jackson, the founder of the Birmingham Rep, to pump life into its moribund annual festival; Jackson's first season brought in the young upstarts Peter Brook and Paul Scofield to shake things up. Jackson soon tired of the low budgets and retrograde attitudes of Stratford, but his tenure laid the groundwork for the arrival of Peter Hall and the creation of the Royal Shakespeare Company in 1960. Meanwhile the most important architectural development of postwar Shakespeare had occurred, the founding of the Canadian Stratford Shakespeare Festival in 1953 in a small railway town in Ontario, led by Tyrone Guthrie. The open-plan auditorium was heavily influenced by Bayreuth.

The location of major arts festivals and their calendar limitations meant that the bulk of audience members must travel to reach them, a circumstance that still applies today, though the journeys are almost always much easier than in 1947. As we know tourism is about incident yet tourists, like wild-game hunters, want to bring trophies home to touch: the memory of their experiences is often commodified. Some aspects of tourism deliberately set out to create memories. Just as family snapshots prompt remembrance of things past, imagined and actual, so souvenirs serve as aides-memoires of travel. But the literal souvenir, as Susan Stewart (1984: 135, 151) notes, by definition destroys its context and becomes a fetish that can never be more than partial, displaying 'the romance of the contraband'. We do not require souvenirs 'of events that are repeatable' but rather of those 'events whose materiality has escaped us'; thus the souvenir is 'a kind of failed magic'. Most travellers now understand this. In a travel-saturated world, a model of the leaning tower of Pisa is no longer an innocent souvenir but a joke that signifies the tourist's self-awareness, is kitsch, ironic and knowing. One of the most notable characteristics of tourism in postmodernity, or 'post-tourism', is avoidance of literal souvenirs and, in substitution, the conversion of experience into lateral material goods: tourists to Paris buy not models of the Eiffel Tower but fashionable clothes and shoes, marking the visit with purchases that back home enable a subtle display of where they have been. Photos and videos of famous or exotic places are of no value unless they include the traveller in the shot, the pictures not only reminiscent cues but material demonstrations that *I was there*.

The accumulation of touristic goods constitutes a personal heterotopia, the archive that materializes memory and that theoretically has no end point apart from the gatherer's death. Though based in individual consciousness and taste predilections, such archives, when they become extensive, often make their way into public museums and theatre collections, where they lose the personal attributes of the collector and stand alone as objective documents. Here we come face-to-face with the great paradox of performance and memory; in Certeau's terms, the tension between the discourses of psychoanalysis and history. If tourism, festivals and all performance are marked by temporal limits, how do we carry back the traces? We can overlay the past on the present (which is the psychology of the self) or we can materialize the past with photos, souvenir programmes and the detritus of the gift shop (which moves beyond personal consciousness to archive a history). In terms of desire I suppose that the second is meant to prompt the first. Lots of shopping is available to memorialize Shakespeare, and has been since the eighteenth century. At the Shakespeare Birthplace in Stratford you can buy Shakespeare watches, earrings, mugs, teapots, ceramic models of Tudor houses, even Desdemona's handkerchief, embroidered with magic in the web of it.

The inadequacy of all methods of sustaining performance experience does not stop the attempt. In the words of Peggy Phelan (1997: 5), psychoanalysis shows that 'the experience of loss is one of the central repetitions of subjectivity'. Why then do we wish to preserve incident? Because we can be so moved by performance that we do not want to release it? Because we want to share experience after the fact? It is its impermanence that makes performance distinctive and exciting, yet we often wish to staunch its loss. There is an ineffable sadness at the heart of touring, and at the heart of spectating, the sadness of not owning the event, the melancholy of its disappearance into memory, a kind of death.

THE HOUSE OF MEMORY

In the pragmatist view of experience, the knower and the known act on each other, subject and object intermingling. Just as the spectacle does not exist without the spectator, so spectation is complete only at the moment of the spectacle. As Pierre Bourdieu (1990: 3) put it in a different context, 'The body is in the social world but the social world is also in the body.' All spectation, even when accomplished in a cohesive group, ultimately occurs in individual consciousness; conventionally phrased, we share the signal but not its reception. Thus any attempt to codify the memory of performance through historiographic methods, accumulating documents and arguing on the basis of evidence, necessarily exists outside the cognition of the spectators. In this sense performance analysis and history are always partial and forms of fiction, just as biography is: the imposition of a perception that is external to individual perception. Thus the job of performance history is to understand and give meaning to the event through social and aesthetic analysis, not to be the sum of the audience's experiences.

Esse est percipi, George Berkeley famously wrote, and Samuel Beckett agreed: to be is to be perceived. We like to think we live in a shared world, not a solipsistic universe of nearly silent imaginings like Beckett's Hamm or Krapp or May. We seek agreed perception, tribal recollection, the discourse of consent. We solicit the perception of others: theatre is a space where the gathered may not know the other but can know that the other is proximate, perceivable, sharing memory.

This is the desire for collective knowledge, a common imaginary, cultural memory. What is cultural memory? It is not actual memory, not individual consciousness. It is a metaphor, a historical and social construct, a way of phrasing our desire for mutual experience. Of course tribes and nations and ethnicities build cultures on collective myths and common premises, even if the premises are contested or false. But such sharing does not mean that every member of the group holds in psychological memory all the important matters that make up group memory; if that were so there would be no need for cultural memory. Cultural memory is another fiction, forged by the centres of power and the careful distribution of knowledge, reinforced by repetition, education and methods of information dissemination – through the ideological state apparatus, the media, cultural hegemony or 'necessary illusions'. Cultural memory is the narrative we accede to. The literary canon is one realization of cultural memory, supposedly created through general understanding but activated by powerful political forces. Theatrical repertory is also a canon, an agreed or imposed set of organized displays on our stages; it is not a chaotic archive but an ordered, certified pact with the past, an official memory.

The validity of cultural memory is tested most clearly in the idea of the museum. There are various types of museums – hundreds of thousands in the world today – and they can frame the works inside them in various ways, but generally speaking they 'masquerade the constructedness of the museum frame as "natural" historical truth or consensus'. As a result, according to Preziosi and Farago in *Grasping the World* (2004: 2), 'Most museumgoers are not prepared (educated) to analyze both the framework and its contents', because museums have traditionally presented themselves as transparent reliquaries of historical or artistic truth. But museums achieve this appearance only by careful staging, so that their contents are read in a particular light. Thus museums are performances, 'pedagogical and political in nature – whose practitioners are centrally invested in the activity of making the visible legible'.

As Stephen Bann (1984) notes, modes of organizing material in museums for two centuries have been polarized between two scenographic practices. The first uses chronological or stylistic progression, whereby objects are arranged along a temporal axis, from the beginning of a period to its end, rooms following each other by centuries, so that the experience of viewing replicates the passage of time and divides the material into demarcated spaces. This corresponds to Certeau's historiographical approach to memory, where the relationship between the past and the present is one of absolute succession. The second scenographic practice arranges objects from a place, historical moment or school in such as way as to create the dramatic effect of the dining hall or bedchamber of a great house, surrounding the viewer with an illusion of being in the past. This impression in the spectator corresponds to the psychoanalytic approach to memory, overlaying the past on the present. Thus we can say with Preziosi and Farago (19) that 'the museum, as a house of memory, contained within itself what became distinct practices such as history and psychoanalysis.'

But if museums are a kind of performance, so performance can be a kind of museum, as I implied earlier. To be precise it is not the performance which has literal museum characteristics but rather the desire to remember it and align it with other performances which leads to cataloguing, critical memory and the tendency to decorporialize the event. We are only too aware that memory is unreliable, that it fades with time, that it distorts experiences and thus distorts our pasts, and can even be falsely implanted. Memory means nothing to outsiders. It inevitably foregrounds the individual; as in my dreams, I am the constant protagonist of remembered events. So I am also the constant protagonist of my remembered spectation. Do I remember performances accurately? Is there an objective standard for remembering? If I am moved by performance, will that affect my memory? If I take notes, will they reflect my psychological experience as a spectator or will they already be part of history writing, an invented narrative? Is there a distance between my personal memory and my professional memory?

One set of answers lies in memory research. In the most relevant situation, a clear relationship has been established between emotion and memory. Generally speaking, emotion at the time of an event tends to intensify memory. In a recent summary Reisberg and Heuer (2004: 4–5) conclude 'there is no question that emotional memories tend to be quite vivid'; in some studies a correlation between vividness and emotionality has been shown to be as high as .90 for fearful events, .89 for sad events and .71 for happy events. Further, emotional events tend to be mulled over, amounting to 'memory rehearsal', fixing the incident strongly into consciousness. Yet some vivid memories of emotional events are completely inaccurate; there is no consistent relationship between emotion and memorial accuracy. Observers of an emotional incident, a car crash, for example, can recount events in great detail, yet video recordings of the incident often reveal those memories to be seriously inaccurate. (Think of the conflicting reports of the John F. Kennedy assassination.) Observers may 'remember' events that never happened.

Part of this phenomenon is explained by what neurological studies call 'flashbulb memory', the tendency to remember a powerful instant as if it had been lit by a flash and then to fill in the blanks with an invented set of narrative connectives, the way we might try to make narrative sense of our dreams. As early as 1959 the Easterbrook Hypothesis, based on animal studies, concluded that during an emotional event *'arousal causes a narrowing of attention*, so that an aroused organism becomes less sensitive to information at the "periphery" of an event'. Extrapolating this to humans is problematic, but some invitation to do so is provided by a pattern observed among crime victims known as the Weapon Focus Effect: 'witnesses to crimes often seem to "lock" their attention onto the criminal's weapon and seem oblivious to much else in the scene' (Reisburg and Heuer 2004: 7). They will remember the gun or the knife vividly but have poor memory of other details, including what the criminal looked like. From this I conclude four related things about performance memory.

1 I am always the protagonist of recollection; though my companions and other spectators may be in my mind, their experiences are irrelevant unless they intruded at the time upon my experience.
2 The more the performance moved or excited me, the less likely my memory of it is completely accurate; this is especially true of foundational performances I witnessed as a young man which impressed me deeply, where memory rehearsal has been frequent.
3 My heightened or flashbulb memory of specific details may well have caused me to create a context for those moments that is independent of what actually occurred.
4 'Playing back' my memory of performance is itself a type of dream performance and thus doubly subject to the predicaments of accuracy.

Memory and performance are complicated by the prevalence of mechanical and electronic recording, but the complications are often not what they seem. Film and video documentation of performance that we once witnessed live offers the chance to re-examine details, to correct memorial mistakes and through replay of specific moments to analyse incidental or subtle effects that we may not have noticed in the original performance. For students and historians such recordings often stand in for presentations not seen in the flesh. But it is well recognized in theatre and performance studies that film and video are always partial witnesses, recording only what the camera can see or the operator has chosen to see, denying the force and atmosphere of live performance: they are transformatively false to what they appear to document (De Marinis 1985). Recordings are evidence of live events but must be used with great methodological care. Films based on plays, like the numerous examples of Shakespeare films, are a different matter, but we must make a crucial distinction between viewing as an ordinary spectator, the movie running from beginning to end, and using the DVD version for teaching or research, where start and stop, replay and slo-mo and frame-by-frame viewing alter the experience substantially. Watching Kenneth Branagh's *Hamlet* in a public cinema, if you have the stamina, is psychologically and phenomenologically similar to watching a live theatre performance; from the standpoint of memory the only significant difference is that we can look at it again. The opportunity for complete review is of great importance to the historian of film and performance, but is not very significant to a spectator on a night out, who is left with the same problem of memory.

FORGETTING *HAMLET*

Is it possible to imagine a world without *Hamlet*? The most famous play in our solar system has been part of western thought for 400 years, and has a reasonable hold on some Asian and African cultures as well. It is a simple matter for journalist-critics, especially London critics, to compare one production or one actor to the last, or one from forty years ago. Ironically the play is manifestly about forgetting. From the Ghost's echoing charges to his son – 'remember me!', 'do not forget!' – to the Gravedigger's memento mori, from Hamlet's refusal to remember his love letters to Ophelia to Fortinbras's claim of 'some rights of memory in this kingdom', the tragedy is worried about the failure of memory, its unreliability, the final forgetfulness of death. And for Freud, as we have seen, the play enacts the terrors of the detour-return, bringing the discarded past into the present, overlaying the forgotten on the remembered, re-biting the protagonist with his unsolicited history. 'There's rosemary, that's for remembrance': if Freud had been a homeopath, that might have been his remedy for sufferers of repressed memory.

I would like to forget *Hamlet*. The endless quotations, the burden of references, the three texts, 'memorial reconstruction', the stories not completed, the phantom presences endlessly returning. But as a paradox from Žižek (2002: 22) has it, if we really want to forget something 'we must first summon up the strength to remember it properly'. Is it possible to remember properly a text and performances that have been so stitched into my memory that they have become part of me? When I think of *Hamlet* can I ever think of the play or only my incorporation of it? I carry into each new production a jumble of reminiscences: of my first reading a half-century ago, of many prior performances, my study of its textual, critical and stage history, its location within western culture, high and low, what I have written and thought about it. I am not a spectator, I am a museum of *Hamlet*.

But even a naïve or first-time spectator, a young person seeing the films with Mel Gibson or Ethan Hawke, is likely aware of some the historical burden. Though the drama may be about forgetting, or trying to forget, its eminence constantly invites considerations of personal and cultural memory: at *Hamlet* we are all guilty cultural creatures sitting at a play.

Perhaps that is why it achieved added significance after the Second World War. In America and Britain the play continued to be seen in the romantic tradition, but things were different further east where issues of historical memory came spectacularly forward (see Kennedy 2001). I think of Nikolai Okhlopkov's 'Iron Curtain' *Hamlet* in Moscow in 1954, remembering the Stalinist years of deliberate forgetting. Or the version by Yuri Lyubimov in the same city, playing for nine years from 1971, which presented a world of forgetfulness, a massive knitted curtain sweeping everybody into unmarked graves. Or the 'electronic' *Hamlet* by Hans-günter Heyme in Cologne in 1979, in which characters videoed one another to prove their own existences; at the end Ophelia, dressed as a racing driver, played Fortinbras, as if no one could quite remember the plot. More important still was Heiner Müller's seven-and-a-half-hour amalgamation of *Hamlet* and his own by-product play *Hamletmaschine* in East Berlin in 1990; during rehearsals the Berlin Wall came down, the state collapsed, the Cold War ended, the Soviet experiment replaced by the spectacularity of postmodernity. We are forgetting everything, the production said – okay, let's forget everything.

One year earlier the Museum of Jurassic Technology was established in Culver City in Los Angeles by David Wilson, a special effects man in Hollywood and a visionary collector. Two years later he opened the Delani / Sonnabend Halls as a permanent exhibition, devoted to Geoffrey Sonnabend, 'neurophysiologist and memory researcher', whose three-volume work called *Obliscence: theories of forgetting and the problem of matter* was published by Northwestern University Press in 1946. Sonnabend, according to the summary leaflet on sale at the museum, 'departed from all previous memory research with the premise that memory is an illusion'. Forgetting, he held, was 'the inevitable outcome of all experience':

We, amnesiacs all, condemned to live in an eternally fleeting present, have created the most elaborate of human constructions, memory, to buffer ourselves against the intolerable knowledge of the irreversible passage of time and the irretrievability of its moments and events.[1]

While Sonnabend did not 'deny that the experience of memory existed', his work claimed that 'what we experience as memories are in fact con-fabulations, artificial constructions of our own design built around sterile particles of retained experience which we attempt to make live again by infusions of imagination'. Through a series of displays and diagrams, the exhibit creates a sense of Sonnabend's life and work, detailing his 'Model of Obliscence' in which the 'Cone of Obliscence' transgresses the 'Plane of Experience': first experience, then memory, then forgetting (illustration 9). Angels and ministers of grace defend us.

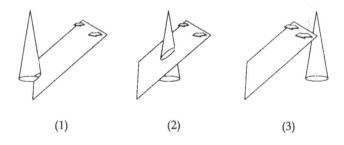

(1)   (2)   (3)

(1) being involved in an experience
(2) remembering an experience
(3) having forgotten an experience.

Illustration 9 Sonnabend's 'Three Steps', Museum of Jurassic
Technology, Los Angeles

The theory of obliscence has a firm connection to the experience of performance, and prompted me to learn more about Sonnabend and his relationship to Madalena Delani, 'a singer of art songs and operatic material' with a short-term memory problem, who influenced his thought. There is only one difficulty: no matter how large the library, you will not find a copy of *Obliscence* in it. The book, Sonnabend, Delani and the theory have never existed except in the Museum of Jurassic Technology. Even the word 'obliscence' is an invention, though it has obvious cognates that give it credibility. The exhibition is a sophisticated – I almost said hoax, but that's not right, it is no more a hoax than *Hamlet*. A gallery of curiosities, rewarding as well as mysterious, it is a memory space which draws in its viewers by silently exposing the constructedness of museums and the nature of their performances. From this standpoint traditional museums might be considered hoaxes, since they customarily hide their historiographic and theoretical principles behind the mist of transcendent art. By exhibiting with a straight face a teasing fabrication, the Museum of Jurassic Technology calls cultural memory into question and leaves us with a sense of displacement long after a visit. The exhibit suggests that memory, both personal and professional, is a desperate grappling with time and incident which inevitably alters the value of experience. In effect the exhibit asks that we not forget it, but what is it we remember?

Is remembering *Hamlet* inevitably false to the encounter of the spectacle? By chronicling performance do we investigate and question cultural value or merely notate the changes that time begets? Is performance history a security against forgetting or a forlorn bell tolling us back to our sad selves? Does history supplant personal memory? Is cultural memory inevitably false to the self? I do not have the answers, but I can summarize what I see as the problems. First, the friction between official or emergent cultural memory and a spectator's personal memory is irresolvable; when the historical encounters the psychological, or the accumulated stability of the archive encounters the fleeting instance of performance, we become uneasily aware of the predicament of time in art. Second, the materializing of personal memory through objects and souvenirs, while understandable as an attempt to recapture past incident, generates further anxiety about the value of experience which escapes capture. And last, recall itself, a private performance of the past in the way that museums are public performances of the past, is subject to so many fallibilities that it might as well be a species of forgetting. We cannot forget *Hamlet* but what is it we remember?

I fear that the ghost of Geoffrey Sonnabend has been presiding over this short essay, a ghost of a ghost, underlining my hesitations about the use of psychology in performance history. I have engaged in this book primarily with the sociological, political and economic issues of spectation rather than the psychological, where I am manifestly tentative. Psychoanalysis was founded on the idea that recollection of repressed trauma, guided and enforced by the analyst, would be healing and liberating for the analysand. But psychoanalysis has been brought to deep crisis by the movement to drug therapy. By asserting that anxiety and depression are the result of cognitive imbalance, are issues in themselves and not symptoms of deeper illness, chemical psychiatry has rebuked the idea of an originating trauma and thus denied the significance of analytic work on memory. The crisis corresponds intriguingly with what was the standard Marxist critique of Freudianism, that it was a bourgeois luxury that from the start placed too much stress on infancy and not enough on social milieu or the exercise of will. The work of memory, whatever therapeutic results it may have, can too easily be accepted as complete in itself. With regard to the spectator, Lacan is obviously helpful in understanding subjectivity, as I make plain in the next chapter, but a memory-based psychoanalytic approach seems simplistic when applied to audiences, who operate both as individuals and as groups. Despite its importance to the subject we know too little about the psychology of the spectator, as I noted before, and what I know tends to be about myself. Like a haunting spectre or repressed ghost scenting the morning air, performance always cries, 'Adieu, adieu, adieu! remember me.' But what is it we remember?

CHAPTER II

Assisting belief: ritual and the spectator

In the early spring of 2004 I travelled to Kerala in south India, the fabled Malabar Coast, the spice coast, the major source of black pepper and exotic spices for Europe from the medieval era. Kerala is a narrow strip of territory that runs from the southern tip of the subcontinent 550 km up its western side, a region of great topographical variety, seacoast, backwaters, rain forest, hills and mountains, lush with vegetation and plantation. Because of its fertility and location on the Arabian Sea it has been influenced by a great cultural and religious mix: in antiquity Aryan invaders, Chinese adventurers, Jewish merchants; Syrian Christians before the fourth century; then Muslim Arabs, Portuguese seamen (Vasco da Gama landed at Calicut in 1498), the Dutch in the seventeenth century, the East India Company at the end of the eighteenth. Historically tolerant to religions and ethnicities, it is common today to see a temple, a mosque and a church sitting side by side, and the portions of the population which are Muslim (25%) and Christian (19%) are much higher than in the country as a whole. There is even a remnant of a Jewish community in Cochin, and the fishing nets on counterweighted poles used there were introduced by the Chinese. Perhaps diversity contributed to the remarkable social condition of the region. The world's first democratically elected communist government, established in Kerala in 1957, helped to create the most equitable land distribution in India, its highest literacy rate (over 90%) and its longest life expectancy (73 years).

The layering of culture and religion in the state has also contributed to distinctive performance modes with antique origins: Kuttiyatam, Krishnattam, Ayyappan Tiyatta and of course Kathakali. I went to begin a study of the ancient ritual performance called Teyyam. I was accompanied by my daughter Miranda, a journalist stationed in Delhi for some years. She was on assignment for National Public Radio in the USA, preparing a report on the wave of farmer suicides then occurring in the same region. Reporters of a different type, our separate projects blended in unexpected ways.

Though I had been to South Asia for extended periods, the earliest in 1973, I am not an expert on its performance traditions, not skilled in its languages nor sufficiently familiar with its social diversity. I came as a cultural tourist interested in widening my knowledge of performance, expecting to achieve only the most rudimentary understanding of what I might witness. I thought of myself as an inexpert anthropologist, in the sense that any engaged visitor is a self-constructed anthropologist, a self-conscious other. I knew then, and stress now, that my observations would be personal, idiosyncratic and possibly inaccurate. How could they be otherwise? Despite these shortcomings, my goal might nonetheless be legitimate if I allowed my limitations to moderate my inferences. My object was to study Teyyam from the outside, using it as a platform to consider the relationship of spectation to belief.

We began in the Wayanad district in northeast Kerala, which backs onto the mountain range of the Western Ghats. On the eastern side of the mountains in the state of Karnataka, drought had plagued farmers for years and thousands had taken their own lives. Now the drought had spread to Kerala, normally a wet tropical environment, and so had the suicides. The problem was simple: commercial suppliers had provided high-yield seed and chemical fertilizer on credit, but the crops had failed and small farmers could not repay the loans, often made by private moneylenders. Shamed in their own eyes and unable to support their households, some took the drastic way out, compounding the difficulties for their families. The chosen methods were both revealing and harsh. A few had set fire to their failed crops and immolated themselves (though not all of those died), a ritual declaration of some power. Most farmer suicides, however, were even more direct in their protest against the moneylenders and suppliers: they chose to swallow the chemical fertilizer that had put them in such a dishonourable position.

Miranda had arranged to visit the leader of the local protests, a poor farmer himself with an impressive intelligence, who was seeking state intervention and debt forgiveness. She also interviewed the family of a suicide and other local people. Some were suspicious at first but gradually welcomed us. (I was accepted without question, since in India it is expected that a single woman be accompanied by her father or brother.) It was difficult to encounter the human pain in the midst of such natural beauty, partly because much of the land appeared verdant and productive. But on closer inspection I saw that crops were failing everywhere, those fabled Malabar crops of coffee and cardamom, pepper and ginger, tea and cinnamon and nutmeg and vanilla. Because the Keralan land redistribution had created many smallholdings, it was not possible for farmers to adapt rapidly to drought-resistant crops; most spice plants need six or seven years to mature, so they were facing a long barren period. My own investigation into ritual performance had been unpredictably contextualized by a contemporary social and economic problem of a serious nature, one that had been met by a ritualized but harsh response.

TEYYAM IS THE GOD

Teyyam (or Theyyam) is a ritual performance mode of north Kerala, concentrated in the Cannanore and Calicut districts[1] which border Wayanad on the west. The consensus of scholars is that Teyyam maintains Dravidian tribal and folk devotional practices, including animal sacrifice, with an overlay of Hindu theology and various other Vedic interventions, effectively fusing a subservient or 'little' culture with the dominant or 'big' culture. Its two most noteworthy social characteristics are its emphasis on lower-caste people (only members of low castes have the hereditary right to perform it) and its freedom to criticize social and caste superiors, landowners and the ruling classes. Indeed one of the most powerful examples of the Teyyam tradition is performed by the Pulayas, an outcaste people with a history of terrible oppression, treated as sub-human by caste Hindus before independence (Pallath 1995: 34). Thus Teyyam can serve as a safety valve for the traditionally subjugated or downtrodden, offering access to a god who listens to their troubles and complaints; 'teyyam' is a corruption of the Sanskrit word 'daivam', meaning god. Sometimes called 'teyyattom', 'the dance of the god', it is performed to entice, appease or celebrate a god, an animate or inanimate spirit, an ancestor or hero.

Whereas Kathakali has courtly origins, a high-caste tradition of performers and sponsors and is customarily acted in or near Hindu temples, Teyyam occurs in shrines (*kavus*) to local divinities on a calendar basis or as celebrations in private houses for liminal occasions such as births, initiations or burials. It shares some obvious techniques with other Keralan performance forms, in drumming, dancing, costumes and the use of chanted narration. In fact Kathakali was developed as a high-art form in the seventeenth century in and around the Calicut court by adapting the methods of Teyyam and other ancient traditions. Both Teyyam and Kathakali use Malayalam, the Dravidian language of Kerala, though Kathakali relies on a heavily Sanskritized variety that is difficult to understand and today is directed towards connoisseurs (and tourists in resort centres like Cochin). A further crucial distinction is that Kathakali, which literally means 'story play', dramatizes the gods and heroes from the *Ramayana* and *The Mahabharata*, while Teyyam is not a story form but uses similar methods to personalize the appearance of the god.

Because traditions of performance vary, sometimes considerably, it is not possible to summarize the procedures of Teyyam comprehensively or to relate the progress of a model. (Ashley and Holloman 1990 give a detailed account of a performance observed in the 1980s but as an example, not a paradigm.) Some sixteen castes in north Malabar perform Teyyams (Pallath 1995: 61) and more than 400 versions are still performed today, with significant variations in form, myth, makeup, costume and musical and performance style (Nambiar 2001: 289). Some use only one performer, others use many; some focus on a single god or spirit, some more; some are part of festivals lasting five days, others occur on one night. Much depends on the abilities of the actors, the finance available and above all the commitment and customs of the sponsoring community. Adaptive forms are created as the social structure changes. In fact the break-up of Keralan matrilineal society after independence and the land reform of 1957 impoverished the old landlords who were the customary sponsors of Teyyam, sending the form into a decline that has only recently been reversed; since Teyyam depends on an oral tradition a number of examples have been forgotten or only partially rehabilitated. In the past artists spent their entire lives dedicated to it; now they tend to be part-time practitioners for a period in their youth (Pallath 89). It's reasonable to conclude that while the materials and styles of performance are similar, the order of events, the gods or spirits displayed and the relationship to the community will vary. Rely on the writers I refer to for greater detail.[2] My question is quite narrow: what do the witnesses believe about the ritual and how does that affect the performance?

The centre of Teyyam is spirit possession. In most shamanistic forms, possession occurs when the god or spirit enters the body of the priest performing the rite who is then entranced, taken over by the spirit, but does not cease being himself. The shaman is overcome by the god, who borrows the shaman's being for the time of possession. In Teyyam, however, the conviction is that the actor (who is not at all a priest or shaman) by artistically impersonating the god or spirit *becomes* the god or spirit. The elaborate costume and makeup contribute to this accord; the theatrical elements of the ritual are used magnificently to establish the god as a reality-in-the-world. Of course theatrical elements inevitably sound overtones that the performance might be an ordinary fiction, a representation of the god's metaphoric presence rather than his or her actuality. Obviously it requires deep, non-rational faith to accept that this low-caste man, dancing on the dirt in a poor shrine compound, is actually for a time a god.

In ritual circumstances it is never possible to judge degrees of belief among devotees or notate statistically how many participants are engaged chiefly by the liturgy or the communal tradition behind the performance. The acceptance of a performed metaphor is itself a variety of belief, so that the meaning and nature of belief is a spectator juggling act. Though belief occurs only within, it can be demonstrated only without; it always has a social consequence. Concerned with other south Indian forms, Clothey (1983: 1) proposes that religious ritual works spiritually through the social, since it affirms 'the participant's identity at the same time as it makes transformation possible'. The anthropological approach to ritual has long been aware of this duality and has tended to suppose that belief is less significant than the performance of belief. Barbara Myerhoff (1990: 247), for example, drawing on earlier work by Roy Rappaport, stresses 'the irrelevance of "authentic" experience in rituals'. Lying is both common and permissible. 'Ritual is a performative genre; one performs a statement of belief through a gesture. That is all that is socially required and all that is of interest to the society. Personal feelings are irrelevant; genuflection is all.' This line of thought, which has dominated the approach to ritual studies associated with *TDR* (*The Drama Review*), finds its clearest expression in Richard Schechner's notion of 'efficacy', whereby the value of a ritual act lies in its proper performance, not in the state of mind or state of soul in the celebrant, participant or witness: efficacy occurs in ritual acts, he writes, 'despite the duplicity, or worse, of those undertaking them'. Schechner's own experience of performing a conversion to Hinduism with mental reservation so that he could study temple rites open only to Hindus, detailed well in *The Future of Ritual* (1993: 1–5), is the anthropologist's classic outside/inside, we/they position, a neocolonial occupation of the cultural landscape of the other, who is often infantilized.

With regard to Teyyam there is evidence that some actors distance themselves from belief. Ashley and Holloman (1990: 136–7) interviewed K. P. C. Panicker, a great Teyyam performer and teacher, who maintained that an aesthetic commitment was sufficient for his work:

I see *Teyyam* as an art not as a belief. As far as my technique is concerned, no one can surpass me. No one can tell from my performance that I am not a believer. I am not a believer. I am a good performer. But I never tell anyone that I don't believe.

Local theories emphasize the deity's authority over what the invested actor speaks and dances in the ritual, but Panicker insisted that everything he did, 'including his possession, came from his own ability, not from an outside power'. Thus he would arrive early for a performance and secretly discover the problems prevalent among the members of the community, using this information later 'to demonstrate the omnipotence of the divinity and to confirm their belief in him'. Similarly during the Teyyam a local assistant would whisper in his ear the names and titles of the important people present so that he could address them personally when they approached him as the god. A devotee might hold that the god will come despite Panicker's state of mind. In some systems of belief, including Roman Catholic doctrine about transubstantiation, the miracle (or magic) can occur even through an unbelieving priest; if the agent is authorized and performs the ritual correctly the god does not mind that he is called by spiritual forgery or counterfeit mentality. Panicker's interviewers recognize that his sceptical approach is not universal or even common among Teyyam performers, but his honesty reveals how even with the best intentions ritual can operate as paternalistic deception.

An action which depends on a secret held in the heart always borders on the ludic, where the significance of the pretence is partly visible and partly hidden. An alert spectator at any performance is engaged in a more-or-less continuous negotiation between acceptance and rejection of what is on show, for the spectator is always asked to consider the spectacle inside a set of beliefs. They may not be organized or doctrinal beliefs, they may amount only to the willing suspension of disbelief, as Coleridge suggested about his poems on the fantastic, they may be nothing more than the conventions of the play or the rules of the game, yet they order the interaction between the seer and the seen. Something more is activated, however, when a sacred performance is premised on confidence in the genuineness of the invisible or, as in the case of Teyyam, the credibility of what would normally be incredible, an actor becoming a god. Then the material sign is asked to signify more than it can sustain, so it can work only if a spectator allows it to move into the self where it is no longer a representation but an object or instrument of the supernatural, the spiritual or the divine. Since the sign moves into belief, ritual is the obliteration of the sign. Schechner and the *TDR* school have tended to neglect this crucial element of spectatorship, and I have more to say about it later.

I AM THE GOD YOU HIRED

Miranda and I arrived in Cannanore after a four-hour drive over difficult mountain roads from Wayanad to the sea. Through a previous arrangement we visited in the early evening A. K. Nambiar, an expert on the folk art and performances of north Kerala. Interestingly our talk was interrupted at one point by observing the women of his home perform a ritual around the outside of the house celebrating the *thirukkalyanam* or divine marriage of Shiva and Parvati, commemorated on 4 April. At about 8.30 our host took us to a local shrine in Azhikode where a Teyyam was about to begin. Nambiar is well-known in Teyyam circles and after introductions to the keeper of the shrine and the important personages who had organized the event, we were warmly welcomed, asked to sit in chairs reserved for honoured guests and allowed to photograph. (Unfortunately I used the wrong digital setting for darkness and only a few of the pictures can be reproduced here.) The preliminary invocations and dancing lasted until 11.00 pm, and were followed by a number of less theatrical ceremonies involving the images of the deity to whom the shrine is dedicated and the preparations and ultimate appearance of (I think) four different actors in sequence. As with Kathakali, the actor's backstage preparations are lengthy, the makeup ground from cake and carefully applied, permitting the time necessary for spiritual preparation. The culmination of the ritual occurred after 4.00 am with two divine possessions, the second continuing into dawn. It was fully light when we left about 7.00, with a few closing ceremonies remaining to be performed.

The first spirit was the peacock god. The actor achieved his transformation in the regular way of Teyyam: his dancing, which was extremely impressive, became faster and faster, he shook to the sounds of the drums as they increased in tempo and volume and the quality of his presence changed as a large red tailpiece was applied. In Teyyam the actor recites or chants the god's story in the third person until the moment of possession and shifts to the first person when he becomes the god. This actor-god accepted the obeisance of his worshippers, blessed them, and in a lengthy section listened one-by-one to their grievances (illustrations 10 and 11). His advice was often disdainful, indicating that the troubles of mere humans were common and insignificant.

The final possession was performed by a different actor. He wore a long skirt of coconut palm over his costume, eventually adding a large flat mask and straw headpiece. He began by killing two chickens. He wrung their necks, cut off their heads and drained the blood into a bowl,

Illustration 10 Teyyam: the peacock god with a devotee, Kerala 2004

Illustration 11 Teyyam: the peacock god with assistants

narrating the god's history the while. Such blood sacrifice, entirely antithetical to Hinduism, is the clearest indication that Teyyam preserves elements of pre-Vedic rites. He achieved ecstatic possession in a way similar to the peacock god. While a large fire was prepared, he listened and spoke to devotees, often laughing at their troubles with a loud 'ha-ha-ha'. According to Pallath (1995: 84), at this point the actor becomes the 'potten Teyyam' (*potten* means idiot or loafer), an aggressive or violent spirit who runs about the shrine yard abusing or reviling the elders, laughing at authority and mocking his superiors, all of which I observed. Using long palm fronds, two men pulled out flaming logs from the fire and set them aside in a pile of other firewood, then swept the remaining hot ash and coals into a neat mound. Arranging the thick grass skirt across his back, the actor lay on the burning coals time after time, his assistants pulling him up – he rose reluctantly – then helping him down again in a falling movement. Each time the skirt caught fire he remained in a casual attitude, crossing his legs as if to show he was not troubled. In Teyyam a ritual of divine possession blends intriguingly with a ritual of social inversion, and the success of the event depends in part on the potten's ability to amuse the crowd by humiliating the local establishment. The invested actor now forced the chief sponsor of the event to kneel in the dirt, addressing him with an abusive language that was half-comic, half-divine. More remarkably, he moved to the new log fire, now blazing, and lay against the flames which set the straw costume alight repeatedly. Devotees stood about the two fires for all of this lengthy action, the obvious highlight of the festival, the firelight eventually blending into sunrise.

In a ritual performance what is the difference between a participant and a spectator? In the early twentieth century the Cambridge anthropologists, all classicists influenced by James Frazer's *The Golden Bough*, insisted that tragedy arose from Greek religious rites and attempted to explain spectation through a similar theory of origins. Jane Harrison held that theatre was born when the first participant in Dionysian rites mentally placed himself outside the spiritual circle: he became a detached spectator, a watcher rather than an accomplice, which she held to be fundamentally divergent conditions. But the division is never so easy: we shift in and out of mental connection to ritual as its movement engages or disengages us. As Eli Rozik (2002: 77) writes in his critique of the Cambridge school, 'spectatorhood is a form of participation'. I was an outsider at this Teyyam, not Indian, not Hindu, dressed in western style, a non-believing witness whose presence was tolerated, yet I was twice invited to leave my seat, come onto the ground and receive the blessing of the gods. Though I thought of myself as an observer, when the actor-god touched me I became a participant. Schechner would agree that belief had nothing to do with it; put more precisely, lack of belief is not a barrier to mental involvement. Participation is not separate from spectation, nor precludes the attitudinal state of spectation. To adapt one of Schechner's own favourite phrases, as a participant I was not a spectator, but I was also not not a spectator. I was a watcher in the midst of devotees, but the devotees were also watchers.

Let us accept that the division between participant and spectator is not a necessary one, that the vigilant spectator is always an assistant at the spectacle. But the question that most interests me remains unsettled: what changes when the spectator-participant IS a believer? Humphrey and Laidlaw (1994) suggest that ritual action is without meaning because we can never discern the actual intentions of celebrants and congregants; only their acquiescence to the prescribed 'stipulation' can be known. The Myerhoff-Schechner view that efficacy is derived from the performative action and not interiority, from liturgical accuracy and not the grace of the god, itself influenced by Victor Turner's idea of ritual as a social process, brings secular performance onto the same plane as sacred performance. The concept has appealed to a number of experimental theatre practitioners in the twentieth century and beyond, including Schechner himself, in part because it suggests that the non-contingent or ideal world is accessible through human ludic activity in the contingent world, whether in a Keralan shrine or a New York theatre.

But our inability to comprehend the cognitive processes of ritualists with any assurance should not blind us to the enormous perceptual change that occurs in the witness as a result of belief. If I, Dennis Kennedy, take the Teyyam actor's blessing as a non-believer in the god's presence, but next to me a devotee performs the same action believing in that presence, as witnesses we could not be more separate. Our division is not the result of an anthropological otherness; despite all our cultural differences I am free to will myself into belief. But as it stands our inner/outer relationships are utterly unlike. If the devotee believes the god is present, then the god is here: bow down before him. If I do not believe the god is present, then he is not: bow down before him with critical curiosity. For the believer the objective falls away into the subjective, and paradoxically both are tangible in the actor-god who passes through fire. For the non-believer the actor in the fire is a mightily theatrical way to end the night-long ceremony. We performed the same action with entirely different significance. As spectator-participants we had witnessed entirely different shows.

And what of Miranda? As a woman she was not invited to take the blessing. She sat in her chair and witnessed a third show, the ridiculous spectacle of her father bowing before a man in a red peacock dress. Yet throughout all of us were thoroughly aware of the underlying theatrical nature of the event. Nambiar told me that the best Teyyam actors, far from volunteer worshippers or humble priests, command high fees, as much as 5,000 rupees a night, a very considerable sum in south India (then equivalent to 500 euro). The divine appears only through the human, and the skill necessary to achieve the appearance must be hired.

FAITH AND BELIEF

In his book *On Belief* Slavoj Žižek (2001: 109–10) points to a distinction between faith and belief. Because belief can be irrational and faith is always so, because both demand an act of will and more than acquiescence, we tend to see them in the same light. But we can believe in something without having faith in it. 'When I say "I have faith in you," I assert the symbolic pact between the two of us, a binding engagement, the dimension which is absent in simple "believing in . . ." (spirits, etc.).' As an example Žižek notes that 'the ancient Jews BELIEVED IN many gods and spirits, but what Jehovah demanded from them was to HAVE FAITH only in Him, to respect the symbolic pact between the Jewish people and their God who has chosen them.' Belief, then, is a perception or state of mind, faith a compounded agreement (though sometimes a one-sided agreement). Can I believe in the Teyyam god without keeping faith with him? Yes. Can I have faith in the spiritual order that Teyyam indicates without believing in the god's presence? Certainly yes. For the congregant, faith (trust) in the congregation's system of belief is not the same as believing in (sharing) the system of belief. Congregants, united in ritual ceremony as an audience, hold faith collectively in a way that no individual does, believer or not.

Similarly we can say that in the theatre what turns a stage fiction into more than a fiction is the connivance of an audience. Though the result is not reality-in-the-world, connivance moves fictional enactment to a state that lies beyond the imaginary and beyond the symbolic. The relationship between a willing, attentive audience and the performance is an agreement which approaches the quality of faith. A temporary agreement, to be sure, but a shared trust nonetheless. Does a performance achieve its singularity, its manufactured or contrived otherness, when this connivance occurs? If so, it is not a matter of suspending disbelief (a double negative that does not become a positive) but of creating belief in (sharing) the embodied intensity of the fiction through absorption with it. In the terms Lacan applies to dreams, in presenting a fiction to an audience the theatre can open the Real that in daily life is disguised by ordinary reality. The Real is of course a difficult Lacanian concept, that order of existence that lies beyond the imaginary and the symbolic. In this context I suggest the Real can be thought of as the almost inaccessible object that is outside the symbolic order, outside 'the big Other', outside language, 'the object of anxiety' as Lacan calls it a number of times in the 1954–5 seminar (Lacan 1988). The Real is thus related to the Freudian trauma the individual necessarily represses in order to operate on the level of the conscious (the ego). As Žižek (2006: 59) puts it, the theatre can allow us glimpses of 'the Real that emerges in the guise of an illusory spectacle'. That is what religious ritual sets out to do more directly, without the social pretext of theatrical performance.

Michel de Certeau, moving closer to Guy Debord than usual, claims that we have become 'a recited society', repeating stories we do not believe in, ascribing them to an authority that is always other. The 'spectator-observer' knows that the images and stories are mere semblances '*but all the same* he assumes that these simulations have the status of the real'. He continues:

Belief no longer rests on an invisible alterity hidden behind signs, but on what other groups, other fields, or other disciplines are supposed to be . . . Citation thus appears to be the ultimate weapon for making people believe. Because it plays on what the other is assumed to believe, it is the means by which the 'real' is instituted (Certeau 1984: 186–9).

Though this is a gloomy understanding of the state of social credence, it underscores how often our thought and activity rely on distension and displacement to make things work. In a different essay entitled 'What we do when we believe', Certeau writes that 'believing is the link, distended, that connects by speech two distant gestures'. Not just of human association but also of god, belief is often displaced onto another who is assumed a believer. A number of anthropologists have noted how common it is for devotees to say 'I don't believe the shaman is possessed but I know that people in the past believed it and I uphold the ceremony for the sake of tradition.' But remembering that belief is internalized, there is no reason to suppose that a ritualist would answer an anthropologist's inquisition about belief honestly, or define belief the same way. 'I have heard that some people believe' permits a position of rational scepticism inside the acceptance of a system of faith. And this applies in the opposite case as well, as Certeau notes: 'In many cases it is the "unbeliever" who believes that the "believers" believe, and this enables him to believe that he is not a believer – or vice versa' (Certeau 1985: 195, 202).

As I have said, most performance operates along similar lines of distended belief, not just by constant deferral (citation) of signifiers, but also by substitution, what Joseph Roach (1996) calls surrogation. For the spectator-participant in ritual performance, however, belief obviates surrogation and makes the action non-contingent, an object-unto-itself. The present falls away into the past (the moment of origin is repeated) and into the eternal (the reiteration is testimony of the moment's continuation). This is why ritual performance is charged with psychic danger, because it proffers visible substance while it flirts with insubstantiality. Schechner's famous definition of performance as 'restored behaviour', outlined in 1985, is not adequate for a believing spectator-participant. Performance which displays the god is restored or 'twice-behaved' behaviour from the standpoint of those outside the belief system. For the believer such performance is doubly present: it is present in its material action, which is a restored behaviour, dependent on reiteration; but also present as ineffable manifestation, which, because it is supernatural or divine, is *always first-time, unrehearsed behaviour*. The god came once and now he comes again: that is restored ritual behaviour. The god came once and he comes infinitely: that is eternal behaviour, a repetition that is always originary. The great paradox of ritual is that its vicariousness, the quality that normally points to the limitation of performance and makes it a minor form of deception, is in the eyes of a believer the very means by which faith is secured. By pressing belief to the extreme, rituals of divine appearance allow us to consider the deepest aspect of spectatorship, its relationship to psychological state.

DO THIS IN REMEMBRANCE

If I know too little about Teyyam, I know all too much about my next topic, the Christian eucharist. I was born and raised a Roman Catholic in America, the son of a pious mother and a severely observant father, sent to Catholic schools all my life and even to a Jesuit university (the University of San Francisco, wonderful for its location in the city and for the years I was there, at the end of the beatnik era). Throughout high school I was an altar boy intended for the priesthood, studied little Latin and less Greek, and at USF was required to read Thomist philosophy and its bedfellow, canonical Roman theology. Naturally I reacted against all this by age twenty. T. S. Eliot famously said that he was an Anglo-Catholic in religion, a classicist in literature and a royalist in politics. For the sake of full disclosure I now reveal that I am a leftist in politics, a populist in literature and an atheist in religion. This may be more than you want to know.

The eucharist (from the Greek *eucharistia*, 'thanksgiving'), in St Paul called the lord's supper and also known now as the lord's table or holy communion, began in the apostolic era with the practice of the earliest Christian communities eating a meal in common, which came to be known as the agape or love feast. The characteristics of that celebration are not fully understood but it is clear from Paul that it was fundamental to the new church. Today it usually follows the pattern established in the early medieval Mass, preserved in similar forms in Catholicism, Eastern Orthodoxism, the early reformed churches and in many more recently established sects. The eucharist is a ritual action which replicates (or restores) the moment of the Last Supper when Jesus, aware that he was about to be betrayed unto death, made bread and wine the symbols of a 'new covenant', instructing his disciples to repeat these gestures as memorial acts. The supper may have been the Passover Seder (the gospels do not seem to agree), and if so the new covenant is an obvious reference to the demolishing of the Mosaic old covenant. The eucharist is the only ritual performance that Jesus directly instituted, giving both words and gestures, its similarity to the Seder notwithstanding.

Given its absolute centrality in the history of Christianity and its apparent biblical authority, it is surprising to learn that the injunction to repeat the ceremony of bread and wine as a memorial deed appears in only one of the gospels, and that in a disputed passage. John does not relate the incident of the supper at all. The synoptic gospels (Matthew, Mark and Luke, so called because they are similar in detail) stress the betrayal and Jesus' awareness of his end; while all three narrate the supper, only Luke (22.19) adds the crucial words that institute repetition, 'Do this in remembrance of me.' But this verse is not present in all ancient Greek versions of Luke, and does not appear in some modern editions of the New Testament. It should also be mentioned that none of the synoptic evangelists (whoever they might have been) was present at the Last Supper, and that the gospels were compiled near the end of the first century. In the most widely held view, Mark is the earliest, written about AD 70, some forty years after the crucifixion; early tradition held it was based on the preaching of Peter in Rome. Matthew and Luke are placed ten to thirty years later than Mark; both rely on the biographical outline he established, with additions taken from a list of the sayings of Jesus. The book of John, probably written at the end of the century by a disciple of John rather than by the apostle himself, is from a separate tradition.

The only reliable scriptural authority for the injunction to memorialize the supper comes from Paul's first letter to the Corinthians, chapter 11, written from Ephesus between 50 and 54 while 'most' of those who had seen the resurrected Jesus were 'still alive' (1 Cor. 15.6). Paul's letters are the most ancient Christian texts to have come down to us. Of them First Corinthians is just about the earliest; only his letter to the Thessalonians might predate it, by a year or two at most. The version of the supper in Corinthians is the likely source for the disputed verse in Luke. I quote Paul's passage from the New Revised Standard Version.[3]

[23] For I received from the Lord what I also handed on to you, that the Lord Jesus on the night when he was betrayed took a loaf of bread,

[24] and when he had given thanks, he broke it and said, 'This is my body that is for [*or* broken for] you. Do this in remembrance of me.'

[25] In the same way he took the cup also, after supper, saying 'This cup is the new covenant in my blood. Do this, as often as you drink it, in remembrance of me.'

[26] For as often as you eat this bread and drink the cup, you proclaim the Lord's death until he comes.

From the standpoint of ritual institution, the most important thing to say is that Paul was not present at the Last Supper either and never met the man Jesus. His authority did not come through the apostolic line but from a vision, or rather audition, of Jesus as the Christ (the Greek *christos*, 'anointed', a direct translation of Hebrew 'messiah'). This vision on the road to Damascus converted Paul from the great persecutor of the new faith to its greatest advocate, the apostle to the gentiles. Verse 23 identifies his knowledge of the event as a memory of a memory; 'received' and 'handed on' are technical terms for transmitting an oral tradition. (He uses the words again later in this letter, 15.3.) He says he received the information 'from the Lord'. We cannot know what that means, or know if he gathered it from one of the surviving apostles present at the Last Supper, but we can assume that the eucharistic account was in wide circulation and already in frequent ritual practice. Paul had earlier taught his brethren at Corinth about it: 'I commend you because you remember me in everything and maintain the traditions just as I handed them on to you' (11.2). Indeed the passage about the supper is a corrective instruction, for he was disturbed by reports that the Corinthians were abusing the supper in various ways, becoming factionalized over its proper order, getting drunk or eating too much or neglecting its symbolic meaning: treating it as a human celebration rather than a divinely appointed rite. (He was also disturbed in the early part of the chapter by apparent violations of gender rules and what seem now to be incidentals such as the length of a man's hair or the need for women to be veiled at prayer, matters that derive from first-century customs in the eastern Mediterranean rather than theological belief.)

One can say almost nothing about the eucharist (or Paul) that is not contested somewhere, and I do not wish to engage in scriptural scrapping. My interest here, though dependent on Paul's text, remains focussed on the ritual spectator-participant. As Paul relates it, the action of Jesus is magnificently simple in gesture and hugely complex in signification. What do the quotations, 'This is my body', 'This cup is the new covenant in my blood' mean? Is the breaking of the bread a prefiguring of his broken body on the cross and the ritual repetition to be taken as a citation of that event? Is the cup of wine itself the new covenant, somehow also representing his blood about to be shed?[4] Are these words and gestures metonymic, metaphoric or literal? Are they an invitation to create a priesthood charged with supervision of the new covenant organized around a ritual supper? Are they a powerful magic that must be managed correctly, as Paul seems to imply in verse 29 ('For all who eat and drink without discerning the [Lord's] body, eat and drink judgement against themselves')? Are they simply a farewell motion from a religious teacher who fears oblivion? Does verse 26 suggest that reiteration of the quoted action is proselytic in itself and an anticipation of the imminent return of Jesus as god?

But 'Do this in remembrance of me', twice said, that seems clear enough however translated. The charge is specific and has two parts: repeat the action of the bread and wine, and repeat it in my memory. The speaker does not say how often it should be repeated, whether it should be part of the Seder or some other Jewish ceremony, or who precisely should repeat it (only the apostles present? any future believer?). Compared to the synoptics Paul quotes Jesus very rarely, so these words in the middle of a reprimand to Corinth have additional value, effectively containing the oldest dogmatic rite of Christianity. But what is the dogma?

Of course ritual practice developed independently of Paul, and other writings from the first century on the matter may have been lost. There is no need to assume that even in its earliest days the ceremonies of the new religion were universally identical, or to worry too much over how accurately they replicated the founding moment at the Last Supper. In liturgy the object is not to imitate the original behaviour but to imitate the prescribed manner of the imitation. About the archaic treatment of the eucharist we can only speculate, as we can only speculate over what primitive Christians believed about the divine presence. What seems crucial from a ritual perspective is twofold. First, were the injunction to repeat the actions of the bread and wine not present, then the Last Supper was simply another event at the end of the life narrated by the gospels, like making the lame walk or raising the dead, and has no necessary ceremonial or institutional consequence. Even if the eucharist were accepted as a sacrament by deduction from the undisputed words of the synoptics, as the church did with the six other sacraments it claims to have been ordained by Jesus, it would not have been instituted *expressly as a repeatable event.* Second, as the eucharist developed, its central ideology was that Jesus comes in body and spirit as god, is objectively present in the bread and wine and *must arrive when the words of consecration are validly declared.* It is odd that god, the omnipotent only GOD of all creation, would have no choice about this, but in Catholic thought he does not; god's grace and love being infinite, he has always already wished it, regardless of our unworthiness. Thus as a ritual the eucharist presents its congregants with both divine authorization and divine attendance. If the first requires a degree of belief (belief in the words of scripture, belief in ecclesiastic and sacerdotal authority), the second requires an enormous leap of faith.

What can it mean to a spectator-participant at Mass to believe that god is actually present in the bread and wine, is consumed by communicants and infuses them with his being? This is not a case of divine possession as with Teyyam, for the priest does not become the god. Though the celebrant's words generate the divine attendance, he is *quoting* Jesus at the Last Supper – borrowing Jesus, not borrowed by him – and receives him as the rest of the faithful through alimentation. On the level of ritual narrative this is all unremarkable, a simple retelling of the story with appropriate signs. But since there is no text in Paul or the gospels that explicitly proclaims god's presence in the repeated action, and since it defies human understanding that god could be objectively present in bread and wine without changing their material substance, the Mass asks far more from its congregants than Teyyam or other rituals of divine possession. We might consider alternative theological views on this, one of the most persistently difficult items of faith in Christianity, but they come down to argument over whether god is present in the eucharist actually, figuratively, allegorically or merely spiritually without miraculous occurrence. Though the substance argument has been the cause of much human suffering and death in Christian history, I think the adverbial nature of god's appearance doesn't matter much from the position of the spectator-participant. What does matter is the disposition of the believer toward the presence, and for that I want to look at the question differently, first psychologically then philosophically.

BIG BELIEF, SMALL BELIEF

What grounds us in any type of belief is the ascription of a superior external substance or force, whether religious, ideological or abstractly philosophical. But this force, which Lacan calls 'the Big Other' – *big* refers to the capital O – is the symbolic order itself, necessarily a subjective presupposition, virtual, incapable of verification. It is what individuals recognize themselves in, 'the ground of their whole existence . . . yet the only thing that really exists are these individuals and their activity, so this substance is actual only in so far as individuals believe in it and act accordingly'. (A transparent explanation from Žižek's *How to Read Lacan* 2006: 10.) The Big Other, the medium of symbolic registration, we might also call the Big Belief. It can exist only if 'some ultimate guarantor if it' exists, but, and this reminds us of Certeau, the guarantor 'is always deferred, displaced, never present in person'. So I distinguish two types of belief, each of them separate from faith. Small belief applies to specific occurrences or cases: belief that my father was my father, that the Trojan War took place, that John Kennedy was assassinated by Lee Harvey Oswald alone. This is the type of belief appropriate to the ritual event, in our case the question of the god's presence. Small belief presumes Big Belief in the guarantor: that parents are truthful, that books are reliable, that the US government did not collude in a massive conspiracy. But since the guarantor is not available it must be presupposed as a mythical founding figure or an impersonal force (history, democracy, a church or maybe only 'I have heard that some people believe'). Thus religious ritual, which depends on and is authorized by small belief, is in turn the prop of Big Belief, which in turn is the foundation of faith.

In this spinning circularity we are closer to Pascal than to Schechner. Schechner would hold that belief and ritual performance are two separate things, while Pascal famously held that the rational, critical intellect that questions or denies belief can be conquered by ritualized force of habit. If you doubt, he advises you do as others have done: 'they acted as if they believed, took holy water, had masses said, etc. *Cela vous fera croire, et vous abêtira*, This will make you believe, and you will be dulled' (literally, 'and will debase you' or 'make you like beasts', i.e. you will act on instinct; *Pensées* 680). What a wager! Perform as if you had belief and Belief will come to you. We might as well go backwards and say that the purpose of ritual is not to prop up Big Belief but to sidestep small belief. Or as Žižek puts it, 'To believe – to believe directly, without mediation – is an oppressive burden which, happily, can be offloaded onto another [the Big Other] by the practice of a ritual' (Žižek 2006: 31).

But what if instead of following Pascal's advice I consciously believe in the ritual without Big Belief? Might I believe in the god's presence in Teyyam or the eucharist *only while the ritual lasts*? What I would then be acting out is not a performance independent of the faith upon which it supposedly rests, nor Pascal's judicious expectation of faith to come. Rather I would be acting out an association that is similar to the connivance of spectators in the theatre or the cinema when they momentarily accept the displayed fiction as more than fiction, an opening to the Real, that other world, or that other meaning in the world, available through dream and fantasy and which is outside my concern for the Big Other. In such a case I would for the length of the observance hold to its requirements not just in outer action but in inner state, and afterwards be free to trim down or even discard that state and return to rational doubt or uncertainty. My belief in the ritual would be stimulated or effected by my assistance at the ritual and remain for the duration of the ritual, absurdly disconnected from Big Belief. This may be how contemporary educated devotees at Teyyam manage to acknowledge the god's appearance, moving in and out of confidence in his actuality. Unlike the monotheistic religions, Hinduism does not seem to demand fervent lifelong faith, but a more relaxed theology does not imply that ritualists are without belief in the ritual's premise.

Small belief appears at first as the deadlock of spectatorship, for belief in the immaterial implications and inferences of ritual is unable to free us from the bonds of watching its material expression or performing its physical gestures. Further, we must admit that believers not only operate on a different level of spectatorship from non-believers, we must also acknowledge different levels and types of belief among worshippers, including the possibility that their belief in the premise of the event is sliding, erratic or temporary, a confused shuffling of small belief and Big Belief. This is a metaphysical conundrum without psychological solution, since individual subjectivity is likely to take precedence over the social or religious identity the ritual endorses.

Paul continues to be seen as the great original thinker of the Judaeo-Christian tradition by theologians and philosophers of different stripes. One of the most intriguing of recent studies, Alain Badiou's *Saint Paul: the foundation of universalism* (2003), centres around Paul's creation of a new intellectual order. For Badiou, another self-declared atheist, Paul's contribution lies in claiming that for the world to change from the ancient order (the order of the Roman imperial war machine) it was necessary to pronounce an overwhelming Belief, that as Jesus defeated death so he offers the chance *for all people* to defeat sin and death. The crucial text is from Galatians (3.28): 'There is no longer Jew or Greek [i.e. gentile], there is no longer slave or free, there is no longer male or female; for all of you are one in Christ Jesus.' Paul insists that all are equal in sin regardless of birth or circumcision, and salvation lies equally available to all through baptism in Christ. But Badiou does not accept the resurrection as fact nor Jesus as god, so what possible meaning can Paul's declaration of universal salvation have for him and other unbelievers? The philosopher, Badiou holds, cannot accept the myth of Christianity, so he must abandon 'the content of the fable' and look at what remains. 'For Paul, it is a matter of investigating which law is capable of structuring a subject devoid of all identity and suspended to an event whose only "proof" lies precisely in its having been declared by a subject.' He finds that Paul's 'universal truth' has three parts:

(a) 'The Christian subject does not preexist the event he declares (Christ's resurrection)' therefore
(b) 'Truth is entirely subjective' and
(c) 'Fidelity to the declaration is crucial, for truth is a process, and not an illumination' (Badiou 2003: 5–6, 14–15).

How different from standard post-structuralist thought. Truth is subjective, yes, but nonetheless it is necessary *to be faithful to one's declaration of truth*. This is holding fast to small belief without Big Belief. Paul believed the Messiah was in the blinding light and voice that knocked him to the ground on the road to Damascus, and from that he grew to belief in the resurrection, and from that to Belief in salvation through faith. But if we deny both Pauline events, the road and the resurrection, we can still borrow the *character* of Paul's small belief, for 'the treasure is nothing but the event as such, which is to say a completely precarious having-taken-place' (54). For Badiou the significance is not whether the event took place but the *declaration of the event*, and that is 'truth'. As he writes in another context, 'there can be truth only in the situation wherein truth insists, because nothing transcendent to the situation is given to us' (Badiou 2004: 122). Admiring this position, Simon Critchley (2007: 48–9) nonetheless objects that what Badiou really means by 'truth' is ethical justification, but as long as we keep Badiou's word in quotation marks we should be able to understand its specific connotations.

Badiou's insistence on the value of declarative fidelity is an antidote to contemporary uncritical relativism, though his emphasis on Paul's universalism may be a bit innocent, even sentimental. In a commentary on the letter to the Romans, Giorgio Agamben (2005) sees Badiou falling into the same trap as the church did in basing its universalism (its catholicity) on the apostle to the gentiles. In contrast, Agamben claims Paul's letters are 'the fundamental messianic text for the Western tradition', emphasizing a connection to Hebraism rather than a Roman universalism. His conviction that the return of the Messiah Jesus was imminent franked his letters with haste and immediacy, made them outbursts of the heart from a proselyte desperately working against the deadline not of his own death but of the arrival of 'the time of the end' (62). For Agamben, Paul's messianism speaks not of the beginning of a new universal era but of the ending of all eras. Paul's own Big Belief forced him to advocate rapid conversion for his followers. He never uses the word *christanos* to describe them but if he knew the term it could only have meant 'disciples of the messiah', not an institutional group. There was no time for an institution, no time for ecclesiastic faith or organized theology because Paul did not anticipate centuries of waiting – and would be astonished to learn that two millennia later he would be called the founder of the world's largest religion, still waiting for the Messiah's return.

But despite their differences Agamben does not deny Badiou's great insight, that for Paul personal commitment precedes identity, that 'the Christian subject does not pre-exist the event he declares'. Or perhaps I should say that commitment and identity, belief and subjectivity, are for Paul interchangeable.

To return to our theme, for the ritualist momentary commitment makes possible small belief in the basis of a ritual performance but can be isolated from faith: in the ritual moment the Big Other becomes irrelevant, the sign disappears into the subject, the symbol into the self. The spectator-participant who consents to the ritual action is liberated from larger obligation: the world and time are only here, only now. It is bizarre to use Paul, the faithful adherent par excellence, to duck out of faith, but here's a final proposition: we can accept in our hearts the premise of the ritual without accepting in our hearts lifelong Big Belief. Ritual is more than performance and more than formal efficacy. It can be personally transformative if we allow it, if we declare fidelity to its event, but the transformation need not be enduring. We can depart a ritual of the god's presence carrying the revelation of the moment, but perhaps only for the moment. Which is why so many are condemned to repeat the moment.

Spectation is significantly enhanced by belief, which changes utterly the interior nature of the watching. But spectation with belief is still spectation, which is to say it is complete only in the context of the spectacle.

ENVOI

I haven't accepted communion in a Catholic church for many decades, not even at my mother's funeral. I obstinately resisted returning to the outward expression of what I no longer held in belief. But I remember very well the adventure of first communion, at St Francis de Sales Church in Cincinnati. In those days Catholics abstained from all food and drink before communion out of respect; in the attached elementary school where we gathered even the water fountains were tied with cloth lest a child forget and ruin the occasion. Though the locations were familiar, in my eyes every aspect of the moment was ritualized. Dressed in a white suit and carrying a marbled white missal, accepting the dry, surprisingly sticky wafer on my tongue, I was saturated with an emotion that I took to be the power of faith. I had been trained to believe in the miracle of transubstantiation, and I did believe, though I understood only that Jesus entered me. At home my parents had organized a celebration and uncle Cliff took me in his laundry van on a beer run. 'Den', he said, 'this will be the happiest day of your life.' Even at age seven I thought that a melancholy forecast, but perhaps he was right in one sense, in Pascal's sense: Big Belief is childlike and capable of sustaining an uncritical happiness. It was the ritual that did it, of course, the Mass with its music and magnificent dramaturgy, the eucharist with its naïve promise of union with the god, all directed toward me and my belief in the divine attendance.

In my middle years when for her sake I accompanied my mother to Mass, she would look at me with grave concern when I did not rise for communion, anxious for the state of my soul. If I was an unbeliever working his way towards atheism, why could I, her only child, not perform a ritual that meant little to me and so much to her? Surely a Pascalian gamble would have been in order. Bow, stubborn knees! Did I resist because I retained some small belief in the eucharist and did not wish to defile it? The god's appearance is not to be trifled with: the heavens open, the actor is aflame. I stood back, ex-communicant, another spectator at the spectacle. What had I gained by detachment and objectivity, by evasions of belief?

Notes

1. INTRODUCTION: ASSISTING AT THE SPECTACLE

1 Martial, *Epigrams* 12.28 and 13.99; Ovid, *Amores* 3.2.3–4. See the commentary in T. J. Leary, *Martial Book XIII: the Xenia* (London: Duckworth, 2001): 163–4; and *Encyclopedia Britannica*, 11th edn. (1910–11), 'Applause', II: 223.

2 Frederick Lees, 'Where fortunes are made by theatre applause', *The Wide World Magazine* n.d. [1890?]: 665–9; clipping in Lincoln Center Library for the Performing Arts, New York (MWEZ + n.c. 23, 508 no. 4). Edward Braun told me that in the Soviet Union verbatim reports in *Pravda* of leaders' speeches at Communist Party Congresses were habitually punctuated with phrases like 'applause', 'stormy applause', 'stormy and sustained applause' and finally 'stormy and sustained applause becoming an ovation, all rise to their feet'.

3 Clipping dated 12 December 1909, in Robinson Locke collection, Lincoln Center Library (NAFR + v. 42: 22).

4 Kabuki actors on tour to New York in 1960 were so unfamiliar with final ovations that they had to be instructed how to bow in curtain calls; see Donald Richie (tr.), *Six Kabuki Plays* (Tokyo: Hokuseido Press, 1963): 105.

5 A history of how audiences appropriated *The Rocky Horror Picture Show* in the US is available at www.rockyhorror.com (accessed May 2008). I discuss spectator arousal in chapters 8 and 9.

6 See www.tonylovestina.com (accessed May 2008).

2. THE DIRECTOR, THE SPECTATOR AND THE EIFFEL TOWER

1 Baudelaire mentions the terms *littérature militante*, *les poëtes de combat* and *les littérateurs d'avant-garde* in a diary entry of 1864, cited in J. A. Henderson 1971: 9.

2 John Goodman on Seurat in *The Oxford History of Western Art*, ed. Martin Kemp (Oxford University Press, 2000): 332.

3 Emile Zola's 'Une nouvelle manière en peinture: Edouard Manet' first appeared in *Revue du XIX Siècle*, 1 January 1867.

3. THE AVANT-GARDE AND THE AUDIENCE

1 Based on box office statements from J. E. Vedrenne to Murray dated 3 February, 19 and 26 March, 2 and 8 April 1906, in the Gilbert Murray Papers in the Bodleian Library, Oxford. See Kennedy 1985: 38–40.
2 Programme for *The Turning Point*, St James's Theatre, 6 January 1913, Theatre Museum, London. On the relationship between stage costumes and spectators, see Kaplan and Stowell 1994.

4. SHAKESPEARE AND THE COLD WAR

1 Herbert Farjeon, *The Shakespearean Scene* (London: Hutchinson, 1949): 114–15; Gordon Crosse, *Shakespearean Playgoing, 1890–1952* (London: Mowbray, 1953): 78–9.
2 Reviews dated 17 August 1955 from *Oxford Mail*, *Star* (London) and *Birmingham Post*, collected with all the notices in the Shakespeare Centre Library in Stratford.

5. THE SPECTATOR AS TOURIST

1 Based on the statistics available in January 2008 on the WTO website, www.world-tourism.org.
2 Figures from the latest *Annual Review* on the Globe Centre's website, www.shakespeares-globe.org (accessed December 2007).
3 *Bankside Globe*, 1973 issue, Birmingham Shakespeare Library archive.
4 David Gates, 'The Bard is hot', *Newsweek* 128.26 (European edn), 23 December 1996: 40–8.

6. INTERCULTURALISM AND THE GLOBAL SPECTATOR

1 Reported by Jean-Claude Carrière in a talk in Los Angeles in 1991.
2 'Tempesto: Sadoshima no rehasuru', interview in *Marie Claire* (Tokyo), January 1987 before rehearsals began (translation kindly provided by Thomas Rimer). I have gone over some of this ground before (Kennedy 2001: 316–19) to make a different point about the visual implications of interculturalism.
3 The exception was Irving Wardle in *The Times*, 19 August 1988. Thanks to the Toho Company of Tokyo for providing copies of all British and Japanese notices of the production.
4 A useful but somewhat different approach to surtitles is taken by Marvin Carlson in *Speaking in Tongues: language at play in the theatre* (Ann Arbor: University of Michigan Press, 2006).
5 The issue is argued in detail in Yong 2005 and in the introduction to *Shakespeare in Asia: contemporary performance*, ed. Dennis Kennedy and Yong Li Lan (Cambridge University Press, forthcoming).

7. THE BODY OF THE SPECTATOR

1 *Birmingham Post*, 13 September 1976. Michael Mullin, *Shakespeare Quarterly* 38 (1987): 355. Gareth Lloyd Evans, *Shakespeare Quarterly* 28 (1977): 193–4. Robert Cushman, *New York Times*, 5 February 1978.

2 Richard David, *Shakespeare in the Theatre* (Cambridge University Press, 1978): 87. Gareth Lloyd Evans, *Shakespeare Quarterly* 28 (1977): 194. Irving Wardle, *The Times*, 14 September 1977.

3 Roger Warren, *Shakespeare Survey* 30 (1977): 179.

4 Robert Smallwood, *Shakespeare Quarterly* 41 (1990): 111. Stanley Wells, *Shakespeare Survey* 43 (1991): 191–2.

9. THE AROUSED SPECTATOR

1 Charles Dickens and R. H. Home, 'Shakespeare and Newgate', *Household Words* 4 (4 October 1851): 25–7. 'Our London Commissioner, no. II', *Blackwood's Edinburgh Magazine* 71.439 (May 1852): 596.

2 Kerry Sproston, Bob Erens, Jim Orford, *Gambling Behaviour in Britain: results from the British gambling prevalence survey* (London: National Centre for Social Research, 2000), 17–28; based on a detailed survey of 7,700 people aged 16 to over 75. Exceptions to the participation averages included lesser percentages by those over 65 and those in full-time education.

3 J. W. Welte *et al.*, 'Gambling participation in the U.S. – results from a national survey', *Journal of Gambling Studies* 18.4 (2002): 313–37; based upon a telephone survey of 2,630 'representative U.S. residents aged 18 or older'.

4 For example, M. E. Cross *et al.*, 'Student-athletes and gambling: an analysis of attitudes towards risk-taking', *Journal of Gambling Studies* 14.4 (1998): 431–9; and M. W. J. Langewish and G. R. Frisch, 'Gambling behaviour and pathology in relation to impulsivity, sensation seeking, and risky behavior', *Journal of Gambling Studies* 14.3 (1998): 245–62.

10. MEMORY, PERFORMANCE AND THE IDEA OF THE MUSEUM

1 I rely in part on Susan Crane's 'Curious cabinets and imaginary museums' (in Crane 2000: 60–80), where the Sonnabend leaflet is reprinted entire (81–90); these quotations from p. 85. Its text is also available on the Museum of Jurassic Technology's website www.mjt.org (accessed May 2008).

11. ASSISTING BELIEF: RITUAL AND THE SPECTATOR

1 For convenience I use the familiar English names. Their new names are Kannur and Kozhikode; Cochin is now Kochi.

2 Other studies include K. K. N. Kurup, *Teyyam: a ritual dance of Kerala* (Trivandrum: Kerala Department of Public Relations, 1986); John Richardson

Freeman, 'Purity and violence: sacred power in the Teyyam worship of Malabar' (PhD thesis, University of Pennsylvania, 1991); and Sita K. Nambiar, *The Ritual Art of Teyyam and Bhutaradhane: theatrical performance with spirit mediumship* (New Delhi: Navrang, 1996).

3 New Revised Standard Version, 1989, quoted from *The New Oxford Annotated Bible*, ed. Bruce M. Metzger and Roland E. Murphy (New York: Oxford University Press, 1991). Words in square brackets are disputed among the most ancient manuscripts.

4 Matthew (26.28) offers a less ambiguous expansion of the words over the cup: 'for this is my blood of the [new] covenant, which is poured out for many for the forgiveness of sins'. Though this text has been preferred in most versions of the eucharist service, recall that Matthew's gospel was written sometime between AD 75 and 100, a generation or more later than 1 Corinthians and well after Paul's martyrdom under Nero about 65–7.

References

Abercrombie, Nicholas, and Longhurst, Brian, 1998. *Audiences: a sociological theory of performance and imagination*. London: Sage.

Agamben, Giorgio, 2005. *The Time that Remains: a commentary on the letter to the Romans*, tr. Patricia Dailey. Stanford University Press.

Ang, Ien, 1991. *Desperately Seeking the Audience*. London: Routledge.

Antoine, André, 1921. *Mes Souvenirs sur le Théâtre Libre*. Paris: Fayard.

Aronson, Arnold, 2000. *American Avant-Garde Theatre: a history*. London: Routledge.

Ashley, Wayne, and Holloman, Regina, 1990. 'Teyyam', in Richmond *et al.* 1990: 131–50.

Auslander, Philip, 2008. *Liveness: performances in a mediatized culture*. 2nd edn. London: Routledge.

Badiou, Alain, 2003. *Saint Paul: the foundation of universalism*, tr. Ray Brassier. Stanford University Press. In French 1997.

   2004. *Theoretical Writings*, ed. and tr. Ray Brassier and Alberto Toscano. London: Continuum.

Balme, Christopher, 2007. *Pacific Performances: theatricality and cross-cultural encounter in the South Seas*. Basingstoke: Palgrave Macmillan.

Bann, Stephen, 1984. *The Clothing of Clio: a study of the representation of history in nineteenth-century Britain and France*. Cambridge University Press.

Barker, H. Granville, 1909. 'Repertory theatres', *The New Quarterly* 2: 491–504.

Barnes, Peter, 1992. 'Working with Yukio Ninagawa', *New Theatre Quarterly* 8.32: 387–93.

Barthes, Roland, 1997. 'The Eiffel Tower' in *The Eiffel Tower and Other Mythologies*, tr. Richard Howard. Berkeley: University of California Press. In French 1964.

Bartow, Arthur (ed.), 1988. *The Director's Voice*. New York: Theatre Communications Group.

Baudrillard, Jean, 1994a. *The Illusion of the End*, tr. Chris Turner. Cambridge: Polity Press.

   1994b. *Simulacra and Simulation*, tr. Sheila Faria Glaser. Ann Arbor: University of Michigan Press. In French 1981.

Baudry, Jean-Louis, 1985. 'The ideological effects of the basic cinematographic apparatus', in Nichols, B. (ed.), 1985. *Movies and Methods*, vol. II. Berkeley: University of California Press. In French 1970.

Beauman, Sally, 1982. *The Royal Shakespeare Company: a history of ten decades*. Oxford University Press.

Benjamin, Walter, 1999. *The Arcades Project*, tr. Howard Eiland and Kevin McLaughlin. Cambridge, Mass.: Harvard University Press. Based on *Das Passagen-Werk*, ed. Rolf Tiedemann (1982).

Bennett, Susan, 1997. *Theatre Audiences: towards a theory of production and reception*. 2nd edn. London: Routledge.

   2005. 'Theatre/Tourism', *Theatre Journal* 57.3: 407–28.

Bentley, Eric (ed.), 1976. *The Theory of the Modern Stage: an introduction to modern theatre and drama*. Harmondsworth: Penguin.

Berghaus, Günter, 1998. *Italian Futurist Theatre, 1909–1944*. Oxford: Clarendon Press.

   2005. *Avant-Garde Performance: live events and electronic technologies*. Basingstoke: Palgrave Macmillan.

Berman, Russell A., 1989. *Modern Culture and Critical Theory: art, politics, and the legacy of the Frankfurt School*. Madison: University of Wisconsin Press.

Bharucha, Rustom, 1993. *Theatre and the World: performance and the politics of culture*. London: Routledge.

Bird, S. Elizabeth, 2003. *The Audience in Everyday Life*. London: Routledge.

Blau, Herbert, 1987. *The Eye of Prey: subversions of the postmodern*. Bloomington: Indiana University Press.

   1990. *The Audience*. Baltimore: Johns Hopkins University Press.

Boal, Augusto, 2000. *Theatre of the Oppressed*, tr. Charles A. and Maria-Odilia Leal McBride and Emily Fryer. New edn. London: Pluto Press. In Spanish 1974.

Boorstin, Daniel, 1964. *The Image: a guide to pseudo-events in America*. New York: Harper and Row.

Borsa, Mario, 1908. *The English Stage of Today*, tr. Selwyn Brinton. London: John Lane, The Bodley Head.

Botstein, Leon, 2004. 'Music of a century: museum culture and the politics of subsidy', in Cook, Nicholas, and Pople, Anthony (eds.), 2004. *The Cambridge History of Twentieth-Century Music*. Cambridge University Press.

Bourdieu, Pierre, 1984. *Distinction: a social critique of the judgement of taste*, tr. Richard Nice. London: Routledge. In French 1979.

   1990. *In Other Words: essays towards a reflexive sociology*, tr. Matthew Adamson. Cambridge: Polity Press.

Bradby, David, and Williams, David, 1988. *Directors' Theatre*. New York: St Martin's Press.

Braun, Edward, 1982. *The Director and the Stage: from naturalism to Grotowski*. London: Methuen.

Brenner, Reuven, 1990. 'The uneasy history of lotteries', in Brenner, Reuven (ed.), 1990. *Gambling and Speculation: a theory, a history, and a future of some human decisions*. Cambridge University Press.

Bristol, Michael D., 1990. *Shakespeare's America, America's Shakespeare*. London: Routledge.

1996. *Big-Time Shakespeare*. London: Routledge.

Brockett, Oscar G., and Findlay, Robert R., 1973. *Century of Innovation: a history of European and American theatre and drama since 1870*. Englewood Cliffs, NJ: Prentice-Hall.

Brook, Peter, 1968. *The Empty Space*. London: MacGibbon and Kee.

1987. *The Shifting Point, 1947–1987*. New York: Harper and Row.

Buford, Bill, 1991. *Among the Thugs*. London: Secker and Warburg.

Bürger, Peter, 1984. *Theory of the Avant-Garde*, tr. Michael Shaw. Minneapolis: University of Minnesota Press. In German 1979.

Carlson, Marvin, 1972. *The French Stage in the Nineteenth Century*. Metuchen, NJ: Scarecrow.

1989. *Places of Performance: the semiotics of theatre architecture*. Ithaca: Cornell University Press.

1990. *Theatre semiotics: signs of life*. Bloomington: Indiana University Press.

2001. *The Haunted Stage: the theatre as memory machine*. Ann Arbor: University of Michigan Press.

Carra, Lawrence, 1971. 'The influence of the director – for good or bad covering the years 1920–1969', in Williams, H. B. 1971.

Case, Sue-Ellen, 1996. *The Domain-Matrix: performing lesbian at the end of print culture*. Bloomington: Indiana University Press.

Cashmore, Ellis, 2005. *Making Sense of Sports*. 4th edn. London: Routledge.

Causey, Matthew, 2006. *Theatre and Performance in Digital Culture: from simulation to embeddedness*. London: Routledge.

Certeau, Michel de, 1984. *The Practice of Everyday Life*, tr. Steven Rendall. Berkeley: University of California Press. In French 1974.

1985. 'What we do when we believe', in Blonsky, Marshall (ed.), 1985. *On Signs*. Oxford: Blackwell.

1986. *Heterologies: discourse on the other*, tr. Brian Massumi. Manchester University Press.

Chambers, Colin, 1980. *Other Spaces: new theatre and the RSC*. London: Eyre Methuen.

Charnow, Sally Debra, 2005. *Theatre, Politics, and Markets in Fin-de-Siècle Paris: staging modernity*. New York: Palgrave Macmillan.

Chinoy, Helen Krich, 1971. 'The profession and the art: directing in America, 1860–1920', in Williams, H. B. 1971.

Chothia, Jean, 1991. *André Antoine*. Cambridge University Press.

Clark, T. J., 1984. *The Painting of Modern Life: Paris in the art of Manet and his followers*. London: Thames and Hudson.

1999. *Farewell to an Idea: episodes from a history of modernism*. New Haven: Yale University Press.

Clifford, James, 1997. *Routes: travel and translation in the late twentieth century*. Cambridge, Mass.: Harvard University Press.

Clothey, Fred W., 1983. *Rhythm and Intent: ritual studies from south India*. Madras: Blackie and Son.

Cohen, Erik, 2004. *Contemporary Tourism: diversity and change*. Amsterdam: Elsevier.

Cole, Toby, and Chinoy, Helen Krich (eds.), 1963. *Directors on Directing: a source book of the modern theatre*. Indianapolis: Bobbs-Merrill. Rev. edn. 1976.

Collett, P., and Lamb, R., 1986. *Watching People Watch Television*. University of Oxford Department of Experimental Psychology.

Cowens, Steve, 2001. *Blades Business Crew: the shocking diary of a soccer hooligan top boy*. Bury: Milo.

Craig, Hardin (ed.), 1951. *The Complete Works of William Shakespeare*. Chicago: Scott, Foresman.

Craik, Jennifer, 1997. 'The culture of tourism', in Rojek, Chris, and Urry, John (eds.), 1997. *Touring Cultures: transformations of travel and theory*. London: Routledge.

Crane, Susan A. (ed.), 2000. *Museums and Memory*. Stanford University Press.

Critchley, Simon, 2007. *Infinitely Demanding: ethics of commitment, politics of resistance*. London: Verso.

Croce, Benedetto, 1941. *History as the Story of Liberty*, tr. S. Sprigge. London: Allen and Unwin. In Italian 1938.

De Marinis, Marco, 1985. ' "A faithful betrayal of performance": notes on the use of video in theatre', *New Theatre Quarterly* 1: 383–9.

1993. *The Semiotics of Performance*, tr. Áine O'Healy. Bloomington: Indiana University Press. In Italian 1982.

Deak, Frantisek, 1993. *Symbolist Theater: the formation of an avant-garde*. Baltimore: Johns Hopkins University Press.

Debord, Guy, 1990. *Comments on the Society of the Spectacle*, tr. Malcolm Imrie. London: Verso. In French 1988.

1994. *The Society of the Spectacle*. New York: Zone. In French 1967.

Delgado, Maria, and Heritage, Paul (eds.), 1996. Introduction to *In Contact with the Gods? Directors talk theatre*. Manchester University Press.

Delluc, Brigitte, and Delluc, Gilles, 1990. *Discovering Lascaux*, tr. Angela Mazon. Bordeaux: Éditions Sud-Ouest.

Dolan, Jill, 1991. *The Feminist Spectator as Critic*. Ann Arbor: University of Michigan Press.

2005. *Utopia in Performance: finding hope at the theatre*. Ann Arbor: University of Michigan Press.

Dombrink, John, 1996. 'Gambling and the legalisation of vice: social movements, public health and public policy in the United States', in McMillen 1996a.

Duncan, Barry, 1964. *The St James's Theatre: its strange and complete history, 1835–1957*. London: Barrie and Rockliff.

Dunning, Eric, 1999. *Sport Matters: sociological studies of sport, violence and civilization*. London: Routledge.

Edelman, Robert, 1993. *Serious Fun: a history of spectator sports in the USSR.* Oxford University Press.

Ehrentrant, Adolf, 1993. 'Heritage authenticity and domestic tourism in Japan', *Annals of Tourism Research* 20.2: 270.

Elias, Norbert, 1978. *The Civilizing Process*, vol. I: *The History of Manners*, tr. Edmund Jephcott. Oxford: Blackwell. In German 1939.

Elias, Norbert, and Dunning, Eric, 1986. *Quest for Excitement: sport and leisure in the civilizing process.* Oxford: Blackwell.

Elsaesser, Thomas, 1995. Introduction to Buckland, Warren (ed.), 1995. *The Film Spectator: from sign to mind.* Amsterdam University Press.

Elsom, John (ed.), 1989. *Is Shakespeare Still Our Contemporary?* London: Routledge.

Elsom, John, 1992. *Cold War Theatre.* London: Routledge.

Farr, Michael, 1992. *Berlin! Berlin! Its culture, its times.* London: Kyle Cathie.

Feifer, Maxine, 1985. *Going Places: the ways of the tourist from imperial Rome to the present day.* London: Macmillan.

Fischer-Lichte, Erika, 1989. 'Theatre and the civilizing process: an approach to the history of acting', in Postlewait, Thomas, and McConachie, Bruce A. (eds.), 1989. *Interpreting the Theatrical Past: essays in the historiography of performance.* Iowa University Press.

1992. *The Semiotics of Theatre*, tr. Jeremy Grimes and Doris L. Jones. Bloomington: Indiana University Press. In German 1983.

Fiske, John, 1987. *Television Culture.* London: Routledge.

1989. 'Moments of television', in Seiter, E., 1989. *Remote Control: television audiences and cultural power.* London: Routledge.

1990. 'Women and quiz shows: consumerism, patriarchy and resisting pleasures', in Brown, Mary Ellen (ed.), 1990. *Television and Women's Culture: the politics of the popular.* London: Sage.

Fiske, John, and Dawson, Robert, 1996. 'Audiencing violence: watching homeless men watch *Die Hard*', in Hay *et al.* 1996.

Fiske, John, and Hartley, John, 2003. *Reading Television.* 2nd edn. London: Routledge.

Flesch, William, 1987. 'Proximity and power: Shakespearean and cinematic space', *Theatre Journal* 39: 277–93.

Foucault, Michel, 1986. 'Texts/contexts: of other spaces', tr. Jay Miskowiec, *Diacritics* 16.1: 22–7.

Fuchs, Elinor, 1996. *The Death of Character: perspectives on theater after modernism.* Bloomington: Indiana University Press.

Fussell, Paul, 1980. *Abroad: British literary traveling between the wars.* New York: Oxford University Press.

Goffman, Erving, 1967. *Interaction Ritual: essays on face-to-face behavior.* New York: Anchor Books.

Goldberg, RoseLee, 1988. *Performance Art: from futurism to the present.* London: Thames and Hudson.

Golub, Spencer, 1993. 'Between the curtain and the grave: the Taganka in the *Hamlet* gulag', in Kennedy 1993.

Grady, Hugh, 1991. *The Modernist Shakespeare: critical texts in a material world.* Oxford: Clarendon Press.

Gussow, Mel, 1996. *Conversations with (and about) Beckett.* London: Nick Hern.

Guthrie, Tyrone, 1964. 'Theatre at Minneapolis', in Joseph, Stephen (ed.), 1964. *Actor and Architect.* University of Toronto Press.

Guttmann, Allen, 1986. *Sports Spectators.* New York: Columbia University Press. 1996. *The Erotic in Sports.* New York: Columbia University Press.

Hamburger, Maik, 1998. 'Shakespeare on the stages of the German Democratic Republic', special section in Hortmann 1998.

Hamil, Sean, 1999. 'A whole new ball game? Why football needs a regulator', in Hamil, Sean, Michie, Jonathan, and Oughton, Christine (eds.), 1999. *A Games of Two Halves? The business of football.* Edinburgh: Mainstream.

Hay, James, Grossberg, Lawrence, and Wartella, Ellen (eds.), 1996. *The Audience and Its Landscape.* Boulder, Colo.: Westview Press.

Hemmings, F. W. J., 1993. *The Theatre Industry in Nineteenth-Century France.* Cambridge University Press.

Henderson, Archibald, 1932. *Bernard Shaw: playboy and prophet.* New York: Appleton.

Henderson, John A., 1971. *The First Avant-Garde, 1887–1894.* London: Harrap.

Herbert, David T., 1995. 'Heritage places, leisure and tourism', in Herbert, David T. (ed.), 1995. *Heritage, Tourism and Society.* London: Mansell.

Hewison, Robert, 1987. *The Heritage Industry: Britain in a climate of decline.* London: Methuen.

Hoberman, John M., 1984. *Sport and Political Ideology.* London: Heinemann Educational.

Hobsbawm, Eric, 1994. *Age of Extremes: the short twentieth century, 1914–1991.* London: Michael Joseph.

Hoerschelmann, Olaf, 2006. *Rules of the Game: quiz shows and American culture.* Albany: State University of New York Press.

Holbrook, Morris B., 1993. *Daytime Television Gameshows and the Celebration of Merchandise: The Price is Right.* Bowling Green, OH: Bowling Green State University Popular Press.

Holland, Peter, 1982. 'The RSC and studio Shakespeare', *Essays in Criticism* 32: 205–18.

Holroyd, Michael, 1989. *Bernard Shaw*, vol. II. New York: Random House.

Horkheimer, Max, and Adorno, Theodor W., 1969. *The Dialectic of Enlightenment,* tr. John Cumming. London: Verso. In German 1944.

Hornby, Nick, 1992. *Fever Pitch.* London: Victor Gollancz.

Hortmann, Wilhelm, 1998. *Shakespeare on the German Stage: the twentieth century.* Cambridge University Press.

Hughes, Robert, 1991. *The Shock of the New: art and the century of change.* 2nd edn. London: BBC Books.

Humphrey, Caroline, and Laidlaw, James, 1994. *The Archetypal Actions of Ritual.* Oxford: Clarendon Press.

Jackson, Steven, 1988. 'Towards an investment theory of sports spectatorship', *Play and Culture* 1: 314–21.

Jacquot, Jean, 1964. *Shakespeare en France: mises en scène d'hier et d'aujourd'hui.* Paris: Le Temps.

Jameson, Fredric, 1990. *Postmodernism, or, the cultural logic of late capitalism.* London: Verso.

Jeffery, David, 1992. 'France: towards *création collective*', in Yarrow, Ralph (ed.), 1992. *European Theatre 1960–1990: cross-cultural perspectives.* London: Routledge.

Jensen, Robert, 1994. *Marketing Modernism in Fin-de-Siècle Europe.* Princeton University Press.

Kaplan, Joel, and Stowell, Sheila, 1994. *Theatre and Fashion: Oscar Wilde to the Suffragettes.* Cambridge University Press.

Katz, Elihu, 1996. 'Viewers work', in Hay *et al.* 1996.

Kennedy, Dennis, 1985. *Granville Barker and the Dream of Theatre.* Cambridge University Press.

  1990. 'Ich bin ein (Ost) Berliner: *Hamlet* at the Volksbühne', *Western European Stages* 2: 11–15.

  1993. (ed.) *Foreign Shakespeare: contemporary performance.* Cambridge University Press.

  1998. 'Performing inferiority', in Bate, Jonathan, Levenson, Jill L., and Mehl, Dieter (eds.), 1998. *Shakespeare in the Twentieth Century.* Newark: University of Delaware Press.

  2001. *Looking at Shakespeare: a visual history of twentieth-century performance.* 2nd edn. Cambridge University Press.

Kershaw, Baz, 2001. 'Oh, for unruly audiences! or, patterns of participation in twentieth-century theatre', *Modern Drama* 42.2: 133–54.

Kiernander, Adrian, 1993. *Ariane Mnouchkine and the Théâtre du Soleil.* Cambridge University Press.

King, John, 1996. *The Football Factory.* London: Jonathan Cape.

Kirshenblatt-Gimblett, Barbara, 1998. *Destination Culture: tourism, museums, and heritage.* Berkeley: University of California Press.

Kott, Jan, 1966. *Shakespeare Our Contemporary*, tr. Boleslaw Taborski. New York: Anchor Books. In Polish 1961.

Lacan, Jacques, 1988. *The Seminar of Jacques Lacan, Book 2: the ego in Freud's theory and in the technique of psychoanalysis 1954–1955*, ed. Jacques-Alain Miller, tr. Sylvana Tomaselli. Cambridge University Press. In French 1978.

Lehmann, Hans-Thies, 2006. *Postdramatic Theatre*, tr. Karen Jürs-Munby. London: Routledge. In German 1999.

Leiter, Samuel L. (ed.), 1986. *Shakespeare Around the Globe: a guide to notable postwar revivals.* New York: Greenwood.

Li Ruru, 2003. *Shashibiya: staging Shakespeare in China.* Hong Kong University Press.

Lowenthal, David, 1985. *The Past Is a Foreign Country.* Cambridge University Press.

Lyotard, Jean-François, 1984. *The Postmodern Condition: a report on knowledge*, tr. Geoff Bennington and Brian Massumi. Minneapolis: University of Minnesota Press. In French 1979.

MacCannell, Dean, 1976. *The Tourist: a new theory of the leisure class*. London: Macmillan.

Macqueen-Pope, W., 1958. *St James's: theatre of distinction*. London: W. H. Allen.

Mainardi, Patricia, 1987. *Art and Politics of the Second Empire: the universal exhibitions of 1855 and 1867*. New Haven: Yale University Press.

Marowitz, Charles, 1986. *Prospero's Staff: acting and directing in the contemporary theatre*. Bloomington: Indiana University Press.

McConachie, Bruce A., 2003. *American Theater in the Culture of the Cold War: producing and contesting containment, 1947–1962*. Iowa University Press.

McMillen, Jan, 1996a. (ed.) *Gambling Cultures: studies in history and interpretation*. London: Routledge.

    1996b. 'Understanding gambling: history, concepts and theories', in McMillen 1996a.

Metz, Christian, 1982. *Psychoanalysis and Cinema: the imaginary signifier*, tr. Celia Barton. London: Macmillan. In French 1977.

Mulvey, Laura, 1975. 'Visual pleasure and narrative cinema', *Screen* 16.3: 6–18.

Munt, Ian, 1994. 'The "other" postmodern tourism: culture, travel and the new middle classes', *Theory, Culture and Society* 11: 101–23.

Munting, Roger, 1996. *An Economic and Social History of Gambling in Britain and the USA*. Manchester University Press.

Myerhoff, Barbara, 1990. 'The transformation of consciousness in ritual performance: some thoughts and questions', in Schechner, Richard, and Appel, Willa (eds.), 1990. *By Means of Performance: intercultural studies of theatre and ritual*. Cambridge University Press.

Naimark, Norman M., 1995. *The Russians in Germany: a history of the Soviet Zone of Occupation, 1945–1949*. Cambridge, Mass.: Harvard University Press.

Nambiar, A. K., 2001. 'Ritual and folk performing tradition in Kerala', in Reddi, B. Ramakrishna (ed.), 2001. *Dravidian Folk and Tribal Lore*. Kuppam: Dravidian University Press.

O'Brien, Geoffrey, 1997. 'The ghost at the feast', *New York Review of Books* 44.2 (6 February): 11–16.

Orme, Michael, 1936. *J. T. Grein*. London: John Murray.

Oudart, Jean-Pierre, 1977–8. 'Cinema and suture', *Screen* 18.4: 35–47.

Pallath, J. J., 1995. *Theyyam: an analytical study of the folk culture wisdom and personality*. New Delhi: Indira Gandhi National Centre for the Arts.

Patterson, Michael, and Huxley, Michael, 1998. 'German drama, theatre and dance', in Kolinsky, Eva, and van der Will, Wilfried (eds.), 1998. *Modern German Culture*. Cambridge University Press.

Pavis, Patrice, 1982. *Languages of the Stage: essays in the semiology of the theatre*. New York: Performing Arts Journal.

1992. *Theatre at the Crossroads of Culture*, tr. Loren Kruger. London: Routledge.

Phelan, Peggy, 1992. *Unmarked: the politics of performance*. London: Routledge.

1997. *Mourning Sex: performing public memories*. London: Routledge.

Poggioli, Renato, 1968. *The Theory of the Avant-Garde*, tr. Gerald Fitzgerald. Cambridge, Mass.: Harvard University Press. In Italian 1962.

Praz, Mario, 1950. Report in *Shakespeare Survey* 3: 118.

Preziosi, Donald, and Farago, Claire (eds.), 2004. *Grasping the World: the idea of the museum*. Aldershot: Ashgate.

Puchner, Martin, 2005. *Poetry of the Revolution: Marx, manifestos, and the avant-gardes*. Princeton University Press.

Quayle, Anthony, 1990. *A Time to Speak*. London: Barrie and Jenkins.

Rader, Benjamin G., 1984. *In Its Own Image: how television has transformed sports*. New York: Free Press.

Rapping, Elayne, 1987. *The Looking Glass World of Nonfiction TV*. Boston: South End.

Redhead, Steve, 1997. *Post-Fandom and the Millennial Blues: the transformation of soccer culture*. London: Routledge.

Reisberg, Daniel, and Heuer, Friderike, 2004. 'Memory for emotional events', in Reisberg, Daniel, and Hertel, Paula (eds.), 2004. *Memory and Emotion*. Oxford University Press.

Richards, Greg (ed.), 1996. *Cultural Tourism in Europe*. Wallingford: CAB International.

Richie, Alexandra, 1999. *Faust's Metropolis: a history of Berlin*. London: HarperCollins.

Richmond, Farley P., Swann, Darius L., and Zarrilli, Phillip B. (eds.), 1990. *Indian Theatre: traditions of performance*. Honolulu: University of Hawai'i Press.

Roach, Joseph R., 1993. *The Player's Passion: studies in the science of acting*. Ann Arbor: University of Michigan Press.

1996. *Cities of the Dead: circum-Atlantic performance*. New York: Columbia University Press.

Rozik, Eli, 2002. *The Roots of Theatre: rethinking ritual and other theories of origin*. Iowa University Press.

Said, Edward, 1978. *Orientalism*. New York: Random House.

Salmon, Eric (ed.), 1986. *Granville Barker and His Correspondents*. Detroit: Wayne State University Press.

Samuel, Raphael, 1994. *Theatres of Memory*. London: Verso.

Sandvoss, Cornel, 2003. *A Game of Two Halves: football, television and globalization*. London: Routledge.

Saunders, Frances Stonor, 1999. *Who Paid the Piper?: the CIA and the cultural Cold War*. London: Granta.

Sauter, Willmar, 2000. *The Theatrical Event: dynamics of performance and perception*. Iowa University Press.

Schechner, Richard, 1985. *Between Theatre and Anthropology*. Philadelphia: University of Pennsylvania Press.

1993. *The Future of Ritual: writings on culture and performance*. London: Routledge.

Schivelbusch, Wolfgang, 1998. *In a Cold Crater: cultural and intellectual life in Berlin, 1945–1949*, tr. Kelly Barry. Berkeley: University of California Press.

Schmitt, Jean-Claude (ed.), 1984. *Gestures*. London: Harwood Academic Publishers.

Senda Akihiko, 1997. *The Voyage of Contemporary Japanese Theatre*, tr. J. Thomas Rimer. Honolulu: University of Hawai'i Press.

Sennett, Richard, 1994. *Flesh and Stone: the body and the city in western civilization*. London: Faber.

Shackley, Myra, 1994. 'When is the past? authenticity and the commoditization of heritage', *Tourism Management* 15.5: 396–7.

Shaw, George Bernard, 1931. *Our Theatres in the Nineties*. 3 vols. London: Constable.

Srinivas, Lakshmi, 2002. 'The active audience: spectatorship, social relations and the experience of cinema in India', *Media, Culture and Society* 24.2: 155–73.

Steir, Theodore, 1927. *With Pavlova Around the World*. London: Hurst and Blackett.

Stewart, Susan, 1984. *On Longing: narratives of the miniature, the gigantic, the souvenir, the collection*. Baltimore: Johns Hopkins University Press.

Tusa, Ann, 1996. *The Last Division: Berlin and the Wall*. London: Hodder and Stoughton.

Tynan, Kathleen, 1987. *The Life of Kenneth Tynan*. London: Weidenfeld and Nicolson.

Tynan, Kenneth, 1984. *A View of the English Stage*. London: Methuen.

Urry, John, 1990. *The Tourist Gaze: leisure and travel in contemporary societies*. London: Sage.

2002. *The Tourist Gaze*. 2nd edn. London: Sage.

Var, Turgut, 1993. Conference report, *Annals of Tourism Research* 20.2: 376.

Vilar, Jean, 1975. *Le Théâtre, service public et autres textes*, ed. Armande Delcampe. Paris: Gallimard.

Wade, Allan, 1983. *Memories of the London Theatre, 1900–1914*, ed. Alan Andrews. London: Society for Theatre Research.

Walker, Martin, 1993. *The Cold War and the Making of the Modern World*. London: Fourth Estate.

Waxman, Samuel, 1926. *Antoine and the Théâtre Libre*. Cambridge, Mass.: Harvard University Press.

Weimann, Robert, 1978. *Shakespeare and the Popular Tradition in the Theater: studies in the social dimension of dramatic form and function*, ed. Robert Schwartz. Baltimore: Johns Hopkins University Press. In German 1967.

Whannel, Garry, 1998. 'Reading the sports media audience', in Wenner, Lawrence A. (ed.), 1998. *MediaSport*. London: Routledge.

Wiles, David, 2003. *A Short History of Western Performance Space*. Cambridge University Press.

Willett, John (ed. and tr.), 1964. *Brecht on Theatre*. New York: Hill and Wang.

Williams, David (ed.), 1991. *Peter Brook and The Mahabharata: critical perspectives*. London: Routledge.

Williams, Henry B. (ed.), 1971. *The American Theatre: a sum of its parts*. New York: Samuel French.

Williams, John, 1993. 'Sport, postmodernism and global TV', *Postmodern Studies* 9: 231–55.

Williams, John, and Wagg, Stephen, 1991. *British Football and Social Change: getting into Europe*. Leicester University Press.

Williams, Raymond, 1989. *Raymond Williams on Television: selected writing*, ed. Alan O'Conner. London: Routledge.

Willis, Susan, 1991. *The BBC Shakespeare Plays*. Chapel Hill: University of North Carolina Press.

Wood, Paul (ed.), 1999. *The Challenge of the Avant-Garde*. New Haven: Yale University Press.

Worthen, W. B., 1984. 'The player's eye: Shakespeare on television', *Comparative Drama* 18: 193–202.

2003. *Shakespeare and the Force of Modern Performance*. Cambridge University Press.

Yeats, W. B., 1953. *The Autobiography of W. B. Yeats*. New York: Macmillan. Originally in *The Trembling of the Veil* (1922).

Yong Li Lan, 2005. 'Shakespeare and the fiction of the intercultural', in Hodgdon, Barbara, and Worthen, W. B. (eds.), 2005. *A Companion to Shakespeare and Performance*. Oxford: Blackwell.

Žižek, Slavoj, 2001. *On Belief*. London: Routledge.

2002. *Welcome to the Desert of the Real! Five essays on September 11 and related dates*. London: Verso.

2006. *How to Read Lacan*. London: Granta.

Index

Plays, films and other works are listed by title

Printed in Great Britain
by Amazon.co.uk, Ltd.,
Marston Gate.